DATE DUE			

THE CHILD AND HIS ENVIRONMENT
IN BLACK AFRICA

Pierre Erny

THE CHILD
AND HIS ENVIRONMENT
IN BLACK AFRICA

An Essay on Traditional Education

translated, abridged
and adapted by

G. J. Wanjohi

NAIROBI   1981
OXFORD UNIVERSITY PRESS
OXFORD   NEW YORK

Oxford University Press

OXFORD LONDON GLASGOW
NEW YORK TORONTO MELBOURNE AUCKLAND
NAIROBI DAR ES SALAAM CAPE TOWN
KUALA LUMPUR SINGAPORE HONG KONG TOKYO
DELHI BOMBAY CALCUTTA MADRAS KARACHI
and associates in
BEIRUT BERLIN IBADAN MEXICO CITY NICOSIA

First published in French in the
Bibliothèque Scientifique of Les Editions Payot,
106, Boulevard Saint-Germain, 75006, Paris
as *L'enfant et son milieu en Afrique Noire:
Essais sur l'éducation traditionnelle*
(© Payot, Paris, 1972);
translated from the *Petite Bibliothèque Payot* edition
of 1972 (ISBN 2 228 33420 0)

Cover photograph reproduced by courtesy
of Nation Newspapers Limited, Nairobi, Kenya.

Published by Oxford University Press, Science House,
Monrovia Street, P.O. Box 72532, Nairobi. Photoset
by Nthawe Typesetting, P.O. Box 67298, Nairobi and
printed by Kenya Litho Ltd., Changamwe Road,
P.O. Box 40775, Nairobi, Kenya.

Contents

v

Translator's Preface

In translating Erny's *The Child and His Environment in Black Africa*, I was guided by the principle that, due to the high cost of production, publishers prefer shorter books to longer ones. It is with this principle in mind that I decided to shorten the work. In doing so I was guided by two criteria: (1) to omit anything not germane to the main argument or which obscured its meaning; and (2) to leave out of the account any repetitive material.

It is on the basis of the application of the second criterion that I have omitted Chapter Seven, 'The Child in the Global Society', for I feel that the content of that chapter has already been covered in the preceding three chapters.

As for examples of the application of the first criterion—these are too many to mention. But the reader can be certain of one thing: all the important elements of the book have been incorporated in the translation. Should the reader desire a more detailed account of certain topics, the rich bibliography provided will come to his aid.

In spite of the abridgement, I feel that there is unity and coherence in this work, a fact I have emphasized in the subtitle of the book where I have 'An Essay on Traditional Education' instead of 'Essays on Traditional Education'. I feel the work hangs together well enough to merit being considered as one essay. Pierre Erny has approved the abridgement.

For the sake of those who would like to compare this work with the original or to use the two side by side, it is necessary to point out that certain sections of the original have been rearranged.

In Chapter Nine, 'Entry into the Universe of the Word', the section 'Teaching and Initiation' has been transferred to Chapter Eleven, 'Initiation Pedagogy and Spiritual Experience', where it replaces section 2 ('Pedagogical Functions'). The former section seems out of place in the original and the content of the latter section is not as detailed as that of the former. For this reason, section 2 of Chapter Eleven has been omitted altogether. On the other hand, section 8 of Chapter Eleven has been dislodged from its original place and given as an appendix. The rationale for this is to separate fieldwork data (which is what the section in question is) from the rest of the work.

Each chapter of the book is self-contained in that full bibliographical information is supplied where possible, even when the original is deficient in that respect. In this connection it is worth while to point out that all the references to J. Kenyatta's book are to the original work, *Facing Mount*

Kenya, and not to *Au pied du Mont Kenya* used by the original author.

The bibliography has also been slightly modified in order to conform to the standard form current in the English-speaking world. A few additions have been made to it, and these consist of items given by the author in footnotes but which do not figure in the bibliography.

The translator has taken the liberty of adding three new features to the book. These are: (1) a key to the abbreviations; (2) a map of Africa giving the geographical locations of the principal peoples treated in the book; and (3) a table giving the distribution of various ethnic groups according to whether they are patrilineal, matrilineal, or bilineal.

As is customary, the translator has appended his own notes whenever he found it necessary to qualify, explain, or expand certain important ideas in the text.

After these preliminary remarks of a purely editorial nature, I would now like to come to the heart of this preface and give my own impressions concerning the importance of this book. The reading of the book has suggested certain ideas to me which I would also like to put across.

Preoccupation with the past—wanting to know the origin of the universe, of life, of man, etc. is in man almost incorrigible. This preoccupation is not confined only to modern, scientifically-minded man, but is also found in traditional man, who used to construct myths and legends to account for his origin or to show what the past was like. Why all this concern about the past? I think there are two answers that can be given to this question, one theoretical and the other practical.

In man, to know simply for the sake of knowing is as natural as eating, breathing, or going to sleep. It is on this premise that man can be said to desire to know the past, and this kind of knowledge is described as theoretical. On the other hand, knowledge of the past can have a practical value: to help man plan for the present and the future. Given all this, the importance of traditional African life which is thoroughly portrayed in *The Child and His Environment in Black Africa* becomes obvious. In this preface, I would like to explore the implications of the African traditional way of life for modern industrialized society and its formal system of education.

There is a story told about a white man who found an African resting in the shade. Immediately, a dialogue between the two got under way, and it went something like this:

White man (W): Why are you sitting here idle instead of working on the land to make it yield more and better crops?

African (A): Why should I make the land yield more and better crops?

W.: So that you can have a surplus for sale.

A.: Why should I sell the surplus of what I have produced?

W.: So that you can become rich.

A.: Why should I become rich?

W.: So that you can have an easy life.

A.: But, sir, I have an easy life right now and feel quite contented with my life as it is. Really, I do not see the need of going to all that trouble.

It would not take a lot of imagination to figure out who came out the winner in this conversation. Whether this story is true or not is immaterial. What is important is the moral it lays before us: not to confuse the end with the means.

In the West today there is almost a complete reversal of the end-means priority as far as life is concerned. One lives, it seems, for the acquisition of wealth, knowledge, prestige, power, etc., and not to enjoy life as such. Sooner or later, these things which are so ardently sought after prove distasteful, and bring about self-alienation and estrangement. The consequence of this is the large-scale suicides and eccentric behaviour that one hears reported in the West. (I deliberately use the epithet 'large-scale' to underscore the fact that these things take place in any society to a certain degree. They are fast creeping into traditional societies, especially African, and unless some quick action is taken, Africa will be no different from the present-day West a few generations from now.)

In traditional Africa, life was joyously received and happily lived. It was received with joy since it was seen as a way of making an ancestor or founder of the lineage relive. Life was lived happily because man enjoyed harmony with nature, and indeed, with the rest of the cosmos. Seeing himself as a part of the whole, the traditional African did not try to revolt against nature or to subjugate it. The lack of scientific knowledge and technology in traditional Africa may be attributed to this attitude towards nature, with the consequence that the African had to make do with the barest necessities with regard to food, shelter, clothing, and so on. His aversion to tamper with nature cost him dear, e.g. in frequent famines and epidemics.

There are those who will find this attitude reprehensible for being anti-Biblical. In creating man, they would say, God gave him the command to rule over nature and to subjugate it. By letting things take their course, so to speak, the African is guilty of the failure to exercise his God-given faculties of intelligence and will.

There is no denying the fact that there is a lot of substance to this accusation. But then what is the alternative to the traditional way of life? If it is modern industrialized society—whether it be in America, Europe, Asia, or Africa—then that alternative is to be deplored just as much.

Mother Teresa of Calcutta, the Nobel Prize laureate for peace in 1979, shocked her audience when she told them that the industrialized world is suffering from 'a different kind of poverty, a poverty of loneliness, of being unwanted, a poverty of spirit'.* At about the same time that Mother Teresa was making these remarks, Dr Mostafa K. Tolba, Executive Director of the United Nations Environment Programme in Nairobi, was expressing very similar sentiments. He said:

> Overdevelopment has led to a rupture of human relationships. The pressure on time caused by earning money to buy what are perceived as needs but which are really wants converted into needs by advertising, means that a man cannot spend half an hour to check up on a friend who is sick. Eventually, he cannot even spend half an hour to check up on a father or a sister or a son who needs him. I consider this inhuman.
>
> Fortunately, these ties are still strong in the underdeveloped world. The children who are undernourished, who are not sheltered, who are not clothed, who cannot read, they at least have that single positive element of having been brought up in a society where human relationships are still viable, where human beings consider themselves as brothers and sisters, and where these ties still pull them together in times of need. My hope is that in the process of development, these values will not be lost as they have been almost lost in the industrialized nations today.**

All this leads to a fundamental question: Is simplicity of life and the fostering of warm human relations incompatible with industrialiation? Is it a question of either/or, or is it possible to have the best of the two worlds? In my view, the second alternative is possible. In order to show how this is so, I suggest that we try to view traditional African society and modern society dialectically, i.e. in terms of thesis, antithesis, and synthesis.

Let us take as a thesis traditional African society which is characterized by respect for nature and by a subsistence economy. In the Western and other advanced countries, this thesis has been transcended by the exploitation of nature and creation of a monetary economy. For reasons already given, both the thesis and the antithesis have shortcomings and ought to be combined in such a way that they form a more acceptable synthesis. The traditional model of society should bring to the synthesis its high regard for human relations, its spirituality and sense of mystery, while becoming more 'profane' as far as its relationship to nature is concerned. By so doing, traditional society will be proving industrialized society right. On the other hand, industrialized society should take steps to humanize technology and to restore the sense of mystery it has lost regarding nature. If it does so, industrialized society will prove traditional society right. The new society thus created could very appropriately be described as post-traditional/post-industrial society. If brought into being, such a society might form the

*Reported in the *Standard* (Kenya), December 21, 1979.
**Ibid.

basis of a culture in which the African contribution might be considerable. It is such a society which L. S. Senghor foresees when he talks about the contribution which negritude might make to a world culture.

One can think of two ways in which a post-traditional/post-industrial society can be created. One way is by getting the industrialized countries of the world to alter their attitudes and ways of life in accordance with the traditional model of society. The other way is to urge traditional societies to learn from the mistakes of the industrialized societies and to plan their development in such a way that technological advancement and sophistication will be at the service rather than at the expense of human values and warm personal relations. I hasten to say that neither approach is easy. Logically speaking, however, the second approach should be less difficult to attain, since prevention is better than cure.

One way in which an industrial civilization dehumanizes people is in the creation of big cities which attract large masses of people. In these cities human relations find themselves at their lowest ebb. Normally, people in these conglomerates are too hurried to find time to help one another, not to speak of conversing with each other; work, production, and efficiency are given a higher value than human relations. Life in the city is one mad rush, very much controlled by schedules and time-tables. Besides attracting people who are genuinely looking for work, big cities very often become refuges for people who want to leave their homes in small towns or in rural areas so that they can exercise, away from the gaze of relatives and friends, certain freedoms they would not dare avail themselves of at home.

In order to make an industrial society approximate traditional society in the enhancement of the quality of life, it seems that more emphasis should be laid on the development of rural areas. To this end, all the educational activities of a country—especially a developing country—should be directed. Tanzania is one of the few countries in the Third World which have realized the possibility and the necessity of marrying the values of traditional life to the advantages and conveniences of an industrial and technological society. Tanzania is trying to make this possibility real by getting all her citizens to live in small units scattered throughout the country. These are the well-known *ujamaa* villages. Thus, the type of synthesis I am proposing is not something which just sounds good theoretically, but something which can be realized concretely. One can only wish and hope that the inhabitants of Tanzania will realize the importance of the communal life of such villages and willingly try to make a success of them. It is to be hoped as well that many other Third World countries will follow the example of Tanzania.

The very noble human values of traditional Africa that we have been examining do not simply happen or crop up from nowhere; they are brought about and perpetuated by a traditional form of education. We must now examine this type of education, and try to see in which way it can inspire the modern school education which has been accepted so overwhelmingly in Africa.

Traditional African teaching comprised three steps: observation, imitation, and explanation. From the vantage point of his mother's back, the traditional African child was able to observe all kinds of objects and activities in his environment. When the child was not on his mother's back, he was either sitting in the shade in the garden, the front yard, or on the hard floor of the house. There, the child was able to manipulate many things that were the object of his curiosity. Once he was a bit older, two years old, let us say, the child began to imitate adult activity. His desire to help his mother to weed led her to make him a miniature hoe. It is through observation and imitation that the son of a blacksmith learnt how to forge iron. It is through the same methods that Nyakyusa youths were able to build their own huts and establish what were called 'age-villages'. Observation and imitation were so much insisted upon by traditional African education that a child who asked too many questions was frowned upon. As for explanation, it was sparingly provided. Adults gave explanations in response to children's questions, but they refrained from giving unsolicited explanations.

Insistence on learning through observation and imitation is found in other traditional societies as well. This is especially the case among the Navaho Indians, whose children learn basket-weaving through observation and imitation of adult activity. The Navaho are reported to have considered the White man simple-minded because of his habit of asking too many questions and uttering many unnecessary things. The idea behind this attitude is the same as that of the African: if one can see, hear, feel, smell, and taste, one cannot help but learn.

The philosopher Thomas Aquinas distinguishes between two ways of arriving at knowledge: (1) *inventio*, or through oneself, and (2) *disciplina*, or through a teacher. Of the two, the *inventio* mode of learning is more basic. It would seem that traditional Africans, by emphasizing observation and imitation, are more closely associated with the *inventio* approach to learning.

By favouring learning through observation and imitation, traditional African education made the child an active and eager participant in the learning situation, thereby making the acquisition of knowledge and skills more efficient. That theory of modern education which views the child's mind as a *tabula rasa* and makes the teacher the fount of all knowledge has a lot to learn from the traditional African method of teaching and learning.

We have just seen that in the set-up of African tradition, a child was an eager and motivated learner precisely because he was the initiator of his own action. His eagerness and motivation were increased even more by the fact that what the child learnt—be it in the social or technical domain—was concrete and real, and touched him personally. With regard to play, traditional African children engaged in many games of their own invention; in them, they used real objects, not ready-made toys as in industrialized societies.

However, the games played by traditional African children led very early to a serious and utilitarian activity on the part of children. This explains why such children became useful members of the community at an early age. In such a situation, acquisition of knowledge is not viewed as something distinct from the application of that knowledge at a later period. Rather, learning is *ad hoc*: each situation is a learning situation. Thus learning was applied to all the aspects of the personality, and sought to develop functionally all the aptitudes of an individual. Given this, it is not correct to say that one educates for life or through life, but that education *is* life itself. Such an education cannot help but be relevant education. Modern formal education, which is often accused of being irrelevant, can take a cue from African traditional education.

In a traditional society, the educative action is shared by all. When children are very young, they learn mainly from their mother; from around the time they get their permanent teeth, they start to learn from older children, who learn from still older children, who have been taught by adults. The adult group is by no means homogeneous, but is divided into various age-grades according to whether one has undergone pubertal initiation, is married, has married children, and so on. A person in a higher age-grade is expected to instruct, admonish, or counsel those in the lower age-grade, and the latter are supposed to listen. Thus, in traditional society, the transmission of knowledge follows a well-defined hierarchical path. The outcome of this is the creation of a sentiment of respect in the pupil of whatever age-grade for his teachers. This is not surprising, since in traditional societies knowledge is regarded as having an independent existence, and as being endowed with a formidable power. The one who possesses knowledge always inspires awe, whatever the domain in which he exercises his knowledge.

Modern education is today plagued almost everywhere by pupils' strikes. These strikes have resulted in people being injured and in destruction of property, not to mention the loss of precious time for learning. In part, these strikes can be attributed to the pupils' lack of respect for their elders—teachers and parents. The pupils refuse to take their teachers seriously, and consider their less educated parents as ignorant and backward. Obviously, there is something amiss about a mode of education which has such an effect on pupils. Here, again, there is a lot that modern education can learn from traditional African education.

As is to be expected, education in traditional African society was in two main areas: technical and moral. In the technical domain, children and young people used to learn from the observation and imitation of both peers and older people. Here, what was learnt or taught included such skills as the procuring of food, the building of houses, and the making of clothes. As is well known, traditional African technology or industry was very limited, contenting itself with the provision of the barest necessities of life. In this sense it can rightly be described as primitive.

Though deficient in technology and material goods, traditional Africa was very strong in moral education. It is due principally to its moral teaching that traditional Africa can be said to owe its survival. If the distinction between individual and social morality is a viable one, then one can say that the centre of gravity of traditional African morality was social. In traditional African society, the children of one family interacted freely with the children of neighbouring families. In such an atmosphere, children learnt to sacrifice their wills and to give in to the wishes and desires of others. They learnt to share each other's problems and misfortunes as well as material things. Children were encouraged—and in some cases even commanded—to invite their friends over for meals. In this kind of environment, children came to learn that the common good should take precedence over the individual good, social consensus over personal will, interdependence over self-dependence. Children were taught that there is more prestige in giving liberally than in making oneself rich and prosperous, the latter attitude being associated with sorcerers. Mutual social responsibility was a virtue that was given a high priority. Moreover, there was a lot of emphasis laid on the right conduct at all times. The distinguishing mark of traditional African society is that a moral fault was regarded with more abhorrence than a failure in the intellectual or technical domain.

I have referred to the prevalence of strikes in schools, and said that they are due to a lack of respect for teachers and parents on the part of pupils. To put it more plainly and directly, these strikes can be said to stem from laxity in if not the total neglect of the teaching of morality in schools. Earlier on, I intimated that pupils are not wholly to blame for these strikes: teachers, too, have their share (and a big one at that) of the blame. Very often it is the teacher's selfish conduct—such as getting pupils to work on his own shamba without any remuneration, leaving school to go to look after his own business, or the misappropriation of school funds—which sparks off a strike in one school or another. Even though pupils as pupils detest and decry the teacher's behaviour, they themselves are likely to duplicate his action once they accede to his position. And so the system perpetuates itself.

If modern society would like to get rid of such evils (or at least to minimize them), it ought to insist on the teaching of morality in schools, and to see to it that it is taught as seriously as, say, mathematics or science. In this it has only to draw from the example of indigenous African education.

Indigenous African education has been a subject of study by several writers,* but in none of them does one find such an extensive and thorough treatment as in Pierre Erny's *The Child and His Environment in Black Africa*. Having lived and taught in Africa since 1958, Erny is well qualified to write the book he has written. His intention has been to study education using as a background the very rich ethnological data of the various African peoples. In my estimation, the author has not only succeeded magnificently in his aim but has, in addition, given us a glimpse into other aspects of African thought—especially its ontology, religion, psychology, and morality. In this connection, I would suggest that one read *The Child and His Environment in Black Africa* in conjunction with the *Dictionary of Black African Civilization*, translated by Peninah Niemark (New York: Leon Amiel, 1974), and *The Dance, Art and Ritual of Africa* (London: Collins, 1978), by Michel Huet, which offer further details and vivid visual depictions of topics touched upon in this book.

I undertook this translation out of the conviction that it is not necessary to swell still further a market already glutted with books, but that we should strive to master and digest the works already in existence, provided, of course, that they are worth their salt. I am firmly convinced that Erny's book belongs to the latter category.

Finally, let me say how happy I was to work on this book during 1979, the International Year of the Child.

Karatina,
Kenya

---

*Cf., for instance, Smith, *Indigenous Education*; Moumouni, *Education en Afrique*; Wandira, *Indigenous Education in Uganda*; Ocitti, *African Indigenous Education*.

Foreword

The present work is the result of an essentially pedagogical preoccupation. The reader will find in it some studies of varying importance on the life of the African child in his traditional environment and the education he receives in it.

My first live and direct contact with the African child took place in 1958 when I was appointed teacher in a rural school in Upper Volta—in a Mossi environment which was still very traditional. The difficulties that I encountered came mainly from the fact that I was still ignorant of the life my pupils led outside the school—a life which obviously influenced them profoundly. It occurred to me that as a teacher I had a duty to undertake a systematic study of the influences which these children were undergoing in their original culture. Later, I had occasion to widen my first experience on coming into contact with urban youth during the two years I spent in Brazzaville. As a teacher I found the conditions of work there very different, but my first impression was not belied: the mentality and form of thought of those young people remained equally impenetrable to anyone who did not understand the cultural background which moulded their existence and personality. I can say the same today about another rather exceptional environment in Africa—that of industrialized Upper Katanga.

Thus there developed in me the desire to be able one day to explain psycho-pedagogical problems from the data of anthropology and cultural psychology. I wondered whether ethnology might not be able to contribute—from its own analyses of the traditional environment and its evolution—to the research of this new pedagogy for which the countries south of the Sahara today feel a pressing need. It seemed to me that to ask questions about the nature, uniformity, and scope of traditional education would not only be of theoretical interest for the ethnologist but would also bring to light a set of problems and data which are very relevant at the present time and which, when studied, might lead to a new view of the work of teachers.

If therefore educational practice with the numerous problems which it raises in the African environment constitutes the point of departure of my research, it constitutes also its point of arrival, the goal to which it tends. I am convinced that in giving his attention first of all to a procedure which is properly ethnological, the modern educator gives himself an indispensable tool for understanding the full significance of the facts of cultural change to which he is exposed and of which he is one of the most active prime movers. M. T. Knapen has written:

It is the urgency of problems of acculturation which has obliged us to undertake thorough researches into the traditional environment if we wish to tackle the new situation in an objective manner, that is to say, by taking into consideration the totality of data, and then of its antecedents.[1]

At the present juncture, the pedagogical problems appear inextricably related to those of development. They can only be posed correctly in terms of a policy of development. Now in matters of education and teaching, the planner finds himself facing the same problems as the economist. In order to work out a plan of action in whatever field, it is necessary to start from an inventory which is as complete as possible of the forces present, of the potentialities, and of the available resources, as well as an accurate appreciation of the way in which they can be integrated into a dynamic of progress or, on the contrary, how they can act as brakes and obstacles by their powerful inertia. The projection and the prophetic vision into the future which must animate any policy of development can only have value and efficacy if they are rooted in a realistic vision of the present and the past. Now, at this level of evaluation of data, the ethnologist is in a position, it seems to me, to make an important contribution.

The question as to whether a properly ethnological study of traditional education presents a research interest for modern pedagogy in Black Africa was answered in the affirmative as early as 1937 [sic] by Jomo Kenyatta, who was to become Kenya's first president. He writes:

The analysis of the educational system as it existed before the introduction of European rule merits thorough study as it presents undeniable practical interest for educators charged with the transmission of Western education to the Africans. The study of the educational systems of other countries like Germany and Japan has helped other countries to understand the mind of these peoples. It has shown the scale of values taught to the young generations, the leading ideas which were inculcated, the virtues and ambitions which were promoted. Therefore, why does one not ask oneself what is the structure of education in Africa? What are its effects on the growing child? Who controls its development, and how?[2]

More recently, Abdou Moumouni, a scientist and educator, has written the following:

Apart from any nostalgia for the past, any romantic longing and sentimental lamentation, traditional African education is a fertile source of teaching and a subject worthy of reflection which forces itself on anyone who would like to view even half seriously the problems of education in contemporary Black Africa. As it is, colonial education was simply set alongside the traditional African education with the former often ignoring and even despising the latter. However, any new concept of education which claims to respond to the present and future goals of the countries of Black Africa, if it is to assume a true, popular and national character must, on the one hand, borrow from traditional African education some of its features and integrate them into its own modern system and, on the other, cohabit with it during a certain period of time while trying to influence it.[3]

In another place this author returns to the same idea:

Traditional African education constitutes a very rich source of teaching. It is a subject of creative reflection, especially in our age when the question of setting up an educational system which meets adequately the needs and aspirations of our peoples is being asked with much poignancy everywhere in Black Africa.[4]

In order to understand what is happening in the mind and heart of the young African today it is obviously necessary to take into account all the influences which he has undergone, and especially those which relate to traditional life. Traditional culture expresses itself in an education which very early shapes the life of those who are steeped in it, so that such modern assets as the school do not become like seeds thrown on fallow ground, but branches grafted onto a tree full of vigour. Traditional education is a part of the basic data, a part of what exists. It is through it that the past continues to be linked to the present and to the future. It constitutes the point of departure, and before thinking of transforming it, one must first take cognizance of it.

One cannot help feeling that in the last analysis the contribution of new methods and techniques, the introduction into schools of a truly experimental method, renewing our view of the child by modern psychology—all of these, no matter how innovative—are not enough. What Africa needs is a philosophy of education. In the present situation it is a philosophy of education which she perhaps lacks the most in order to overcome the anarchy, the absence of central guidelines, the lack of a total view. It is here that one sees the most striking contrast with traditional education which is based on a coherent view of man, an authentic anthropology.

In an extreme case, the ethnological point of view, no matter how comprehensive, must be surpassed: education is perhaps not only transmission of a culture, but also respect, admiration and silence when witnessing the blossoming, the revelation of human beings. Black African thought excels precisely in emphasizing this aspect of things.

In studying traditional education two different points of view can be adopted. One way is to situate it within ancient Black African culture, within its own dynamics and in its world of values, and to refrain from judging it otherwise than with reference to the goals which it pursues, and the human ideal which animates its. Another way is to place oneself firmly in the situation of cultural change, and then one is inevitably led to assess the educational contribution of the traditional environment with respect to present pedagogical needs, arising from the adoption of a new way of life and of entrance into 'industrial civilization'. The first approach is that of the ethnologist: it is the only one which can render justice to an ancient pedagogy by seeking to understand it from the inside. The second is that of the modern educationist: in the present circumstances it is the only one which is useful and effective, for by taking into consideration the processes of acculturation which are at work everywhere, it helps us to avoid an artificial problematic.

In the present work we shall deliberately limit ourselves to the ethnological aspect of things.* But even if our purpose is not to analyse them here, the complex phenomena which arise from the meeting of cultures constitute the background of our study. One thing is certain: if the ethnologist makes an inventory, in the widest sense of the term, of the constants and the orientation of an educative tradition, if he determines the functions and meaning which its diverse elements assume in the totality of culture, if he evaluates their social and psychological scope, the human training given in traditional environments appears nevertheless indissolubly tied to the former state of the societies in question. But we know well: all that belongs to the past, at least virtually. Through their young people, traditional cultures today aspire with all their power towards a modern, technical, and industrial civilization, and show themselves very eager to assume the consequences which this transformation entails. Are they not on the point of being carried away by the same irreversible current which not so long ago submerged the peasant societies of Europe? By its importance the qualitative jump accomplished by the people we describe as primitive can only be compared to the neolithic revolution resulting from the great discoveries indispensable to the security and development of the human species. As in the latter case, the path to modernity calls for an extremely thorough restructuring whose scope and implications cannot be exaggerated.

We see in the undeniable fact of this accelerated evolution, which neither our regrets nor our nostalgia will stop, the inevitable point of departure of

---

*Given what the author says elsewhere (see pp. xx-xxi, 14-15), it would at first sight seem that he is here contradicting himself. However, that is not the case. The declared intention of the author is to use ethnology as a starting-point for the study of traditional education. By saying 'we shall deliberately limit ourselves to the ethnological aspect of things', the author simply means that he is not going to study any other discipline (beside ethnology) as a basis for studying traditional education; by these words the author does *not* mean that he is going to study ethnology apart from, or at the expense of, education.—Transl.

all pedagogical reflection. Not to take it into account, even in a study of traditional education, would be to surrender to sterile 'archeologism' and 'ethnologism'. It is not at all a matter of seeking to preserve or safeguard that which has decayed, of reviving a dying form of culture, but of seeing how far the taking into account of the *terminus a quo* of the current processes helps us to understand them better, to attenuate their disintegrative character by softening the passages and transitions, and above all to promote the emerging syntheses.

The inventory and evaluation of indigenous education plainly constitutes only one aspect among others of the pedagogical research which one would wish to see conducted. Cultural anthropology can clarify the way in which problems are posed and suggest ways of solving them. But its contribution can only be valid once it is set alongside that of the other human sciences, and in particular those of demography, sociology, psychology, and economics. In the present state of our societies the great options in terms of which decisions must be taken clearly belong to the political domain. The ethnologist cannot have any other claim than that of being an auxiliary in the service of a project which is beyond his competence. It would, however, be a pity should the leaders fail to recognize the role which he can play.

Unfortunately, Africanist research in its present form offers us only a very fragmentary documentation on the child, on traditional pedagogy, and on the manner of personality integration. It is above all the American anthropologists who have emphasized these questions, though they have hardly extended their investigations to Africa. There exist some thorough studies on these questions by Kidd, Franke, Raum, Ritchie, Read, Fortes, Vincent; then there are the works of Griaule, Béart and Centner on games; of Zahan on infantile societies, of Zempléni-Rabain, Levine, Knapen, Ortigues, Parin and Morgenthaler on the relation between education and psychology, as well as innumerable contributions scattered through monographs and journals. If life histories are still rare, the autobiographical novel constitutes an outstanding literary genre in the neo-African production, particularly precious for anyone seeking to understand from the inside how a given cultural milieu succeeds in modelling a personality. In this respect the narratives of Laye Camara,* of Bernard Dadié or of Sheik Hamidou Kane are typical. However, any attempt at a synthesis of this kind will for a long time rest on an incomplete foundation.

My most ardent wish is that this work may contribute in its own way to the search for a more adequate educational theory, one which provides more human solutions to problems.

Lubumbashi, April 1971

*This is the correct name for the author. However, the inverted form (Camara Laye) has become customary.—Transl.

1

Introduction to the Study of Traditional Education

The ethnology of education occupies only a limited place in the usual pre-occupations of European researchers. It is, therefore, useful for us first to define the concepts to be used later in this work and the perspective in which we intend to place ourselves. On the other hand, a plan of general studies in traditional education itself poses serious problems of a methodological order. Given the cultural diversity of Black Africa, the validity of these problems is not evident. Before coming to the heart of the matter, we shall therefore stop to examine some points on method.

1. THE CULTURAL FUNCTIONS OF EDUCATION

René Hubert has defined education as:

the totality of action and influences voluntarily exercised by a human being on another human being, in principle, by an adult on a young person and oriented towards an end which consists of training the young person in various attitudes which will help him to attain the goals of his adult life.[1]

In spite of the very extensive character of such a definition, it does not entirely cover the semantic field of the term 'education' as it is used in cultural anthropology. The latter puts less emphasis on the individual action of one human being on another than on the global influence that the society, by its entire way of life, exercises on those it seeks to integrate into itself. The accent is shifted from the relation of person to person to the all-encompassing relation which unites the individual to the culture which he conveys with greater authority the more he progresses in its assimilation.

From the point of view of ethnology, education has three functions to perform with respect to culture of which it is only an expression, a function.

Dynamically considered, education is first of all the transmission of a heritage from one generation to another. It aims at assuring a continuity, at being the instrument by which civilizations perpetuate themselves. Through education, members of a society, who are also the carriers of that culture, make sure that the behaviours necessary for the survival of the latter are learnt. In some ways education appears like culture itself—transmitting, perpetuating, and actualizing itself in a new generation. It avails itself of

1

everything—its organization, its resources, its genius—in order to ensure its perennial character. Thanks to education, children become, as they grow up, the carriers, the representatives, then the instruments and mediators of this culture. Education is a process of transmission and—even if they are not aware of it—parents and elders act in a coherent way as transmitters of culture. It is a collective means through which, according to H. Marrou, a society initiates its young generation into the values and techniques which characterize the life of its civilization. Education is therefore a secondary and subordinate phenomenon with respect to the latter and takes the form of a résumé or digest of that culture.[2]

Secondly, education can be considered statically. As such, it appears as the heritage and the equipment that the individual receives in order to be able to integrate himself into his community. Thanks to it, he is provided with a language, a body of knowledge, a scale of values, a general framework of thought and reference, a sensibility, an 'ethos', and a *savoir-vivre*.

Finally, even in the most traditional and stable civilizations, education is seen as a factor of social change. The mental universe of a generation is never quite identical to that of preceding or future generations. Secondary institutions, in the sense in which A. Kardiner understands them, act upon primary institutions, and especially the modes of socialization. At the same time that the child becomes a carrier of culture, he also becomes a transforming factor in that culture. But where formerly there were only small cleavages there are today real rifts. By putting people in contact with new books, languages, techniques, ideas, and projects, the school becomes an accelerator of evolution and a powerful factor of socio-cultural transformation.

2. THE LEVELS OF EDUCATION

In this type of education, as seen by the anthropologist, one must not accord a privileged position to any one of the levels at which it is practised, nor to any one among the institutions which support it, not even to any of the ages at which it is administered. It is the general educational economy which is the most important, the overall orientation, the guideline, the underlying model.

One can never insist enough on the fact that a good deal of the education given by adults to children takes place without either side realizing it. One educates more by what one is than by what one does. One might be tempted to place outside the sphere of education the whole activity of child-rearing, all the care that the mother lavishes on the child, all her tokens of tenderness and attention, on the claim that the mother has not the slightest awareness at that moment of acting as a teacher. The relationships which exist between the mother and child are just lived either in joy or in anxiety;

they are not thought about. One can even say that the moment one begins to think too much about them one is falsifying them. But we are well aware today that the climate which prevails during these first exchanges counts more in the development of personality and takes place at a more fundamental level than all which will be added later. The attitudes adopted are not arbitrary. Both the care and feelings which accompany these attitudes are culturally determined in their form and expression.

As the child grows, the influence of the environment makes itself more explicit. It is a time of deliberate training and learning meant as such. The young man is sensitized to an ideal of conduct—to what is good and what is bad. But this education in values would have no meaning if it did not rest on a much firmer rock of behaviour, attitudes, and judgements which are taken for granted in a society. In imparting technical training or in demanding a certain type of moral conduct, the adult becomes aware of his educative role, for he judges the child to have reached the stage of understanding, of receiving instruction, and of submitting his conduct to direction.

Indigenous education reaches its highest degree of consciousness at initiations. The ritual integration into the world of adults must be followed and completed by the divulging of a certain type of knowledge, aptitude and behaviour. The individual must be proved, i.e. tested and strengthened in preparation for what awaits him. It is through the teaching given at initiations that the ideal values of a society appear most clearly. That does not mean that they are taught under the form of a code or a catechism, or explained rationally. Teachings of this kind are not absent: it is only that they appear very secondary. It is more by making the child live intensely the moment of accession to adult life—through symbolic and ritual situations—that the traditional culture hopes to make the child weigh the importance of that moment for himself and for the society. Initiation rites seek to touch him more at the subconscious than the conscious level. The meaning of these rites is not always clear to its protagonists; nevertheless, they are judged to be essential and indispensable. The will to educate, therefore, appears more explicit than the specific content of the education given.

. . . .

The distinction, inherited from psychoanalysis, between a conscious and unconscious level is expressed in different formulations in cultural anthropology: for example, one will speak of what is implicit or explicit, latent or manifest, of an overt or covert culture, of the necessity of a true 'deciphering'. But more illuminating than these bipolar notions, it seems to us, are the tripartite distinctions between formal, informal, and technical learning that have been proposed by Hall.[3]

Formal education seeks to impose—through admonition and precept—

the models which the teacher himself has never questioned. When he corrects the child, saying: 'Don't do that', he does not give reasons to justify his prohibition, and often he would be hard put to give the underlying reasons for his position. The tone of his voice itself indicates that in such a situation there is only one correct way of acting, and to act otherwise is unthinkable. There is no middle position between what is good and what is evil, between what is true and what is false. The child acts, experiments with different ways, makes errors, and is corrected. There is action on the part of the child as well as on the part of his mentors. This type of learning calls for emotional elements, for to violate formal norms is to interfere with the very foundations of social life.

Here we are right in the domain of custom and tradition which have their own way of ensuring their survival. In the eyes of their purveyors, formal systems are identical with nature. What is done here is good and natural. One learns with surprise that there can be other ways of proceeding, but one thinks they cannot be anything but unnatural and socially unviable. Depending on a given culture, tradition exercises a greater or lesser pressure on its members, and the obligation to conform imposes itself in differing degrees. Tradition is characterized by the fact that the influence of the past takes precedence over the exigencies of the present and future. There results from this a rigidity which is not devoid of advantages, for the individual has a clear, coherent and precise image of his life and society even as regards permissible deviations. Each knows what he can expect of others and what others expect of him. Formal systems are tenacious and resistant to change. Their function has analogies with instinct in animals. Formal systems represent what is the most consistent, the most fixed, and the most solid in a culture, the foundation which carries all the rest.

The principal agent of *informal* education is the model or pattern which is made use of imitatively. Here, the pupil alone is active through his openness to exterior impressions and through his effort to conform. There exist systems of conduct which are extremely complex in their details and in the way in which they are transmitted. These pass from one generation to another without anyone realizing that they are being learnt, that they are governed by laws, and without anyone being able to show the ways in which this transmission takes place.

Education becomes *technical* when there is an explicit transmission based on the logical analysis of the ongoing processes. The teacher acts on the pupil and his ability depends on his knowledge and power to analyse. This mode of learning reaches the highest degree of consciousness. The content is so straightforward that is can—should the need arise—be recorded in writing or on tape, and practised in the absence of the teacher. Emotion is almost absent and resistance to change is slight.

These three ways of learning are never found in a pure state, but overlap and mingle. However, it is important to find out which one predominates in a given situation.

Seen as a whole, the education of a child appears thus as an extremely diversified process which brings to bear agents and means of a varied nature according to a precise chronology. But the diversity is co-ordinated and forms an organic whole. Any interruptions may appear heterogeneous in relation to one another, but they depend on the same enviroment and they are bearers of the same cultural affirmation. Homogeneity results from the complementarity of these intrusions and it can only be evaluated at the very end of the process. The study of the elements which constitute a pedagogy can only have meaning in a functional and teleological perspective. Each contribution must be considered in relation to the ultimate goal pursued—the construction of a psychological system capable of a triple integration: personal integration, which is the ability to gather together the multiple influences which exert themselves on the unitary self from outside; social integration, which allows an individual to participate as an active member in the life of the group to which he belongs—recognizing it as his own and in turn being recognized by it; and finally, cultural integration, which makes of the personality the living expression and the adequate conveyor of a way of life, of thought, and of being in the world.

3. CAN ONE SPEAK OF A TRADITIONAL PEDAGOGY?

That one can speak of education in traditional Africa is evident, even though this is sometimes doubted; but to what extent can one also speak of a pedagogy, in other words of an elaborate, explicit, coherent, and systematic way of thinking about education?

The education given by a society—and which is in keeping with the model of humanity which it seeks to promote—may pass unnoticed at the conscious level as forming a total and integrated system. As we have said above, the mother can treat her child according to certain norms without realizing that her actions belong to a global design regarding the young person—a design which greatly transcends her individual consciousness. But at the level of collective mental structures that ethnology has to decipher and describe, even the most automatic educational practices conform to a certain general orientation. They tend in the same direction and mutually reinforce each order in order to achieve the formation of an integrated personality according to a given image. From the fact that there is in any culture a kind of organizing schema, one can already at this level speak of a pedagogy while admitting at the same time that it is of a very diffuse and unconscious nature. Beyond the action that one individual exercises on another, one adult on a youth, one must consider the global influence that a society exercises, through its whole orientation, on those whom it seeks to integrate. Now this influence regularly works in a coherent manner *as if* it were consciously devised for this purpose.

But the African tradition is also a vehicle for highly explicit pedagogical thought. The attitude of parents towards children, of older children towards younger ones, and in general of adults towards youth, is codified and expressed in numerous maxims and aphorisms that one quotes in order to justify such and such a way of proceeding or such and such an intervention. Through such maxims and aphorisms one can predict the existence of an explicit pedagogical goal and of a true philosophy of education in a given society.

The Balari* say in their proverbs:

—When collecting the leaves of a spinach dock one must take care not to break the plant.
—If you punish a child let it be with moderation and do not speak about it afterwards.
—It is sometimes necessary to give a child a slap, but afterwards the hand should go behind the back.
—There is no good education without strictness.
—One gets nowhere by violent actions.
—The education of a distinguished man started at the age when there was only a little scrap of material for a loin-cloth.
—The stream follows such a tortuous course because there is no one to guide it.
—He who makes you walk the longest makes you see more of the country.
—The young crack nuts with hammers bequeathed to them by their elders.
—The bell which rings has first passed through fire.
—The child must obey his elders.[4]

Any collection of proverbs among the Balari abounds in these pedagogical maxims. The forthright statements of one proverb must be corrected by those of another, and one thus arrives at a very subtle view of things. The existence of a true didactic literature such as the one collected from among the Chagga by B. Gutmann shows that there exists in traditional societies a teaching which is socially codified and which is given on precise occasions.

One can therefore affirm the existence not only of education but also of pedagogy in connection with traditional Africa. But we have a popular pedagogy based on oral tradition and one which bears a very strong impregnation by the socio-cultural environment. Such a pedagogy is tied by that very fact to a manner of thought which manages to rise only with

*This group and other major ethnic groups are to be found on the map, page 188. We have tried to be as consistent as possible in the use of these names, though some alternative forms are listed on the map and on the table, page 189.—Transl.

difficulty above the tangible and above the largely unconscious mental structures. All this does not take away anything from its systematic character; on the contrary, it reinforces it. Each human group expresses itself fully in the modes of socialization which it invents. There is an extremely intimate connection between a given pedagogy and the type of society to which it corresponds. The forms of traditional education as they still may be seen today correspond on the one hand, to what is most characteristic in each ethnic group, but on the other hand, are closely related to all those forms that operate in pre-industrial peasant societies.

There is a tendency to neglect traditional education to the extent to which pedagogy is identified more or less with school. Now the latter is an institution which can acquire—as nowadays—a central importance but one which remains contingent, representing one specialized body among other possible ones. It is the whole environment which has educational importance. Whatever the kind of society considered, children assimilate the models of social behaviour, the ideas on family life and existence, the systems of values with relation to socio-economic factors to a much greater measure, both in extent and intensity, outside the school than inside it.

4. BIOLOGICAL MATURATION AND SOCIAL INTEGRATION

The African tradition seems to distinguish three major stages of childhood. The first one corresponds roughly to the time of breast-feeding; the second stage extends from the time of weaning—a period associated with the appearance of milk teeth, continuing up to the appearance of permanent teeth; the third stage goes from that point to the onset of puberty. Because it is biologically based, this tripartite division is almost universal. (It is necessary to note, however, that the time of breast-feeding is very often extended up to the end of the second year.) The criterion of sexual maturity serves to determine the time when society confers full rights and responsibilities on its young members, and introduces a new cycle which leads through marriage and especially procreation to complete adult status.

The stages of education are very closely connected to age gradation. The terms used to describe the person vary as one passes from one category to another, and with them also vary the dress, the activities, the demands made of him, the attitudes adopted in his regard, and the training to which he is subjected. On the other hand, these steps are characterized by the particular incident of some aspect of the life environment. During the first stage the child is evolving almost exclusively within the mother's domain. With weaning, generally speaking, the child is for the first time plunged into a much wider environment within the extended family. The parental figures only emerge a little in comparison to the other immediate members of the family, and it is the other children of the same age and especially those of the preceding age-group who quickly assume a preponderant importance. With what elsewhere used traditionally to be called the 'age of reason', there begins, in Africa, a time of apprenticeship and of participation in group tasks which lead the children to organize and situate themselves in a new way, individually and collectively, with respect to their parents and to adults in general. Finally, initiation rites—where they exist—place the individual on the fringe of his normal environment for a shorter or longer period. The society as such severely reasserts its control over its youth, and delegates for this purpose people of unquestioned competence to act as guides and initiators.

Education related in this way to the social status of the person does not stop with childhood or adolescence, but represents one stage in a larger scheme which accompanies an individual from the cradle to the grave. It is permanent and gradual, and each new stage of adult life—marriage, birth, the initiation of the first child or the marriage of the last, accession to an important social role, old age—corresponds to an increase in knowledge, new rights and duties, a reinforcement of being, and sometimes a real illumination. When a Gikuyu woman has a daughter who has reached the age of initiation, she offers gifts to the other women in order to be taught her new duties and become a member of their group.[5] Among the Bambara, a person normally passes through a whole chain of societies of initiation until with the last one—and thanks to the rites involved—he has reached a true transformation in God who assures him of immortality at the end of his spiritual journey and mystical ascension.[6]

In such a perspective, old age will not be something tragic; there is no fear of growing old, no fear of time. The termination of fecundity and onset of old age do not cause any perturbation, crisis, loss of interest, feeling of impotence or of decline. Quite the contrary: one's prestige increases; he has new roles to play which are specific to this state; new sentiments are born out of a reinforced contact with the invisible world. 'Among the Lovedu, the old men and women always have something new to do and to learn. These years bring them added influence, a fuller life, and greater satisfaction.'[7] The ritual aspects increase in importance in those functions which are reserved for them: they become counsellors, doctors, initiators, family priests, guardians and specialists of deep knowledge, of tradition, of legends, of history, of divination, interpreters of mysteries and dreams, masters of ceremonies, mediators between the living and the dead, and between men and the gods. It is they who know how to handle adequately the maxims of jurisprudence and wisdom and to understand their full significance. The pedagogy which is directed to the child—the only one to be considered here—must be situated in this vaster and more complete totality, embracing the whole life and marking its stages. The initiation model is found in particular in all the institutions that might be qualified, without committing an anachronism, as 'lifelong education'. The passing from age to age is for everybody the occasion for continual improvement. To grow old is to climb the ladder; it is not to go down.

More than any other period of human life, childhood is marked by all kinds of rites: one finds them even before conception in order to call forth fertility, during pregnancy, at birth, at the shedding of the umbilical cord, when the baby is able to sit or stand up, with the first and second dentition, at weaning, with the appearance of the secondary sexual characteristics, with the first menstruation or ejaculation—in a word, during all the major stages of biological maturation. The most apparent, and the most outward, function of rite is to give value to the tokens of these stages and to assume culturally those moments which are naturally decisive in order to make them stages of social growth, and thus to place in a rigorous diachronic framework the education given by peoples who often have no very precise temporal references, and for whom the notion of absolute age is to a certain extent irrelevant. Society superimposes on the biological cycle its conceptions of man which determine social evolution. A cultural discontinuity comes to graft itself onto the natural continuity. The former gives value to the moments of change and transition, and divides human existence into stages.

These facts make us see that basic to any education whatsoever, there is a particular way of perceiving and understanding man—his genesis, his development, his presence in the world, the goals he is called upon to pursue. In this sense one can speak of an anthropology, that is to say, of at least an implicit philosophy of the person, and of a *paidology*, a conception of the child.

The principal feature of this *paidology* rests in the fact that it is more lived than thought about, that generally speaking, it is not possible to receive it ready-made from those who practise it. It must be guessed at and extracted through deduction from the totality of facts which concern the child either proximately or remotely. At the conscious level, important material is provided by the popular wisdom of 'So they say', of aphorisms and proverbs. The analysis of the language which the adults direct at the child or which they use in his regard—stories, riddles, songs, and lullabies—can also provide multiple clues about the way the child is perceived and about the things with which he is symbolically put in touch. The educative practices, on the other hand, help to reveal the way in which the reality of the child is lived existentially. Finally, the rites which mark the first years of childhood so as to indicate the different stages of growth are the privileged gateway to the underlying ideologies.[8]

To the extent that an anthropology—or even a cosmology—expresses not only the thought but also the manner of existence in the world peculiar to a culture, it determines the great axes according to which education is going to organize itself in its most profound and decisive form. From the more or less unconscious images that one has about the reality of the child flow fundamental attitudes that exercise a structuring action on the personality. From more or less unconscious images that one has of the infantile reality are derived fundamental attitudes which exert a structuring action on the personality, and in which one can rightly see the centre from which the elaboration of the social character will radiate. It is the very being itself of the child that is perceived by traditional man differently from the way it is perceived by modern man. Pedagogy, it is true, only rarely pushes its investigations up to the level of the implicit and lived *paidology*. It is in fact to the extent that one leaves one's culture that one becomes sensitive to the variations that the image of man undergoes, to the differences of emphasis that give value to or minimize certain aspects of it from one environment to another. One of the principal services that ethnology can render to the science of the child and to education is to show the relativity, not only of methods, but also of basic attitudes which might appear most obvious and most natural.

5. TRADITION AND MODERNITY

All cultures evolve, sometimes impelled by inner dynamism, sometimes under the influence of external factors. All have adopted in an unconscious manner foreign elements which they have assimilated, either continuously or at certain privileged moments of their history. Nothing could be more false than to present traditional cultures of Black Africa as monolithic, static, non-evolving, and shielded from all external influences. History and ethnology stress the probably decisive incidence of paleo-Mediterranean cultural elements on the greater part of the continent. The life of the great Sudanese empires and of the Bantu kingdoms experienced moments of social and political effervescence resulting in regroupings which went far beyond a purely tribal setting. As early as the eighth century the pressure of Islam was making itself felt in the very heart of Africa; that of Europe and Christianity exercised itself on the coastal regions beginning in the fifteenth century. The slave trade had repercussions on the demographic, psychological, and social plane which are difficult to evaluate, but whose disintegrating effect must have been considerable. During the last century, the European conqueror encountered an Africa which was fundamentally different from that of the great empires: it had turned its back on the desert in order to open itself to the influences coming from the sea, and that represented a considerable change at the economic, psychological, and social levels. The present problems of cultural change have therefore a very long pre-history.

On the other hand, one finds within traditional societies a differentiation which is often very marked. There exist a multiplicity of castes; of statuses; of professional, religious, initiation and secret groups; of age-sets, of associations for mutual help. And with each of these elements there are associated specific norms of conduct, moral rules, models, behaviours, pedagogies. Latent or overt conflicts are everywhere available for analysis. Collective constraint exercises itself in various degrees; the individual can enjoy an appreciable margin of freedom. If cultural models have changed through time, pedagogical systems belonging to different ethnic groups must not be considered as being such monolithic realities as to force all personalities into the same mould. The image that classical ethnology gives of indigenous societies is generally founded on an optical illusion: when one studies a culture other than one's own, one is especially struck by the great laws of structure which govern it; the researcher tries to define average behaviour, a 'modal' personality, but often omits to indicate the possible variations and differences which are socially admitted. If there exists a kind of correspondence between the aims of education and the needs of the society, this does not at all exclude the possibility of distortions and conflicts. In certain Congolese societies conflicting situations are customary and habitual, leading to palavers, unending disputes and the crumbling of clans. The energy spent in trying to maintain tradition shows that it does not enjoy undisputed prestige, and that it does not unambiguously meet the aspirations of everybody. A. Métraux writes: 'Among the primitives there is doubt and uncertainty about every question; for each rule there are exceptions; and against each rule there are transgressions. It is just this relativity which is the most human element.'[9]

However, in comparison with those of industrial societies, the internal homogeneity and the coherence of relatively isolated groups spread over an immense continent with a small population density and based on agriculture used to be, and still are, of quite another nature and strength. There, human life follows well-marked paths. Everyone has a clear understanding of the role he must play. The child can construct an exact image of his future life as an adult. He sees rigid models, and there are only slight variations from one generation to another. One knows where one is going; one has only to allow oneself to be led. Except in extraordinary circumstances there is nothing unforeseen, no novelty or chance. Education is given according to well-defined goals in the perspective of a society which remains nearly the same. The stages to be traversed are clearly marked and are the same for all. The past is a sure guide for the present; the view is more retrospective than prospective, and it is from the past that one finds adequate models to conform to. Education is founded on a vision of man and on certain attitudes regarding the world and life, on a system of values enjoying a high degree of coherence. Whilst in rapidly evolving societies old people feel more maladjusted to their environment the older they become, the older generation is, on the other hand, better integrated and feels more at ease in gerontocratic traditional societies where all is based on an experience and knowledge whose slow transmission in an essentially oral mode is socially controlled and excludes any short-circuiting. Culture is the object of a progressive assimilation whose destination is reached only with age.

At the level of concepts, we have opted for the preferred usage of notions of tradition and custom. To qualify a type of education as traditional is to associate it with a specific type of culture, with a particular type of life. [10] As in the case of Europe, Black Africa has known, alongside peasant and village life founded on elements of civilization which knew nothing of the scholarly transmission of knowledge, types of urban or aristocratic life much more contaminated by outside influences. In the Niger Valley, at the height of the Mali and Gao Empires, there existed an educational system based on Islam and associated with a school organization going from the Koranic school to the University. (This system is, by the way, still in existence.) Often, these external contributions have been juxtaposed to the traditional reality without really transforming it.

The types of education which interest us here are found in a fairly well-defined cultural context where the village constitutes a true spiritual community, where the general picture formed by institutions, beliefs, usages and techniques ensures the cohesion and the moral and social equilibrium of the group. The pedagogical problems posed by the introduction into traditional Africa of a modern school go beyond the narrow limits of an acculturation where two fairly similar cultures would meet, as in the case of the Sudan when the Arab influence made itself felt, or when the Portuguese first established themselves in the Congo.

Just now we are witnessing a much more profound and radical transformation similar to that to which the European peasants were subjected during the last century, and which tends to touch in very differing degrees all the societies which have so far remained traditional. To view a civilization in these terms is to oppose it to another one which is the product of mechanization, of industry, and of the human concentrations implied by the latter. André Siegfried has written:

We have here a transition which can be called fundamental because it does not go from one historical period to another but from one age of civilization to another. Splendid progress had taken place from prehistoric times until the 19th century, but for all that, the material conditions of rural life had changed but little. This was a pre-industrial age which had lasted since the beginning of the neolithic age, expressing itself in the persistence of the village community with its peasants and artisans living side by side and for each other in an almost closed economy. The consequences of this situation were in all respects almost those of an asepsis. It is into this social order, perhaps ten or twenty millenia old, that the machine—for it is with it that everything came—made its appearance, upsetting the then known methods of production and manufacturing, knocking down barriers, bringing together the most diverse societies, opening doors and windows.[11]

This analysis of the European situation can be literally transposed to Black Africa. The differences between the two continents in this regard have come about in less than a century. The colonial conquest undertaken under the impulse of industry coincides with the time when in Europe the traditional civilization started to undergo a profound disintegration. The expansion of industrial mechanization has transformed not only the material conditions of life but also people's modes of thought. It is a whole spiritual world, an order of symbols, of beliefs, of customs and activities which, after having survived since time immemorial, suddenly crumbles. Obviously, it is only in opposition to industrial civilization that the notion itself of traditional civilization acquires a unity and a meaning which up to that time used to be concealed by the diversity of cultures.[12]

Modern society as it has emerged in Western Europe or in the United States has, according to P. Fougeyrollas, four principal characteristics: development of industrial production thanks to mechanization, predominance of writing as a means of expression, growth of the bourgeoisie, and development of a national consciousness.[13] Relations of equilibrium and harmony between man and nature give way to relationships of domination and of enslavement one by the other. The urban agglomerations become the crucibles of modernity where inter-human relations undergo depersonalization and where one witnesses the phenomenon of people being turned into 'masses'. For one who goes from the rural area to the city, tradition ceases to be, in the words of P. Fougeyrollas, 'the unseen substance of daily life' as in the village community; 'it becomes that from which it has separated itself in order to find another existence; it becomes precisely what one calls and understands by tradition because one has taken with respect to it an irreversible distance'. In the final analysis tradition can be defined as 'the totality of relationships of equilibrium between man and nature, and of hierarchical relations between persons of the same community and this in a setting innocent of the great technological transformations'. Where it allowed a comparison with other cultures, tradition necessarily ended up rejecting what was different. The state of the present transition can among other things be characterized by the fact that the comparison becomes habitual and often leads to the choice and adoption of foreign cultural models.[14]

6. CULTURAL UNITY AND THE DIVERSITY OF BLACK AFRICA

Black Africa contains numerous and different ethnic groups, cultures, and traditions—each one using pedagogical methods of its own in order to bring about the formation of a specific type of personality. Given these divergences can one lump into one study the education given in the Niger Valley or in the Chad Basin, that of more urbanized populations of the Gulf of Benin, of the mountain people in the Cameroons or of the herdsmen of East Africa, that of the Central and Southern Bantus, of Islamized peoples living at the edge of the desert and along the coast of the Indian Ocean? Is the very general point of view we intend to adopt legitimate? Is the use we are making of the notion of indigenous education pertinent? In a properly ethnographical perspective such an assimilation would rightly appear hazardous. On what conditions can it become meaningful?

Between what is common to all the educational systems and what is particular to each one there is a wide margin for effecting different re-groupings with respect to affinities of structure that one discerns among them. One can undoubtedly detect numerous traits common to pedagogical systems of peoples without a written language or of those without an urban tradition. This is so because the purely oral character of the transmission of cultural wealth as well as the intimate symbiosis existing here between man and nature orient the education given to childern in a precise direction. The criterion which allows us to consolidate the various educative traditions of Black Africa is neither essentially geographic nor essentially racial: it is of a cultural order. The cultural unity of Black Africa can be affirmed in perspectives and at levels which are very different. Now if there is a domain where it reveals itself with particular force it is that of childhood education and socialization, and all the more as one goes back to infancy. It seems to us possible to identify an important collection of common traits, if not a true unity of structure. The same elements are found in most systems and are often arranged in an identical manner. Diversity comes above all from the relative weight which is given to the elements in question, the way in which they are emphasized and justified, and from the importance which sets them apart. One is permitted to extract constants provided that one avoids hasty generalization, that one takes into account the whole diversity, and indicates the departures from the general pattern. With respect to Black Africa, it would be necessary in particular to take into consideration the existence of domains and areas of culture which constitute so many intermediate gradations between ethnic particularism and Africanism.

Let us recall what was said earlier, namely, that the point of view we want to adopt ultimately is that of the pedagogue and not of the ethnologist.

Our aim in this study is to being together an ethnographical documentation which is as wide as possible, to make a kind of inventory in order afterwards to ask ourselves in a later study in which way the data thus collected concerns the modern educator in his work and research.

Now if the psychology of the African people is in fact very diversified, if taken in detail the methods of socialization used by the traditional environments vary considerably from one people to another, one nevertheless notices that *the problems of education are posed everywhere today in fairly identical terms*. It turns out that in a pedagogical perspective, the basic knowledge of the common cultural background is much more important than that of the ethnic variants. Tribal particularism cannot serve today as an adequate framework for research in modern pedagogy. Even in the positions taken by a number of thinkers and politicians who seek to promote the use of African languages for teaching, one generally finds a definite concern to go beyond the narrowness of local idioms. In young states where a national consciousness has not yet emerged, the opinion of leaders is above all sensitive to factors of unity and distrustful with regard to any divisive forces. A school built to cater for national unity will often be given the mission to go beyond, if not to fight, tribalism, the ethnocentric attachment to regional peculiarities. Obviously that does not mean that used correctly these elements cannot reveal their great richness at the level of cultural foundations. In the same way that the unity of the various types of traditional life bursts apart when confronted with industrial civilization, indigenous education presents a relatively homogeneous front when it is standing face to face with modern education.

Such is, it seems to us, the global context which not only justifies our approach but also calls forth a reflection which, though based on local data, raises itself to a level where the problems in question can be tackled as a whole.

2

Ritual Pedagogy

When one thinks of the education given in traditional Black Africa, the image of initiation rites immediately comes to mind. To think this way and stop there would be very wrong, for traditional education in Africa covers a much wider field. Besides initiations, there are other rites which touch on education. In the eyes of a Westerner, these rites are no more than temporal benchmarks of growth connected with the anthropology and religion of the people who practise them; they are devoid of any real meaning. Yet these rites constitute for the African tradition an integral part of pedagogy as well as its most essential and fundamental aspect, to such an extent that to omit them or to evade them voluntarily is inconceivable, and would lay the individual open to the danger of not being recognized as a 'man' by the society.

For the purpose of this study, we shall begin with an examination of the rites themselves and the functions which they perform: identification and recognition of the child when he is born, the marking out and consecration of the different stages of growth and development, integration in the society and participation in the life of that society which receives and accepts him as a member. As we proceed with this study, we shall keep in mind the anthropological background to which these ritual gestures and acts have reference, for it alone can confer meaning on them. Then, finally, we shall seek to understand the sense in which these rites have educational value and meaning.

1. RITE AND IDENTIFICATION

When, during a post-natal rite, the family group gives a name to a baby born within it, it confers on him an identity, recognizes him as a member, giving itself as well a means of exercising control over him. The name constitutes a privileged part of the social personality the essence of which is to be communicated, and by which man is for the most part delivered over to the service of others. Ethnography reveals the different ways in which a name can assert itself, and the different meanings it carries in various societies, families, or even individual cases. It also shows how varied can be the names given to an individual in order to express, on a synchronic level, all his relationships to the paternal and maternal lineages as well as to the age-group; on the diachronic level this expresses the transformations which the individual undergoes and the successive stages through which he passes.

But in the African tradition the anthropological significance of a proper name goes beyond a simple designation unrelated to the individual. In general, the name is not arbitrarily chosen from a pre-established list, but gives itself—so to speak: *the child is born with a name*. It is not a simple question of inventing a name but of discovering, revealing or detecting the right name capable of defining the being of the child. Should the immediate family make the mistake of giving the new-born the wrong name the child will, according to many African peoples, fall sick or cry incessantly in order to show that it is placed in a false situation which must be revised. It is not simply a matter of conferring an identity on the child, but rather of establishing an *identification*, an interpretation of the signs which enable his immediate family to declare *who he is* by giving him a name; in other words, to recognize him by relating him to a personality already known.

Very often the finding of the right name is not such an easy matter. At birth the child is thoroughly scrutinized in order to discover the similarities he might have to a dead related adult or to a previous child who is no longer living of the same mother. Premonitions and dreams in which the mother might have seen ancestors following or touching her or asking her to drink must also be brought to bear. The soothsayer is consulted. The name—or at least one of the names to be given to the child—must take into account any significant coincidences that have been brought to light, either by using the name of the dead again or by finding a wording which will affirm in one way or another that 'he has come back'.[1]

Quite often there is established a kind of dialogue with the powers of 'the beyond' concerning the child's arrival. Even before conception, the woman has recourse to some of them in order to obtain fertility. And during the whole time of her pregnancy, she must be on the lookout in order to discover—from imperceptible signs and events—words addressed to her through which invisible powers counsel her and give her orders and injunctions. To name the new-born child according to something seen as significant for the mother amounts to acquiescing in the intervention of the invisible powers, telling them that the content of their message has been understood, and that one agrees to place the child under their patronage.

The major conclusion to draw from the above account is that in addition to God and the parents, others are involved: ancestors, spirits, and divine hypostases, whose roles are most difficult to define. Certain popular sayings lead one to think of a true incarnation or even of reincarnation. Another type of explanation refers to a plurality of spiritual priciples of man which, dispersed at his death, meet different fates. Some of these, however, seek to return and resume life within the same kinship group. It can also be said that from an ancestor the child inherits—along with his name—something of his social personality, his individuality, his identity, his place and function within the clan—parameters which help others to define him. Finally, one can see in this protective power a kind of patron in the other world, whose earthly representative is the child, impregnated with his vital force. In either case, the aim is to assure to the invisible ones a certain· survival by allowing them to integrate themselves into the earthly existence of the present living generation which, in the eyes of the Black African tradition, is the only one endowed with complete reality.

As can be seen, the inheritance which the child receives from his forbears transcends the purely biological order: it touches the spiritual being and most intimate aspect of the personality. But in a dynamist ontology where the forces of life represent not an attribute but the very essence of being, the influences to which a man is subjected by the protective powers are inherent in his nature and constitutive of his personality. The child can only understand himself with reference to the whole system of forces which upholds him and allows him to subsist. When something acts on him, it is not simply a passing influence, but is part and parcel of a continuous and durable stream of fertilization and animation. In this respect, the action of the father on the son does not consist uniquely of procreation and of giving existence to, but implies a continual incubation of the vital force of the father on that of the son in order to develop it and make it thrive. In the same way the intervention of an invisible force in the emergence of a new life marks it indelibly and determines its individuality.

Beyond the different explanatory models that can be envisaged, the African tradition sees in the child more than a *tabula rasa*, a virgin soil, a formless clay which is waiting to be fashioned. For those who receive him, the new-born baby is already *somebody* that one can identify, and in whose countenance one can recognize features sometimes of those near and dear, and sometimes of mysterious and dreadful powers. The child comes into the world with his personality—a personality amplified, regenerated and reanimated through its contact with the divine world where it is endowed with a higher knowledge and will. He is, as many African peoples say, an 'old man'. But all these qualities are still hidden, walled in and contained, as it were, in a closed vessel. After the physical birth, his individuality seeks to be born, to manifest itself in the broad daylight, and to pierce through the vessel which hides it. Seen in this light, education will be seen as one of the arts of midwifery. Coming into the world may be said to be a series of births, extending through childhood.

2. RITE AND ENTRY INTO THE WORLD

Let us now consider one after the other the rites which successively mark out human life from its early beginnings. What is the anthropological significance of these rites? What is the aim of the society in so solemnly legalizing the moments in which the progress of the child to greater maturity manifests itself?

The underlying idea to which one must return constantly appears to be that of 'souls' or of the priority of spiritual principles with respect to their entry into the visible world. In most traditional civilizations, it is considered self-evident that in coming into the world, human individuality must emerge from a beyond, a world invisible, but nevertheless quite close. In being born here on earth, the child loses, little by little, the consciousness of its prior existence, and acquires only slowly that of being an individual of this world. He begins by feeling a stranger, but by and by he establishes close ties with those around him.

Being born must therefore be thought of in terms of the category of passage. To come here is to leave the beyond; it is to be in transit, to change one's state. Being born here means dying up there, and at the end of life, the opposite is true: to die here is to be born up there. In civilizations which put emphasis not only on what endures in man but also on what 'goes and returns', perhaps even on a literal reincarnation, human life is seen as obeying a cyclical principle. Childhood, like old age, constitutes a intermediary or transitory stage, a period of progress. While the child tries to free himself from the control of the other world, the old man prepares himself to return there. At the centre of the social structure there are adults, i.e. men who are completely integrated here below and who, by their fertility, assure the continuation of the cycle of life. In the case of the rites of death, we see a progressive departure take place, with the individual passing through the state of 'defunctus', of being deprived of function, before assuming the status of ancestor. In the same way, at the time of birth, the accession into the world of the living takes place gradually.

Man, in his earthly condition, is characterized by his materiality. It is through his body that he has assumed the form of life which is his lot here below. It is through his body that others perceive and recognize him. The body is above all a screen, a veil, an opaque object which human individuality must pierce in order to reveal itself for what it is. The body represents the most transitory element of the person. However, far from being looked upon as a prison, it is seen as an instrument through which one communicates with others and participates in the life of this world which is basically good. The body is a means of self-expression whose maturation allows the personality to emerge from the other world, and whose decline forces that personality to return to that other world.

The continuity of bodily development does not exclude an alternation between periods of accelerated growth and stagnation, between leaps forward and long moments of apparent inertia. But it is not the physiological stages in themselves which determine the social growth of a child.

In the cutting of the umbilical cord of the child or in teething, the society does not see mere signs. These things indicate that the child is maturing, becoming stronger, developing a clear will to live, becoming more and more adept at living with others, so that it behooves the society to recognize him and to accept him more fully as a member.

In a sense, the cultural order is clearly separate from the natural order. Human life is a succession more of social roles and statuses than of phases of organic development. The further the individual progresses in life, the more vague the link between the biological and social stages becomes, and this is especially true of puberty.

In the process by which the new-born becomes a man, we can see two elements. On the one hand, we notice that even though human individuality is given at the very first, it needs, in order to reveal itself, a body which is subject to all the slowness of biological maturation. On the other hand, the society keeps a watchful eye on the development of this mysterious, ambiguous and veiled being that is the child, attempts to identify him, and wonders whether he is going to cling to and accept with a firm will the new type of life which has been offered him or whether he is simply going to be a passing phenomenon. Will he be capable of becoming a full member of the society to which his birth has destined him? To this 'stranger', to this marginal being who has hardly left the other world, and who is still steeped in a certain cosmic vagueness, the society alone can bestow a status, a human countenance, as the child goes on revealing himself. Only the group can define the child as a person and give him a social dimension.

At each stage of development, the child gets farther and farther from the world of his origin, and as this happens, the group makes a gesture of acceptance and proceeds, by means of a rite, to integrate the child into the world of the living. At birth, the child passes from the maternal womb to the house—which represents a still-closed universe of family life and society. A period of seclusion is imposed on him and his mother, and it lasts until the umbilical cord has healed. The first appearance of the child is celebrated by taking him outside—to the yard, to the small alleys of the village, to the crossroads, to the market-place, i.e. to the points of social life and the shapes of the human world. Through walking, the child is able to get away from his mother and to enter into contact with his immediate surroundings. Through his first dentition, the child demonstrates that he can henceforth take part in the solid nourishment of the adults. By being weaned, the child severs the psychological umbilical cord which has hitherto bound him to the maternal figure.

With the second dentition there appears in the body an undeniably adult element which signifies that the time has come for the child to begin to participate fully in the common tasks and to receive clan and tribal marks— tatoos, scarifications, mutilations—which signify, after the manner of trademarks, the child's kindred. Finally, with the onset of sexual maturity, the person becomes capable of procreation, that is to say, of fulfilling that social function par excellence: to insure the continuity of the group. Where they exist, initiations solemnly introduce the young to the life of the group in its fullness. Initiations are not isolated phenomena, but come as a coronation of rites. Although rites differ somewhat from one ethnic group to another, they have a common aim: to integrate the child into his community and to give him the place which he will occupy as a person during the different stages of his development.

3. RITE AND OPENING

Still veiled in the beginnings of his earthly existence, the child appears— like a grain or shoot—as a complete potentiality. Whereas the child is nothing in actuality, he is everything in potentiality. He is completely drawn towards his realization, his fulfillment, his development and his manifestation. Encapsulated as he is in his perfection, being enclosed in his richness and wrapped up in his cocoon, the child is like a perfect microcosm which is shut off from the outside world, inaccessible, but sufficient to himself and happy.

The child's primal indistinction is often translatable in terms of bisexuality, androgyny, or sexual non-specificity. This indetermination appears in different forms in the various cultural traditions. In the Niger Valley, and in particular among the Bambara and the Dogon, there are elaborate speculations about the androgynous nature of the child, corresponding to that of the mythical beings of the beginning of the world. At birth, each human being is double, 'twin', at one and the same time male and female physically and spiritually. The 'twin' principle, postulating a fundamental duality, is realized in the cosmos by the 'sky-earth' opposition and it is reflected in the person by the separation of the sexes—which is necessary for the multiplication of the species. The body of the child is ambivalent: the boy is female by the possession of the prepuce, and the girl is male by having a clitoris.[2] One can therefore understand how in these Sudanic societies sexual mutilations are explained: the circumcision and excisions which remove the prepuce and the clitoris confirm the boy and the girl respectively in their proper sexes by getting rid of the contrary principle. These operations, therefore, bring about a profound change at the level of the person and establish in a decisive manner a natural difference between the child and the adult.

So long as the child grows androgynously, encompassing the two contrary elements which make up the two contrary poles of human nature, it enjoys the interior plenitude and harmony which enclose him in himself like a monad which has no need to look outside itself for anything lacking in its nature. In this context, sexual mutilations appear as operations having an irreversible character, and cause a break, a definite imbalance in the person by depriving him of a part of himself, and thus obliging him to seek outside himself—in human society, and above all in a member of the opposite sex—the element which he needs in order to complete himself, and to fill the emptiness which he feels within. By making marriage desirable and possible, these ritual operations are creators of family and society. The loss of primal perfection—physical and spiritual—must be compensated for by social and cultural development.

From the words and songs used during circumcisions, it is evident that while ridding the boy of his femininity, one opens up his mind and frees him from ignorance, lack of understanding, and opacity. The Magwanda and Bapedi say to their initiates: 'Until now you have been in the darkness of childhood; you were like women and knew nothing.'[3] In this respect it is necessary to recall that the most profound type of knowledge—and by the same token the most obscure (by virtue of being unfathomable)—is that connected with sorcery. We are touching here on what one might call the nocturnal kingdom of knowledge of which woman is the representative par excellence. This type of knowledge appears as wisdom in reverse, and it is impure, dirty, and evil.

For the Bambara, man, in his natural state, in his childish and uncircumcised condition, remains infected with a congenital vice called the *wânzo*, which fouls the spirit, covers it as if by a veil, and blocks the knowledge of both oneself and God. It is opposed to a full understanding of the person at the social and religious level, and prevents self-mastery and the understanding of the role of pain. In a sense, all of human development can be looked upon as a struggle against the *wânzo*. The rite of circumcision lends help to this struggle by making part of the *wânzo* flow into the earth with the blood and by provoking, through pain, an illumination and purification of the spirit. This obscuring principle is intimately connected with the femininity of the androgyne, which appears as a defect of masculinity as shown by the presence of the prepuce.[4]

The state of perfection which the child enjoys endows him with a particularly sharp knowledge and a true gift of vision. This is how he is pictured in many popular tales. But the child does not normally manifest this superior knowledge which inhabits him. However, though perfect in their essence, children are limited on the social level, and are the prisoners of their own integrity. The child enjoys such a perfection that he retires within himself, thereby becoming incapable either of understanding or leading a social life. Being complete, the child has no need of others. The child's self-sufficiency must be cut through, mutilated; he must be made to thirst after something other than himself, and through pain be made to open up to others. Among the Bambara and the Dogon, it is the purpose of the mutilations to signal access to social puberty.

But once the leap is made, man experiences all the pulls and vicissitudes of social life. He keeps in his heart the memory of the state of paradise which he used to know, and this generates in him nostalgia for the lost unity. It is only through a difficult initiatory climb, through a long education that the child will find again in God plenitude, knowledge, and wisdom. These will cause an inner joy in the harmony regained. Such is, at least among the Bambara, the theme of the society of the *Koré* which aims at theomorphosis, the transformation of the initiated into God. But in a more general way, one can say that it is with age that one acquires the experience, wisdom, and knowledge of esoteric matters. In a certain sense, these allow the old in traditional societies to enjoy a plenitude similar to that of the child.

All these anthropological themes—pre-existence, passage, original perfection, etc.—explain in what sense society intervenes in the unfolding of human existence by means of rites; they explain the significance of these rites, how they are to be viewed globally, and how they possess considerable educational value. All this belongs perhaps to the passive aspect of things where the child is the object of the group's attention. There is, however, a positive aspect where the child appears as a subject operating very actively within the group.

4. RITE AND PARTICIPATION

The child possesses a particular nature which he owes to his plenitude and to the position he occupies in daily life. He appears as an inchoate being, having not yet attained maturity, as a developing being which is essentially a forward movement, an impulse, a project, a virtuality in search of actualization. He is a man in the state of nature, not yet changed by the society, naked like the first human beings, without a feeling of shame, ignorant, unconscious of his condition and destiny, with an intact body and an intelligence which is still opaque and veiled. He is *small*, and because of this he is often compared to midgets, those hairy beings which populate the savage world, and which are made to intervene at conception and in foetal life.

Through analogy, traditional thought associated the child with quite another element which enjoys a similar status to its own in the universe, that is to say, to all that which is in a state of commencement, beginning, germ, genesis; to all that is in the process of self-formation, of being born, of maturing, of growing. He resembles the grain, the bud, the young shoot, the young vegetation at the beginning of summer; he is born of a woman fertilized by a man who is himself born out of the earth fertilized by the sky through the help of rain. He is related to the spring which shoots up from the sides of the earth, and like the king who is crowned, like the word which comes out of the mouth, the house which builds itself, the object made by a craftsman. The relations are likewise extended in time: in being born and in growing, the child reproduces the beginning of the universe and of space as recounted in myths and cosmogonies, those narratives of the beginning of the world. They are related to primordial beings, those which populate the original waters, or emerge from them, a humanity still dumb, wailing, inarticulate and naked, prior to the invention of agricultural work, clothes made of fibres, and speech. The stages of growth and socialization recapitulate those of human evolution.

As P. Tempels has shown, African ontology rests essentially on the idea of force; in other words, it views being dynamically. According to this ontology, it is not enough to say that being is endowed with force, that it *has* force as an attribute or a necessary accident. It is necessary to go as far as to identify the two and to say: being *is* force; force constitutes the very essence of being. From this point of view, the integration of the child in the cosmos is realized analogically not only at the level of thought but also at that of the dynamism which constitutes the thread of things. Mutually related things react on one another. If the symbol of the child, of gestation, and of birth is applicable in some way to the whole of cosmic reality, this affinity with the world makes it possible to act on the world.

Being efficient by his very being, the child's presence will justify itself each time he does something such as making an object, handling grains, bringing in the new harvest and eating some of its first fruits, or celebrating the first appearance of a new-born child. In artistic, agricultural, and cultural life, appropriate ritual functions are assigned to children. In the performance of certain ceremonies, children are not only subjects but also agents. Analogically speaking, they are integrated in a network which embraces everything, but where each one remains in the place or compartment assigned to him, where each one is organically connected to the others in an immense spider's web a single thread of which cannot be touched without causing the whole network to vibrate.

On the social level, the child represents a force because it increases his lineage in number, power, and prestige. The child represents richness par excellence, and is the symbol of vitality, abundance, and prosperity. His birth is a reminder to everyone that life continues and that the family perpetuates itself. Thanks to the child, the living can hope to enjoy the prerogatives attached to the ancestral state, and to be joined to the future generations of the social group which alone gives meaning to the survival of the dead. The child is a mediating force, a dynamic link which strengthens the alliance ritually concluded between the lineages at the time of the marriage between two of their members; he is the connecting link between the members of the wife's family and that of the husband. He is the proof that the exchange has been successful, fruitful. Without children, the matrimonial bond loses its significance and is liable to dissolution.

The incomplete character of his integration into the society, his marginal status, the persistence of his ties with the other world, prevent the child from enjoying a complete participation in the life of the group. However, these aspects do allow him to fulfil specific functions (connected with his particular nature), above all on the ritual and symbolic level. This makes the child indispensable and irreplaceable for the good functioning of the social organism which draws from him its power of rejuvenation and renewal and uses him as it uses the old men—as a mediator with the beyond.

5. EDUCATION AND THE REVELATION OF THE HUMAN BEING

According to the spiritual perspective of the African, the child cannot be reduced to what is earthly. He cannot be explained simply in terms of the interplay of biological or environmental influences, since he transcends both. He is at once the reflection, revelation, and emissary from the other world, from heaven, from the divinity. He possesses a supplementary dimension which makes him an irruption and manifestation of the sacred, a bridge between the earth and the beyond. He is born with a ready-made personality, an intelligence, and a will. He has a whole past behind him, a past which becomes present once again, making him an especially important person.

In the outlook proper to traditional anthropology, the important question is not to know how man has *become* what he is, or how a child is supposed to forge his character, but rather how an individuality which is given a priori, determined in its nature even before it appears, leaves its own shell and manifests itself to the world. The problem of human personality is not one of edification but of epiphany or revelation. It is less the problem of the society's active intervention than of receiving the child and providing the best conditions of development for this being to which it has nothing to add because it contains the potentialities necessary for its self-affirmation. It is not a question of moulding the child as if he were a formless clay, but of placing him in a favourable environment, of being attentive to his needs, and of fulfilling his desires.

E. Beuchelt reports the following from an informant of the Niger valley: 'The character of a Bambara is like the land which he inhabits; each year it is alternately humid and dry; it has always been thus and will never be otherwise.'5 Given the linear conception of time, the child is at the beginning no more than a principle and pure potentiality. He becomes a human being only slowly thanks to the action of the environment which causes the differentiation of his organism; then at death the person becomes decisively immobilized in his destiny. Life seems as an itinerary, a way which one traverses in one direction.

On the contrary, in the cyclic perspective—which is the case among Africans—it appears that the personality is always present, only that it changes state according to the passage of time. Sometimes life gathers itself, so to speak, and sometimes it disperses itself. Sometimes it contracts and sometimes it expands. Sometimes it hides itself and sometimes it manifests itself as in the case of vegetation which changes appearance according to the season. Life is not a unique and unrepeatable event: it is an ebb and flow, a systole and diastole, a perpetual recommencement.

In the vision of things where the family community is at the centre of perspective and gravity of all cosmic and human reality, one does not emerge from matter and from the social nothingness; one only becomes someone to the extent to which he integrates himself in a group. Socialization and becoming a person are synonymous, not in the psychological sense familiar to us, but at a level that we might describe as ontological or ontic.

The essence of ritual pedagogy is to touch the child, not in his intelligence, behaviour, conduct, or affectivity, but in his proper existence; it is to make him pass from the state of nature to that of culture, and thus lead him to his true destiny. Rite intervenes at the level of the insertion of the individual into a society which alone, according to African tradition, is capable of giving the individual the status of person and of leading him out [educere] from his marginal state and making him accede to the human condition. We are here right at the heart of education—of that societal action which aims at taking man from his original state in order to lead him progressively to something else.

From the study of the roles played by rites in traditional African societies, we notice that their perception of reality is different from that commonly found among Europeans. To be sure, this is not a difference of essence, but one which arises from emphasizing and favouring certain elements. In both cases, the point of departure is the same: the everyday observation of human behaviour. But whereas the modern scientific tradition concentrates on discovering how things happen, in describing minutely and explaining all the manifestations of growth and of the mental life of the child, the African tradition is less sophisticated in this regard. However, the latter strives to go beyond sensible appearances in order to reach significations which are to be found at a deeper and more hidden level— that of being. What is available to the senses must be seen correctly and in all its subtlety; but it is only a sign, and as such it must be surpassed, since it does not exhaust reality. When the child changes outwardly at the time of dentition or puberty, that is of interest only insofar as these bodily and mental modifications help to characterize the change which is taking place or becomes possible at the level of the person itself. The purely psychological dimension is always transcended by the ontological apprehension of things. Thus, whereas the modern European would ask himself: 'How does the child act at such and such a stage of his development?', the traditional African would ask: 'Who is the child? What is the child at such and such a stage of his development?'

All the Western clinicians and psychologists who have worked in Africa have emphasized this predominance of an ontological perception of the person among traditional Africans. For example, where the European sees sentiments or pure subjectivity, the traditional African sees beings or external forces. To the latter, evil appears as an aggression by a foreign power for which the individual is not responsible. Instead of saying: 'He commits evil', one will say: 'He is inhabited by evil', or 'He *is* evil.'[6] One tends to reify or even personify the great movements which agitate the human heart. Behind each fact, writes D. Westermann, the Black man tends to see, not a cause, but a being which causes.[7] This realistic character of African thought manifests itself also in the way in which one represents knowledge, conceived of as a kind of entity in itself, objectifiable independent of the subject, subsisting by itself. All this gives the impression that knowledge is something which, on the ritual level, can be appropriated through the taking of certain foods in a ceremonial meal.[8]

It seems to us that ritual pedagogy takes its originality and specificity from its claim to act at the level of being itself. In that it conforms to a fundamental requirement of Black African thought. By its highly symbolic character, rite signifies what it realizes and carries in itself its own meaning. In that way it can be said to 'instruct'. But we must not forget that initiations are rites before being instructions, or more exactly the teaching aspect which they contain has a ritual dimension.

Traditional education thus fits into a precise human framework made up of mental and social structures, attitudes, and intentions. Numerous studies on Black African religion and thought have shown that the way in which the traditional African perceives the world and reacts to it is different from that of other cultures, and it displays quite a remarkable degree of homogeneity. It is to this background of the conception of the universe and of the place that man occupies in it that one must refer in order to understand how such an environment has managed to elaborate a *paidology* which is implicit, diffuse, latent, lived rather than thought about, a complex of ideas, images, and underlying emotions; the way in which one apprehends and conceives the very personality of the child, the dynamic which is proper to him, and by that very fact the demands the society makes on him in the domain of education. As G. Gusdorf has written: 'The training of a man, if it is to be understood precisely as the coming into the world of a personality, as the establishment of this personality in the world and in humanity, becomes a phenomenon of cosmic dimension.'[9]

3

The First Discovery of the Other
or The Heritage of Early Childhood

The first discovery of the Other takes place through the maternal figure and its substitutes. But already in the establishment of this primitive relation between the infant and the mother, cultural modalities intervene in a decisive manner in order to emphasize more or less strongly one element or one type of experience. The nature of the care bestowed on the child and the emotional atmosphere in which it is lavished determine the configuration which will serve as a mould for the first impressions that the child will receive from his environment and for the first outlines of his personality.

I

The practices of child rearing and the educational attitudes appear most 'homogeneous across the African continent during the long period of suckling. It would, however, be false to speak of a uniform model for, as research has shown, among each people, even in each region or family, women proceed in slightly different ways. Here we shall concern ourselves only with the general orientation which seems to be suggested by a comparison of the various particular traditions.

The African mother is seen not only as the one who feeds but also as the one who soothes through her breast any tensions of the child. She stands ready to satisfy immediately his needs and wishes. The mother is essentially a presence, a reassuring and pacifying proximity. She is offered to him without an intermediary, directly, in the intimacy of a relation which knows nothing of distances—spatial or temporal. Normally, the child does not have the opportunity to experience solitude or abandonment, however briefly, for at the slightest cry he is consoled beyond his demands.

The mother is thus placed in a predominantly passive role. She allows herself to be possessed, and even to be ruled, by the child. It is rare for her to stimulate him or indulge in a little endearing play, or specific expressions of tenderness with him, or even to speak to him or coax him, thus showing herself to him as a person with her own reactions. She shows her affections by accommodating herself to the child, by keeping herself attentive to him, protecting him and providing him with whatever he asks. In the eyes of the child, the mother is less a personal subject than an overlapping being, completely good, easy to manipulate; one which can be used as an object, but with respect to which one is dependent as a mistletoe is on the tree which supports it, water on the vessel containing it, the egg on the hen.

If it is true that the mother provides the only environment the baby knows during the first few months of its life, she is replaced, little by little, for short periods and for the lesser maternal functions, by various substitutes, female retainers in aristocratic circles, elsewhere by older girls or women from the immediate environment. The human environment of the African child is more diversified than certain descriptions would give one to understand. He receives an extremely abundant and diverse social stimulation. The African child passes from hand to hand or even from back to back, and sees himself surrounded by many familiar figures. The traditional modes of behaviour very early put him in a vertical position and furnish him with an ideal vantage point for observing a universe thickly populated with human faces. His visual and social field is enlarged much more precociously than in cultures where the cradle is in use.

In practically the whole of Black Africa, weaning constitutes a critical period as regards the mental and physical health of the child. It is generally characterized by its lateness—usually at the end of the second year—and its suddenness. On a properly dietary level weaning is generally prepared for by a gradual and even precocious habituation to adult food. But on the psychological level the change takes place so quickly that the child interprets it as an abandonment. Suddenly, the mother becomes active, puts him at a distance, and refuses to give him the breast which has become not only a symbol of appeasement of hunger but also of all security. It is not rare to see a baby separated completely from its mother and sent to the home of another woman of the family for some time. Even if he stays with his mother he must learn how to adapt himself to certain of her demands, and to take rebuffs and refusals. He must relinquish the privileged relation which until then he has enjoyed with the maternal figure and in which he has found a source of extraordinary happiness. He is now asked to become a child like the rest within the group of brothers and sisters in the wide sense of the word. There thus takes place in weaning a real reconstruction of the relational universe, not only that of the baby but also that of the mother.

The stage at which weaning takes place varies, but generally speaking it is fixed in relation to the resumption of conjugal relations after a long period of post-natal continence. There is thus a causal link and often a temporal coincidence between the father's return to the scene as the mother's sexual companion and weaning. As a general rule, weaning takes place, at the very latest, when the mother becomes aware that she is again pregnant. It is not therefore as in Europe where the birth of a new baby determines the mother's change of attitude. This sudden change seems more arbitrary to the child since he cannot see clearly who is gaining from the change nor with whom he must compete for her attention.

Weaning plunges the child into the life of the group. After the forced relinquishment of the exclusive and affectively charged relation with his mother, he finds himself with numerous figures of adults and peers who receive him with love to be sure, but who can offer him only very neutral kinds of relations in comparison to the previous one. In a number of cases, therefore, the child goes through a period of perplexity and painful mental paralysis, not understanding what is happening to him, and losing thereby a taste for life. He becomes more frail, his psycho-motor development stagnates, and he becomes susceptible to infectious diseases, anorexia and malnutrition. Even his behaviour begins to show regression. A number of cases have been described as a true trauma of weaning. But, normally, life once again takes the upper hand. Faced with the inevitability of being kept at a distance, the child must gradually resign himself to the situation. Slowly he begins to take an interest in going to visit other figures, especially his age-mates.

Going by the present ethnographic documentation, it can be said that this schema of the first relational experience between the mother and child appears largely correct, leaving aside rare exceptions revealed by a detailed study of diverse ethnic traditions. There are, however, differences—sometimes quite considerable—in the intensity of either the mother-child relation during the lactation period, or of the sentiments which prevail at weaning. Formally speaking, identical elements of child-rearing are found more or less everywhere, but it is essentially their affective aspect which is subject to variations. Now, one must ask: What image of the Other is the child able to derive from these experiences which are all the more fundamental as they are the first to impress themselves on his psyche?

II

Initially, in the eyes of the baby, the maternal figure appears not as an individuality which is clearly delimited, but as a *mater magna*, an enveloping femininity, all-powerful and 'numinous', with which only the bonds of a total and parasitic dependence are possible. A more objective perception of the mother as a concrete person can only emerge slowly as the ego and consciousness become differentiated. But in the beginning, the Other, the outside world, and in a certain sense even one's body and one's ego are only experienced through the image of the mother. The way in which the child perceives her is going to colour and determine his whole vision of the world: if he finds her good, all will appear well; if he finds her bad, all will seem hostile and threatening.

With regard to the African child, this kind of relationship, which can be described as primitive, goes beyond the European norms due to the fact that in the former case the mother does not seek to promote in the child experiences which would help him to differentiate between what belongs to his ego and what is foreign to it. Nursed on demand, time is not structured by expectation, or by the alternation between full and empty periods. The closeness between the two beings does not allow other things to become objects of affection and to take on substance. United to the mother as the parasite is to its host, the limits of his individuality are, in the eyes of the baby—and perhaps also in those of the mother herself—more confused and fluid. There develops between the two a strong empathy which reveals that on the fringes of their co-existence an intercommunication subsists. The mother is like a great container who continues to be as one with the child. Psychologically, the umbilical cord is late in getting severed. Much more than in Europe, the child makes one think of a young marsupial, or an extra-uterine embryo, to use the expression of the biologist Portmann.

Waiting, frustration, putting at a distance, are reduced to a minimum. The Other is essentially gratifying, good for curling oneself up in, good to eat, a paradise where nourishing milk flows perpetually, an immobile and tension-free plenitude. Once certain difficulties have been surmounted, the child grows rapidly, happy, in full bloom, acquiescing to life with all his being, widely open to all influences. It is this image which most observers report about Africa. Undoubtedly, the figures around him multiply, but they also assume maternal functions, and they identify themselves with the image of the 'big mother' which, by that very fact, does not endure any serious competition capable of cutting into it. The character at once so intense and so prolonged of this first relation which seeks to exclude any other experience and above all any unfavourable impression of hunger, solitude, or exile, deliberately leaves the child, one might be tempted to say, unprepared in his sensitivity to the inevitable separations and frustrations which are going to come up at the time when, engrossed by other things, the mother will be obliged to put an end to this symbiosis and sever the bond which until then united her to the child.

Weaning constitutes a decisive moment, a solution to continuity. The mother changes her attitude. Objectively, to the extent that the child stays near her, she remains very attentive indeed. But it is not on an objective mode that the drama is played and that the child perceives the mutation. It is his symbolic universe which is turned topsy-turvy. What was good suddenly becomes frustrating, productive of anguish, and therefore 'bad', 'mischievous'. What was close and warm becomes distant, strange, and cold. If everything changes, will not the mother who was good to eat become 'poisoned', even devouring? She used to accept him and now she seems to reject him without the child perceiving what can be the cause of this reversal. Accustomed to a totally gratifying attitude, he feels the frustration, even if objectively it is minimal, as an attack on his integrity. This sudden solitude is to him unendurable and takes away his zest for life. He is missing only one being and all is depopulated.

The child has a slow experience of the inevitable ambivalence of everything and every situation. Instead of discovering progressively, by stages and with care, that there is in everything a mixture of good and evil, he has, during the first long and intense phase, experienced an unshared sort of happiness, which is going to make him feel very strongly the least changes in the relation with the mother, whatever be their nature, form, or real significance. The first serious encounter with frustration in the domain of inter-human relations can take the dimension of a catastrophe, of a trauma. In an extreme case, it is equivalent to the complete downfall of a marvellous narcissistic universe. It seems to us that ultimately it is less related to the modalities of weaning than to those of suckling which in an extended manner set up the maternal breast as the source and symbol of all security, of all pleasure, of all appeasement.

The opposed experiences of gratification and frustration which in Europe alternate from the beginning are, in African child-rearing, introduced successively. The latter creates a discontinuity in the perception of the Other of which weaning constitutes a highly sensitive turning point. Instead of promoting a synthesis, it juxtaposes two opposed and irreconcilable ways of grasping reality. As for those who are the subject of this child-rearing, there will be no mean between the gift of life and the abandonment which annihilates it, between plenitude and nothingness, between total security and metaphysical threat. The symbolic register on which the drama is played is that of food, of 'orality'. It is in the breast that the child used to see the source of his happiness; from now on it is in its refusal that he will experience unhappiness and solitude.

A prolonged breast-feeding accustoms the child to dependence vis-à-vis the maternal figure. Weaning—which comes more or less suddenly to put an end to it—leaves the child's personality dissatisfied, making him adopt regressive attitudes; it reawakens in him nostalgia for the past, and does not encourage him to develop a greater autonomy. The affective neutrality which will henceforth characterize interpersonal relations and the accompanying feelings of ambivalence often give support to a real climate of insecurity which prevents frustration from becoming an element of progress, adaptation, development, and transcendence. Instead of stimulating the child and making him go forward, it cuts off his wings and induces him to seek in the past the image of a state of beatitude without either tension or conflict. However, the processes of socialization to which the child is subjected do not allow sentiments of dependence to crystallize on the relation with a mother who becomes more and more distant. These sentiments will have to look for a new point of fixation, and transfer themselves *to what the mother symbolizes*—a closed and secure universe, which can only be that of the extended family or the clan.

As generally practised, weaning therefore constitutes an experience which in a sense is negative, even traumatic, but one which is necessary for the social integration of the child. Up till now, the child has remained enclosed in a reciprocal relation where elements pertaining to nature and food have been predominant. From now on he is going to be introduced into the enlarged group which is the carrier of culture where the father and his substitutes are going to take on more and more important. Weaning represents two types of universe: of intimacy and of sharing. But the child cannot pass from one to the other on his own strength or at the end of a spontaneous maturation. He takes the step reluctantly. He is thrown into the world of socialization which at first seems hostile and isolating. One can see a certain parallelism between this type of weaning—which is predominantly oral—and the Oedipal one of the European child, with its sexual symbolism. Later we shall see that structurally, the two appear to have analogous functions. But while the first develops in the individual sentiments of dependence necessary for adaptation in a social environment where the group imposes itself as the central reality, the second aims at guiding the person towards his inner autonomy.

When the child is separated from his mother, partially or completely, there begins for him a period of life whose psychological co-ordinates are particularly difficult to define. Up to that point, the mother has served as an intermediary in his relations with the collectivity, thus as both a link and a screen. By effacing herself, she leaves him alone in the midst of a greatly enlarged social field, face to face with numerous but rather indistinct figures. She plunges him—albeit in varying degrees, according to the social group in question—into the clan bath where he will be able to move around more or less freely within a multitude of fathers, mothers, and brothers in the classificatory sense. All this happens at an age when his European counterpart is wedged in the vise formed by the parental couple and from which it is normally impossible to escape. As a maxim of the Ngoni says: A child belongs to the whole village; everyone can take care of him or correct him. From the very beginning the child is introduced into a mode of socialization of an enlarged collectivity.

Globally, the second infancy appears as a turning-point in which the child is made to completely restructure—sometimes painfully—his relational world and to identify the figures which he finds around him. The great importance to be accorded to weaning, as it is generally practised in Africa, to a child who is already advanced in age comes from the discontinuity, the sudden break that it introduces into his life on the level of relations with other people, from the experience of solitude and perplexity which it forces him to go through, and from the considerable effort which it demands of him in order to resituate himself in the social sphere. The educational roles are going to multiply but without contradicting themselves, for in a homogeneous society all the influences that the child undergoes bring him different aspects of the same cultural affirmation.

On the most fundamental and primitive level of personality formation, the practices of child-rearing current in Black Africa lead the child to experiences of the Other in ways which are profoundly different from those that a young European normally encounters. The contributions of this period are determinant in the sense that they impress on the developing personality a decisive orientation. Once an individual has obtained a working knowledge of one type of relationship at the beginning of his life, once a schema of conduct is erected and integrated by his organism and a style of life adopted, he expects that all the subsequent relations he will establish with people and the exterior world should follow the same model. Are the attitudes that the environment adopts towards the young child capable of being related organically and functionally to the elements which will intervene during the second and third infancies, or even during adolescence, in such a way as to constitute with them a coherent whole endowed with a precise cultural significance? How is the education given at more conscious and diversified levels going to prolong, corroborate, bend, and give nuance to the first orientations impressed on the personality? It will be possible to sketch out answers to these questions as our study progresses.

4

Vertical Integration in the Lineage

'A man is his kinship.'
—A Serere proverb

'The way through which I have come is not a bad one.
The way of kinship is long, but it is not a bad way.'
—A circumcision song of the Bambara

'It is to his father or his mother that the rat owes his long tail.'
'Chew maize as long as your teeth are good; as long as you have your father and mother, take advantage of their help.'
—Balari proverbs

Entering the world, man is first a child of someone. The most immediate relation in which man finds himself is that which, through his mother and father, unites him vertically to ancestors, real or mythic, and gives him a place in a lineage—a series of successive generations going back link by link to the principle of all life. The attitudes of close relatives with regard to the individual can only be understood by referring to their respective place within the kinship group, to the immanent structure of the latter and the ideology which supports it—a set of data which evidently is not without pedagogical significance. It is this first type of integration and the educative modalities which belong to it that we must now consider.

1. THE LINKS OF KINSHIP

In traditional Africa, the kinship system regulates most of the social relations. The type of communication which it represents and the exchanges which it creates between individuals and groups occupy a privileged place in both Sudanic and Bantu societies. It is the extended family group which constitutes, independently of the systems which govern it, the basic cell of society, the fundamental moral person, and the most immediate educative environment. Lineages and clans appear to those concerned as organisms in the strongest sense of that term, having a reality not only social but also biological and ontological, subsisting by themselves and seeking to perpetuate themselves, animating and uniting their members by the same blood and by the same life, conferring on individuals a sense of belonging and a human status. Whoever is cut off from it reverts into nothingness. The lineage often appears as a reservoir of 'names', of social personalities, so that it is always the same figures which return. It forms a closed system of communicating vessels, so to speak, to which one can only belong through the right of birth, and where are found joined together the living, the dead, and the individuals yet to be born, those on and under the earth, provided only that they are descendants of the same ancestor. The group of the living is only a momentary incarnation of an immanent group which gathers together all the departed members and those yet to be born.

Like a cell of a living body, the individual cannot be conceived of as an autonomous element, for he is by his whole being dependent and bound up with others. He is and will always remain subordinated to his ancestors, be they living elders or dead ancestors, for they are the channels through which man is united to the source of all power and life: children of the same divinity, the same current of vital power which animates the universe in order to propagate itself even to the last creature. One can only maintain oneself in existence by placing oneself within the field of forces to which one is destined by being born in a given lineage. The ancestor is all the more powerful for being more remote, because then he is closer to God. It is from this idea that the principle of seniority which governs the whole of the society is derived. The status of a person is not governed uniquely by considerations of age or of primogeniture, although it is closely connected with them. The social body is organized hierarchically in terms of criteria which signify at the same time vital power, knowledge and prestige. The father, the patriarch, the chief, etc. give life to those who depend on them, as they are the condensors and dispensers of vital forces. By themselves these people are nothing, for they only represent and transmit. Their authority is all the more firm and total for its foundation is situated beyond the moral and social level; that foundation is at the very level of being and vital force. As L. S. Senghor writes: 'It is the participation in divine reality which, in the final analysis, makes the family.'[1] The living depend on the dead through whose intervention life is communicated to them. But the dead also depend on the living who allow them to remain active, to use that force of which they are the trustees, to attach themselves to the present generation and to function as transmitting channels. Not to have any descendants is to be isolated at the level of lineage, and by that very fact to be socially non-existent.

One will therefore educate the children first and foremost with regard to the life they are destined to lead within the family and as members of a group in which the incentives to social action ought to take priority over those which are personal, and which can only be conceived of in terms of the collectivity of which they are an integral part. Within a social structure constructed and cemented in this way, submission of descendants to the ancestors is the only conceivable and socially acceptable attitude. The greatest moral and religious offence consists in not recognizing authority, the status and rights of parents and their mythic extensions—the ancestors. One will strive to promote the values, not of independence, but of social interdependence.

At the level of interpersonal relations the predominance of the social manifests itself in that the way one behaves towards others is determined less by their personalities than by their respective statuses. Custom prescribes how the husband and wife, parents and children, brothers and sisters, older and younger brothers, uncles and nephews, in-laws, those belonging to the tribe and strangers, ought mutually to treat one another.

Can they speak to or look at one another? Can they eat together? Must their speech be respectful or informal? In which terms should they address one another? Such are some of the questions which are meticulously settled in advance, and thus partly abstracted from individual good will and spontaneity. Traditional societies tend to emphasize certain cleavages, for example, between the world of men and that of women, between that of the young and that of the old, between professional groups, age-sets, classes and castes in such a way as to diversify, but also to stereotype, behaviour.

The consistency of the nuclear family and the roles which have fallen to it vary considerably from one ethnic group to another.[2] However, the centre of gravity of the organization of kinship is not found at the level of the married couple but at that of the extended family and the lineage. Marriage is a *rapprochement* of two kinships for the purpose of procreation in which, in the most extreme case, the two partners play only an instrumental role. The intimacy of the couple constitutes to a certain extent a threat to a system which distrusts a small family for fear that its strength will be prejudicial to other bonds. Sexuality is a matter for the group, not for individuals. Its affective or sentimental aspect is of course present, but it is not determinant, and must not, in principle, manifest itself externally. The unity of the couple is not seen as an ideal to be promoted in a global system which aims first of all at the strengthening of clan alliances and at fertility. The practice of polygamy contributes even more to de-emphasizing the unity of the couple.

In the context of the African family, as has already been mentioned, one notices everywhere the rarity and poverty of affective and verbal exchange between husband and wife. This comes as a great contrast to the very rich dialogue between brother and sister and between mother and son. Even though the maternal bond is the very foundation of the alliance, and therefore of kinship, as representatives of different lineages, the spouses remain strangers to one another. 'The most frequent form of communication between the married couple', it has been noted in the Ivory Coast, 'is indifference.'[3] In varying degrees, this observation can be applied to all

African societies, whether patrilineal or matrilineal. Since sexuality is first of all communication, it does not need language, whereas the cohesion of lineages requires language.[4] The limitation imposed on the verbal exchange within the couple appears as one of the most certain means of preserving the unity and interest of the social group as opposed to those of the cellular family.

The example of societies where, as among the Somba of North Dahomey, the baby girl is, from the moment of her birth, the 'wife' of someone, but where before marriage, there exists also between a young man and a young woman other than his 'fiancée' a great deal of freedom in the expression of attitudes and sentiments, has led L. Thore to write the following:

> The society does not always and under all circumstances prohibit intimacy and the expression of sentiments between man and woman but only in the durable form of union which it recognizes and sanctions: marriage. Alongside the prohibition of incest, there exists a prohibition of sentiments—or more exactly—of the words which express them and without which their development is impossible. This prohibition acts in the opposite direction of the first one. All takes place as if the cultural models limit maximally the verbal exchange between a man and a woman where sexual exchange is allowed and officially consecrated by marriage. However, this verbal sexual exchange is allowed in consanguineous relations where the prohibition of incest is applied. Sometimes, as among the Somba, a group tolerates a more liberal conduct during the period between childhood and adulthood where one plays, so to speak, at becoming a man. But as soon as the 'game' gives way to more serious things, then the group must intervene in order to sanction a particular form of durable exchange; the group distinguishes carefully their exercise.[5]

But in this matter one should avoid committing a serious error. To say that the traditional African family is not founded on the values of intimacy between husband and wife and on the couple's aspiration to unity is not at all equivalent to saying that sentiments of love do not exist. On the contrary, it has been noted that there do exist an esteem and affection which unite the husband and wife from the very beginning of their marriage, and especially later on. Among the Bushoong, for instance, where girls generally give their consent to marriage, J. Vansina has shown that the intensity of these sentiments could be such as to lead one of the partners to commit suicide in cases of a lack of response from the other partner. In this ethnic group, lack of sexual attraction or of affection is very often the cause of the breaking up of the family.[6]

In a patrilineal society, the wife is tied to her husband both as a spouse and as a begetter; in a matrilineal society, only as a spouse and this obviously makes the relationship more fragile. A stranger in her husband's house in both cases, the wife makes herself accepted only gradually as she bears children. An observer has humorously summed up the situation of the different members of the traditional African family, saying: 'A man seeks the company of other men, loves his sister, and sleeps with his wife.'[7] The ideal family is founded on harmony and love, but at the same time it is recognized as a norm that there are latent antagonisms behind mutual identifications, the ties of blood and comradeship; however, different recognized procedures for coping with these antagonisms exist. Many societies maintain a strict organization where the relations between members take place smoothly in a climate of security and stability. Others, however, have always lived in an atmosphere of perpetual conflict.

In traditional societies the cellular family has meaning, but does not exist as a value. The vertical father-son or mother-son axis always takes precedence over the husband-wife axis; it is a carrier of an ideal of continuity within the lineage, and it overshadows the values of intimacy and independence which emerge as soon as the couple—a horizontal reality—acquires a sociological consistency of its own. It is in this structural predominance that we must see one of the most solid bases of aspirations towards polygamy which characterizes almost all African societies.

The practice of polygamy has evidently very profound educational consequences. It allows the wife to maintain a prolonged post-natal continence, and induces her to live together with her young children in the same hut where the father comes but rarely. In this case the married couples are less affectively united with one another. One could even say that they are 'less married' than in monogamous unions. As a consequence, the vertical wife-child link is going to exceed in intensity the horizontal wife-husband link. In this connection, M. T. Knapen has written the following about the Kongo woman:

> Since affectively she is only weakly drawn towards her husband, her whole attention is reserved for her child. It is not enough to say that she loves him: she *needs* this child as a being to which she can give herself with all her affective power.[8]

The 'amorous' life of the wife goes through alternate phases: sometimes it is more passive and oriented towards her husband, sometimes it is more active during long periods when it is concentrated exclusively on the child. This life is governed by the law of all or nothing as it is revealed by the study of interpersonal relations among Black Africans.

In a vision of the world where fertility and the need for self-perpetuation are as fundamental for the individual as for the lineage, it is not surprising to see the child become a central figure, eagerly awaited and received with joy. By his coming the world is renewed, and the primordial history recounted by myths becomes actual: he is the best testimony of the return of that cycle which unites human life to that of nature. The desire to see a large posterity is not only of a psychological and social order, but is rooted much more deeply in the way in which human and cosmic reality is conceived.

2. THE CHILD AND THE PARENTAL FIGURES

In spite of the great importance of the relations among peers, the 'parent'-child relationship remains the pivot of education. And whenever, on the more conscious level, education is being thought or talked about, it is the vertical influence of the elders which is being referred to. As for the horizontal axis, it is considered simply as the support of an education which is less conscious and less clearly perceived.

Parents very often have a keen awareness of their educative role. Among the Bushoong the parents themselves make toys or miniature houses for their children. The parents show them how to play house and allot them small chores even though they know in advance that they will have to do them over themselves. There is an initiation riddle which asks: 'My father has not taught it to me, my mother has not taught it to me, what is it? The sexual act.' This answer implies that the parents are supposed to teach their children everything else.

In spite of all the other influences that exert themselves on the children, it is on the nuclear family in particular that the main responsibility of socialization devolves, for in the eyes of the Bushoong it is only there that the elements deemed necessary: authority, watchfulness, regular and extended teaching—are to be found.[9]

Among the Tallensi a great deal of importance is attached to the identification with the parent of the same sex, especially from the age of five or six onwards. The child is defined as the son or daughter of so and so, and he identifies himself completely with his family in speech mannerisms. He will be heard to say: 'This is our dog. This is our child. This is our wife.' Very often a boy resembles his father in a striking manner, having adopted his behaviour, his posture, his aspirations, his cast of mind. A given type of character endures in the same family from generation to generation.[10] Even where, as among the Nyakyusa, the village is not inhabited by the men of a single extended family, but by those of the same age-group, the lineage is still very important, creating a true interdependence of interests, but, above all, of ontological links. In certain ethnic groups the subordination to the lineage is constant, whether in important events of life or in routine daily happenings.[11]

Social rules impose the same conduct towards all the individuals of the same group. Particularly in matters of kinship, the classificatory nomenclature tends to elicit the same type of relationship between a person and a whole range of other individuals. However, to say that the child has several 'mothers' and 'fathers' does not mean that the mode of relation which he has with his aunts and uncles is of the same affective intensity as that with his real parents. For instance, the authority of the true father will always take precedence over that of the child's paternal uncles. It is also possible for sentiments of kinship to override those of the family. For example, it has been noted that among the Bete the mother may not punish her child in the presence of paternal relatives. She has to wait to be alone with the child to punish him for a misdeed.[12] When it is said that all the members of the family have the right to advise, blame, correct, or reprimand a child, it is necessary to qualify this statement in terms of the hierarchy of rights which flows from the nature of the bonds of parentage which unite him to the adults in question.

Due to the biological link which unites the baby to her, the mother naturally occupies an absolutely unique and privileged position in his regard. This is particularly true in the areas where, as in feeding, no one can substitute for her without damage to the baby. But the moment this relation ceases to serve a vital function, it is terminated and the child is oriented towards a more global type of relationship with the family as a whole. And from that moment on, the child's education is taken over by the elders of his lineage as a whole, not just his father and mother, but all his older brothers and sisters in the widest sense. The human environment is large enough for other figures to substitute themselves for the father and mother so that after weaning there no longer exists an exclusive dependence on one particular person or on the couple, for it is at this time that dependence on kinship begins to assert itself strongly. Children are the common property of the group. 'That the child is carried on the back, is it not the sign that the parents leave him behind them?' ask the Bambara.

The practice of sending one's children to other members of the family or to friends is observed in a large number of ethnic groups. In a rural environment the child's arrival in the family of relatives or friends is considered not a burden but a favour, for his contribution to household chores and watching the herds is highly welcome. Wealthy households may thus receive many children into their care—in the hope that they will be better fed, better dressed and helped with dowry payments when it is time to marry. Nowadays children are exchanged between town and country primarily for the sake of proximity to a school.[13] But the fact that attending school leaves them little time for work has thoroughly transformed the spirit of this custom.

When a grandmother or aunt living alone expresses the desire to have a child go to stay with her, one cannot refuse her request without offending her. The child is thus put in contact with the largest possible kinship group, and learns to see beyond a small family group. This kind of separation is seen as promoting a good and firm education. It is for this same reason that among the Muslims children are entrusted to marabouts for instruction, and elsewhere to respected masters, outside any parentage.[14] In looking at the *curriculum vitae* of African students one is struck by the fact that most of them have, at one time or other during their childhood, been raised by uncles, aunts, older brothers, grandparents, and sometimes by friends of the family or, during schooling, by even more remote 'tutors', etc.[15] The reasons behind this practice are many: the family structures themselves, especially in matrilineal societies, the great instability of marriages in certain areas, the belief in the educative importance of separation—for the child is thus enabled to fit himself into and adapt himself to a succession of different environments.[16]

It is worthy of note that the separation of children from parents or other family figures does not result in dramas or serious emtional reactions: the global society context in which the child lives does not, it seems, allow him to become deeply attached to specific persons, especially after weaning. The child is instilled with the sentiments of belonging and identity, not with respect to a limited family constellation, but a much larger entity.

Be that as it may, a more thorough study in the domain of psychotherapy has shown that behind an apparent indifference, the African child can be very painfully affected by this kind of separation just like children everywhere.[16a]

In conclusion one can say that if the whole group of elders assures the education of the young, then the roles, the responsibilities, the authority, and the educative models are distributed over a large number of people and assumed collectively but not indistinctly. The atmosphere thus created does not favour lasting affective relations. The child must accustom himself to interpersonal relations which are virtually ephemeral and unstable. Quantitatively enriched and oriented towards a large number of people, these relations are by that very fact weaker, more diffuse, and less pronounced than where they develop within a more limited family circle. As a compensation, the relationships of negative valence and educational errors are also attenuated. If the child does not get along well with a member of his family, even if it is his own father, he has the chance of escaping from his domain. He is not tied to one person either for his happiness or his misery. L. V. Thomas has written concerning the Diola that: 'In the life of the child there are only a few events. From the time the child can walk until he becomes useful, he is more or less left to fend for himself, coming home only for meals, and growing in an affectively dull atmosphere.'[17] This observation is true of many an ethnic group.

3. THE MOTHER

Once the child has been separated from its mother through the weaning ordeal, it develops very differently according to whether it is a boy or a girl. The girl will continue to stay around her mother until the time of marriage. Very often, she lives in the same hut with her mother, gradually learning how to participate in the mother's chores. The close watch kept on the daughters contrasts markedly with the freedom of movement and action accorded the boys. These differences of treatment reflect, in the final analysis, a way of dividing up and ordering the universe according to the two great categories: masculine and feminine.

The woman is seen essentially as a donor of life, and as we learn from the Dogon, one cannot separate her sexual activity from that of feeder. Through the food which she prepares and the water which she draws, she sustains the life of her husband, and in so doing she can be said to assume the role that used to be occupied by her husband's mother. The wife is even referred to as the 'mother of the husband'. The respect that a child feels towards his mother will be transferred, through marriage, to his wife. In general terms, a very strong attachment—even a fixation—exists between mother and child, so that an insult to the mother will be deeply felt. [18] But as a certain familiarity between the two is possible as opposed to the relations with the father, ambivalent sentiments can give themselves full vent. [19] Mothers will have a tendency to govern the lives of their grown-up children and to interfere in their family affairs. 'You will be able to have many wives, but remember, you will never have more than one mother', [20] a Baila man is told during his wedding. Among the Lovedu, the husband's mother appears as a dominant figure in the home, watching over the sexual life and the pregnancies of her daughters-in-law, intervening in the care given to the babies, deciding the right time for weaning, etc. The moral authority of mothers remains considerable, even though the family structure does not give them any legal authority. [21]

The matrilineal structure will tend to bring the man and his mother close together, exalting, as L. de Heusch tells us, the life given by the mother at the expense of that conferred by the wife, so that the husband remains somewhat a stranger to the social fate of his own children. [22]

It is quite evident that according to ethnic traditions, the relation of children to their mothers takes on a very different colouration. In the domain of modesty and language, one very often finds a very great reserve between the children and their father, and a very great familiarity with their mother. Among the Gusii, where education is mainly the responsibility of the mother, and where the father is more or less confined to some disciplinary roles,* one can make the following classification of the relation-

---

*I feel that here the author is making a spurious dicotomy, since education, understood in its widest sense, can also be effected through discipline.—Transl.

ship between parents and children: between the father and daughter there reigns an extreme reserve, whereas between the father and the son this is much less. Intimacy appears when we come to the relationship between the mother and son, reaching its peak in the mother-daughter relationship. [23] Generally speaking, one can say that the Gusii mother is closer to her children and is more tolerant than her husband with regard to deviant conduct. But for all that, she tries to avoid showing too much affection.

Among the Bushoong, a mother's sentiments towards her daughter are strongly manifested. The mother uses her daughter as a refuge, and a strong feeling of dependence is established between the two. With the boys the mothers are very open—even in sexual matters—whereas the sons must treat their mothers with great reserve. [24] On the other hand, in Rwanda, the tenderness which unites the mother with her adolescent sons can express itself in words and caresses, whilst such demonstrations are much more rare with the daughters. [25]

Among the Fulani of Gwandu, the affection for the mother is considered to be of a totally different sort from that felt for the father. In this connection, language distinguishes between 'true' love and love 'by necessity'. One loves one's father because it is he who gives one animals and, with them, social status, but the child is not quite certain that his legal father is his biological father, whereas with the mother there is no doubt whatsoever. [26] Also, among the Gikuyu 'children are more attached to their mother than to their father, since it is she who nourishes them and looks after their clothes. It is in her they confide when they are in trouble. If the matter requires the intervention of the father, she takes them to him and explains the situation. She tries to reconcile the two in case of a conflict.' [27] As a Dogon proverb puts it: 'For the child, the mother is worth more than the father.' A particularly intimate relationship is established between the mistress of ceremonies of the Chisungu female intitiation rites and the Bemba girls who have passed through her hands. She will function as godmother and midwife to these 'daughters', and may even receive their confessions when they are in childbirth. Her role is not only that of protector, but one of teacher as well: she gives guidance on child care, she may punish the young woman, and it is to her that questions about sexual life may be addressed. In this her function is opposed to and complementary to the mother's, for the latter is uneasy about mentioning such things to her daughter, and her attitude is predominantly one of leniency. [28]

4. THE FATHER AND FATHERS

If the pre-eminence of the maternal role is incontestable during the whole of early childhood, the subsequent role filled by the father is in general more varied and more difficult to define. This situation is explained by the fact that the paternal universe is entirely cultural, while the maternal universe rests on functions which are rooted more deeply in nature.

If the mother is perceived as the one who produces and transforms food, the father, on the contrary, is seen as the one who controls and distributes it, first in a raw state to his wives, then in a prepared state to the members of the family and to visitors. The ideal aspired to by every Bantu boy is to reach a social status in which the abundance of food will allow him to eat to his satiety every day and to distribute it liberally. The traditional chief, in particular, is referred to as the 'father' of the people and the one who 'nourishes' and 'nurses' his people. In many languages, 'father' also denotes 'master, owner'. Given the strict division of labour, the father, or at least one of his substitutes, has a moral obligation to participate in educating the young man, for only he can undertake training into matters related to the male world. Among the Fulani of Gwandu, the boy becomes economically productive at the age of seven, and remains under the absolute authority of his father until he is about fourteen or fifteen. [29] The young Bantu, as described by A. Richards, is dependent on his father not only for food, but also for the payment of bridewealth and the establishment of his own herd—in a word, for all that is socially valuable and assures a good start in life. Most often, the father is kept away from the birth and from the baby at the early stage; many traditions forbid him to touch or even to see it. But even within a given ethnic group the conduct of the father is not as easy to describe as a coherent whole as is the case with the mother. Depending on the individual, the father can sometimes manifest utter indifference, and sometimes great love and attachment towards the male child, openly showing his tenderness, taking him in his arms, and hearkening to his every word. During early childhood, generally speaking, he has no customary educative functions as such. With regard to the female child, the father will almost remain a stranger, as there are many rules which limit or forbid their contact and mutual expression of sentiments. The female child has first to find her niche among her peers before she can establish solid relations with the paternal figure.

Be that as it may, one should avoid one mistake: even where the father is physically far from the child, he will be surprisingly close through the conversations of the mother who never ceases to talk to the child in the 'name of the father'. This is no doubt due to the fact that the paternal figures enjoy great symbolic importance. Besides the personality of the father it is the paternal function which has a determinant influence on the formation of the child's personality.

However, as the child grows, the educative role of the father becomes more and more important, and at the level of responsibility, he always appears to take a place second to none even in a matrilineal society. Since, in the latter, a man's children do not belong to his own lineage but to that of the mother (unless she is a 'slave', as is the case among the Kongo), it is the male parent who is closest to them by blood (in principle the maternal uncle) who is the chief holder of authority in their regard. In matrilineal clans, a young man is conscious of being a stranger in his father's lineage, and he knows that regardless of age he can, in case of need, always find in the maternal kinship group another home ready to receive him. But the fact that fathers are always preoccupied with the health of their children, and will leave no stone unturned if the latter fall sick—and this for the fear of being accused by the members on the maternal side of neglecting them or of 'eating their heart'—shows that it is on them that the essential responsibility of education, the safeguard and protection of the children against any malevolent action, devolves.

Whatever the case, the bonds which unite an individual with his father bear a close relationship with those that unite him to his maternal uncle. According to the classical model, the father-son relationship in a patrilineal society contains an element of tension and hostility, whereas the nephew-uncle relationship is warm and tender. In the case of a matrilineal society, the relations are reversed.

Let us now examine a few cases of paternal attitudes. Among the Dogon, the boys come under the rule of the male family members as soon as they are weaned. Fathers take their sons to work and to the communal house. [30] As the boys grow, the learning of characteristically male activities multiplies, and the men strive to keep them from feminine influences which would hinder them from becoming manly. Particularly at the time of the second dentition, the boys are forbidden to play with girls, to eat with their mothers, or to be around where food is being prepared. [31] Their food is purposely reduced so that left to themselves and to their hunger, they will be obliged, through their enterprise and self-reliance, to procure themselves the additional food which they require.

During initiation among the Yondo of Sara, the role of the father is paramount: he decides when his son is mature enough to take part in it, chooses the man who will look after him and gives the initiate a new name in which he expresses the thought most dear to him. [32] Swazi children are taught to consider their father as the legal and economic authority. One can hardly exaggerate the extent of a son's obsequiousness in dealings with his father. They work for him, consult him in all things, speak of him as 'chief', and swear by his name. From early childhood these youngsters learn to obey their father, and even married sons never consider themselves free of his authority. As long as they live in their father's house, they are supposed to turn over to him whatever they earn. For their part, the fathers must provide the cattle and goats necessary for their sons to procure their first wives, they must make sacrifice in their names, and be responsible to the courts for any faults committed by the sons while they are living with them. [33]

The rights of succession are not always connected with primogeniture. Among the Nyarwanda and the Rundi it is the son chosen by the father at about the age of fifteen who is made the future head of the household. The childhood period is thus passed with latent rivalry among the brothers. Once the decision is known the resignation of the other sons is only apparent. The Tutsi father, especially, seems a distant and unpredictable power.[34] Among the neighbouring Bemba, where a strict application of primogeniture renders impossible any favouritism, the father appears as one on whom affection can be conferred. The case of his substitute, the oldest brother, will be the same, since he will have been spared the rivalries, and will naturally assume the father's role. Among the Tallensi, only those who have the status of father enjoy juridical and ritual authority. But as long as the father is alive the oldest brother, who represents all his brothers, cannot enjoy any prerogatives or sacrifice to the ancestors.

Through the control which he exercises, and the state of dependency in which he keeps his sons, the 'father', in the widest sense of the term, inevitably arouses sentiments of revolt among them. It seems that various societies are perfectly aware of the rivalry this situation creates, and in spite of the outward filial piety expected of the young men, opposition and suppressed sentiments of hostility can develop among them. The dispositions of custom, however, seek to forestall and neutralize these negative and competitive attitudes of the sons against the father.

Among the Tallensi, a man cannot eat with his first-born son or daughter. The aim of this prohibition is to maintain the distance between them. This prohibition and others like it will be broken solemnly at the end of the ceremonies which mark the father's funeral, when the son inherits his father's powers. But, as long as the father is alive, the son has only limited possibilities in a subsistence economy. The rites and myths which express these typical Oedipal sentiments constitute so many social mechanisms which at one and the same time help to neutralize them and make them culturally productive. The revolt felt by the son cannot come to the surface, as it would touch the very roots of existence.[35]

5. THE MATERNAL UNCLE

Whatever the type of family, the maternal uncle nearly always plays an important role. Very early the child finds himself caught between two poles of attraction—the paternal lineage and the maternal lineage—of which the father and uncle are respectively the representatives and carriers of authority with respect to the child.

Among the Serere people, the child soon finds himself being pulled between the paternal and maternal lineages. But, as H. Gravrand writes, at first sight, the greatest importance is accorded the maternal lineage, and that is why the Serere society can be described as matrilineal. However, taking other elements into account, this society would be better termed bilineal, the maternal lineage predominating. This double belonging no doubt engenders conflicts of authority and multiple tensions. The personality of the father can be so strong as to make the maternal uncle count but little. In case of conflict between the father and the mother's brother, it is the one with the greater dynamism and support who will finally carry the day. The primacy of the uncle is counterbalanced to a certain measure by the control that his nephew can exercise over him; for the latter will inherit from him and he has therefore to make sure that his cousins do not squander his substance before his uncle's death. The internal conflicts of lineage are always ready to explode, and sometimes they do so openly, but there do exist adequate pyschological ways and means of discharging them.[36]

Among the matrilineal Kongo, the triangular father-mother-child constellation often offers only a reduced unity and intimacy. The father's educative authority is tempered by the possibility that the children have of appealing to their maternal uncle. The child is thus made to oscillate between two poles, and this enables him to exercise, if need be, a real blackmail, to play on sentiments, and thus to escape in the extreme case from any true authority.[37] Experience shows that in a matrilineal society a father can still have tremendous influence over his children. Among the Bushoong, for example, the father displays his children to everyone and boasts of their merits. Later, he will reward their every success at school or in hunting with a present. As for the children themselves, they exaggerate their father's qualitites, excuse his faults, show him everything they make, and always ask for his advice. But for all that the sentiments which unite them are not strongly expressed outwardly. The reserve and distance are greater in the case of the daughter, but even there, the attitudes are quite positive. It is for this reason that Vansina has described the Bushoong as a 'daddy's boy' society, even though, legally, the father has only a modicum of authority over his children, and has only one way of penalizing their bad conduct: a curse. As for the relation between the maternal uncle and nephew, it seems to be founded on a reciprocal envy; attempts at bewitchment are supposed to be frequent, and it is the father who defends the child in case of quarrels with his uncles. It is not, therefore, surprising that the son prefers to stay with his father whom he esteems and towards whom he feels a complete loyalty, even though he knows that he will never inherit from him.[38]

In the Tonga country, the young fathers play with their children and sometimes allow small boys to join in their meals even when they are only four or five. The fathers are not at all strict with the sons except when it is a question of taking care of the animals. On the other hand, they deal with their daughters only through their wives, especially as regards sexual matters. The mother has warm and close relations with the daughters, whose confidant she is. However, the mother is a stranger to her sons, who work and live with the men. In this society—which is predominantly matrilineal—the paternal side is represented by a well-defined figure—the father—to whom one addresses oneself in a personal way. The relations with the maternal side are, however, more diffuse. Conflicts of belonging are nurtured among the children, the father fearing their being drawn too much to the people on the maternal side, and he sometimes tries to stop them from making visits there.[39]

Despite the position of authority that the maternal uncle occupies, he intervenes only rarely in the education of his nephew. He is essentially an ambiguous figure: he can either act as the one who extends the sentiments of the mother, or the one who has authority over her. Maternal uncle and nephew are consanguines par excellence, being physically interdependent to a very high degree. There exists a belief that the blood shed by the son of one's sister puts the individual in danger, so that the boy can not be circumcised or have his ears pierced without the authorization of his uncle.* Similarly, the curse uttered by the maternal uncle is particularly dreaded.[40]

The following expressions regarding the uncle have been collected from among the Kongo and Teke youths:

—Maternal uncles are as gentle as mothers;
—They are loved because they are of the same blood as the mother;
—They represent for children a second mother and a second father;
—Children love the maternal uncle because he is the first or second mother (depending on their age) who has the misfortune of being born a man;
—The maternal uncle loves his nephew; the nephew is almost like his child;
—Certain uncles have the same feelings of tenderness and sentiments as the mother; they treat their sister's children better than their own fathers treat them.

However, one-third of the youths interviewed in Brazzaville stressed the disagreeable qualities of the avuncular figure:

—Children don't always love their uncles because most of them are wicked and stingy, preferring to satisfy their sons' tastes rather than those of their nephews;
—As the head of the family, the uncle is often avaricious, and he is generally thought to be a sorcerer; consequently, the children fear him;

*This was exactly the case among the Gikuyu of Kenya, where the uncle demanded a goat as a condition for granting the permission in question.—Transl.

—Rarely does one love his uncle, for he appears to be severe, evil and unpardoning.

In patrilineal societies such as the Kissi of Guinea, the child derives all his legal existence from the fact of his belonging to the paternal kinship group. However, it is his uncle who will give him his first dog, his first hen, the first land that he will be allowed to cultivate—all things which will elicit in the boy the joy of possessing something of his own. Among the patrilineal Bambara, the maternal uncle has the function of compensating for paternal severity, complimenting the child, lavishing gifts on him, and giving him advice with mildness and kindness, free from the rivalry underlying the father-son relationship.[41]

In a patrilineal society, therefore, the relatives on the mother's side do not confer any advantages or legal rights; but, at the same time, they do not enter into competition with the individual. On the contrary, it is with them that an individual can give free reign to his emotions. The only type of sanctions they can impose are ritual or moral, not legal. However, L. de Heusch has classified the characteristics of this structure into three categories: one egalitarian, where relations of familiarity prevail; and two asymmetrical types, one where the nephew either enjoys such privileges that he becomes in a way superior to his uncle; the other where, on the contrary, he recognizes the superiority of his uncle. De Heusch has shown that in a matrilineal, just as much as in a patrilineal society, the elementary social cell is the same. Without ever eliminating completely the paternal function, matrilineal societies at a given time bring about the transfer of authority from the father to the uncle—these two being holders of symmetrical positions with respect to the child and the mother, and both constituting obstacles to their intimacy. In a matrilineal society, however, the relationship with the father is never quite free from rigidity, and that is why one never finds in it the perfect relationship of relaxation or of affection that one often finds between the nephew and the maternal uncle in a patrilineal society.[42]

6. THE GRANDPARENTS

In every society grandparents appear as important educative agents in the domains which do not bear directly on productive activity. They play a positive role—even a primordial one—on the level of social integration. They serve as a link between the past and the present. It is often in their homes that the child goes to reside after he is weaned or when at four years old 'he begins to notice things and to ask questions about them.'[43] When this happens, he is considered to be too big to continue sleeping in his mother's hut. It is the grandmother who is often most competent in treating the child when he gets sick. Quite often among the Gikuyu, children used to spend more time with their grandparents than with the parents, and it was not rare that they refused to go back home.[44] The home of the grandparents serves as a possible place of refuge and protection, and it is with them that the children have the best taste of affection, tenderness, indulgence, confidence, security, and liberty.*

With regard to the generation of parents which stands at the centre of the social system and which constitutes by its fertility the essential pole around which the cycle of life is organized, those of grandparents and grandchildren occupy a symmetrical position, more marginal, the latter having hardly left the other world, and the former getting ready to return there. One notices that in opposition to the relation which unites a child to his parents, his relations with his grandparents are characterized by a sort of equality, connivance, tacit alliance, frank talk, and an urge to make jokes. For the Gikuyu, they belong symbolically to the same age-group, and ritually they stand on the same footing.[45]

Among the Kissi, the grandfather-grandson identification is still more accentuated by the fact that the latter is given the name of his paternal grandfather, and thus symbolically assured his survival.[46] ** Among the Ambo it appears that the child is told: 'Go and play with your grand-mother.'

Asked about their sentiments towards their grandparents, the youth of Brazzaville gave the following answers:

—My heart bleeds with good stories from her;
—I experience a feeling of debt towards them;
—A certain feeling of indescribable joy wells up in me;
—I relive the beautiful evenings of the dry season with my grandparents.

7. CONCLUSION

From the description of family life in the traditional African environment, one can infer apparently contradictory statements. Taken individually the child—and to a much greater extent the group of children—enjoys a freedom and an independence of conduct and of movement which are remarkable. One certainly notices an astonishing freedom, but this should not make one forget the enormous constraint that the child undergoes.

*It is perhaps for this reason that the children raised at the grandparents' among the Gikuyu seemed to be quite spoilt.—Transl.

**Among the Gikuyu, this is easily explainable. In that society, traditionally and now, naming children is strictly based on lineage. Thus, the first-born son will bear the name of his grandfather on the paternal side; and if a girl, that of the grandmother, also on the paternal side. Because of this, the grandparents and the grandchildren consider themselves 'spouses'. Hence, the familiarity between the two generations.—Transl.

He finds himself steeped in the kinship group but without the nuclear family losing its rights. If it is easy for him to avoid particular figures, certain adults (his relations and others) still exercise considerable control over him.

5

Horizontal Integration
in the Society of Equals

Once weaned, the child is not only plunged into a considerably enlarged world of adults, but he is also entering progressively into the society of equals made up of small groups or bands which will later become real institutionalized age fraternities playing an important role in education and in all traditional life. It is to the modalities of this horizontal type of integratin that we are going to devote this chapter.

1. FROM THE PEER GROUP TO THE AGE-GROUP

Very early, all the children of a village or a neighbourhood intermingle. Individualities co-exist; activities are at first parallel; then, little by little, they begin to intersect. Finally, with a rapidly acquired maturity, they become common to all. Within the society of children there is thus set up a kind of mutual education which operates more or less outside the adult world. Without exaggeration, one can see in that society the preponderant factor of socialization in a traditional environment. Character traits which show that the child fits into the group are encouraged, and it is worrying if he keeps to himself or shows no interest in common activities.

Already before weaning, the mother is assisted in the care of the young by older children, especially big sisters, and by the small girls of the neighbourhood. The smallest children are always surrounded and carried about by those who precede them immediately in age. Sometimes, as among the Ngoni, 'day care centres' are organized at the village level. These centres are under the supervision of old women who oversee all these young girls, more or less recognized 'nurses'. The importance of the relationship which is thus established between an older child and a younger one emerges when it is seen as a form of intermediate relation meant to prepare for the transition from the vertical to the horizontal axis of integration. The responsibility of the older child is real. He gets used to having to account to an adult for all that happens, and he is reprimanded for the least incident. The younger children look to him for assistance and protection, and in return he has a right to their obedience and service. He can, if need be, inflict punishment on them. From a relationship constituted exclusively of tenderness and attention at the beginning, one passes very quickly to the more complex relationships where, certainly, these sentiments remain fundamental, but where they are modified by rights and duties inherent in the age hierarchy, and by the tensions which inevitably arise.

Like the family society, that of peers is also built on the principle of subordination of the younger children to the older ones. Age connotes knowledge and authority. It regulates social obligations and the norms which govern the style of greeting, dressing, eating, comporting oneself in public and participating in rites. Within the society of children, age introduces strict differences even to the point of forbidding one age-set from playing with another age-set, for example. Often, the older child is for the younger one the most absolute master against whom he has neither right nor recourse of any kind.[1]

As the child advances in age, his life becomes enmeshed with that of the peer group where he will often have the experience of taking part in games, rites and common tasks. From his immediate seniors the child will learn much more than from his parents. As soon as he is severed from adults, the child will have to correct certain attitudes of obstinacy, caprice or domination left over from his early childhood. To get himself accepted and to gain the esteem of the others, the child must learn to make concessions and to forego certain things which his mother would allow, but which would prejudice him vis-à-vis the other children. This initiation into the collective life is often slow, even painful, particularly in cases where he has not yet recovered from the weaning trauma.

In a society, the more the models which arise from the system of age-sets are emphasized, the earlier the child is drawn into the horizontal types of organization. It is thus that from the age of five, the young Ngoni are strongly integrated in the society of boys of their own category. They become independent in their choice of games and occupations. The indication that they have received a correct education is that they are capable, by the time they get their permanent teeth, of going to live in a common dormitory, away from their parents.[2] The young Fulani described by Saikhou Balde begin to organize themselves into *yirde* from the age of four or five.[3] As K. Weule has said: 'Among the populations around Stanley-Pool, the boy leaves the women's house early in life and goes to join the other boys. They live in a common house, gather their own firewood from the forest, and cook their own meals.[4] In contrast, it is noted that among the Chiga of Uganda or the Kissi of Guinea, children remain with adults until the age of five or six, and they are not even entrusted to older children before that age.[5] Going to stay with other members of the family after weaning often constitutes a transition between the maternal house and the common dormitory. Thus among the Ambo the boys between the ages of four and eight sleep at their grandparents'. Then they go to live in dormitories in groups of two to five to a hut.[6] In an age-set group organized into a real educational institution, the child finds a different environment from that of the family, an environment where learning about social life can take place outside the too narrow ties of affection, belonging, and dependence. In the atmosphere which he breathes there is contained in germinal form that which will characterize his public life as an adult.

2. FROM CLASS TO AGE FRATERNITY

As J. Ki-Zerbo writes: 'Black African society is essentially an initiation society of age-sets, of the successive preparations and integrations of one generation after another.'[7] In fact, in a cultural context where each stage of growth corresponds to a particularly clearly defined status, where the transitions are marked by rites, and where the principle of seniority determines in an important way the organization of the groups, one can expect that the bonds uniting the members who, by their degree of seniority, occupy an identical position vis-à-vis the society as a whole, will be held in great esteem. A system becomes established within which individuals of the same age category come to have a recognized place. Schurtz, the first to show the great importance of these forms of organization, saw in them an attempt to contain sexual life by seeing that the times when sex is freely indulged in are followed by others when it is strictly regulated. Frobenius explains these forms of organization by the very diversity of stages through which the life of the spirit necessarily passes.[8]

The division into age-sets and fraternities tends to structure the whole social body, including the world of children and of young people, eliciting at each level appropriate traditions. The object of this division is to engender between contemporaries and peers a spirit of equality and attachment born of the same common formation and needing to express itself through a mutual confidence and through the obligation of mutual assistance. To the most immediate natural associations—such as those due to consanguinity—are opposed classes based on age.[9] As the groups of relatives are structured according to a vertical pattern, while the age-groups follow a horizontal model, it turns out that the contrast of the two structures is expressed by a real opposition between two axes, the one counterbalancing the other, until they finally arrive at a more or less harmonious equilibrium. Through family ties an individual finds himself joined to people of different generations within the framework of a limited social unity. Through the ties woven by the age fraternity, he enters into relationships with peers in a larger geographical area: the village, region, and ethnic group.[10]

The phenomenon of the age-set and the institutions which derive from them are, in general, more important for boys and men than for girls and women. In virilocal regimes, the boys constitute the element of the population destined to remain on the spot, to take root, and to constitute the stable part of lineages and clans. The girls are destined for exchange, for sealing alliances between two families, thus to disperse far from their original environment and their childhood companions. The bonds of fraternity cultivated during youth have, for men, an important functional significance during the rest of their lives, whereas this is rare among women. In general, the boys enjoy the freedom of coming together and playing common games—a privilege not enjoyed by girls who are more tied to the house and to domestic chores. While still in paternal villages, girls must begin to prepare themselves for the role of strangers.

Where age categories are clearly delimited, a person is subjected to an inevitable discontinuity during his life, since the society expects him to change his conduct each time he changes his status. Even though age fraternities aim at levelling off the inequalities created by clan, caste, or class cleavages, this egalitarian tendency cannot work fully where societies are organized according to social statuses. The young nobles receive a special education in their princely courts. In South Africa, initiations are often scheduled when one of the sons of the chief reaches the age to be' initiated, and he plays a special role in the ceremony. During his youth, he will certainly participate in common games, but the others will treat him with special respect.

Organization into age groups can bring about a truly communal life led within special institutions: common dormitories, youth houses, associations, 'clubs', and temporary villages. Very often these institutions lose their *raison d'être* at the time of marriage, but they can continue as political, military, or initiation regroupings. These create the most fully developed fusion of minds and wills. It is rare that they serve as a basis—as they do among the Nyakyusa—for the building of the society as a whole. Their educational significance can hardly be overestimated. Senghor says that the age fraternity is essentially a school for citizenship, that the education given and the discipline which reigns there ensure the cohesion of Black African society.[11]

3. THE INCIDENCE OF SOCIETIES OF CHILDREN

While age categories are found everywhere, and play an important role as a principle of social division, organized age-groups—and especially fraternities—are not universal, and vary from society to society.

In the case of the Nyakyusa, the boys graze their fathers' cattle between the ages of six and eleven, during which time they reside with their parents. Children of from five to ten families are found together in the pasture land for several years. They choose a leader and make rules for governing their life. One finds there the nucleus of a future village community founded on the criterion of age. At around the age of eleven, two changes take place:

they leave the animals in the care of younger boys in order to devote themselves to agriculture; at the same time they leave their fathers' houses and go to start a new village.

In fact, when the number of children in a village of married men becomes large enough, the children receive from their fathers the necessary land for constructing new huts. These are built on the fringes of the adult world. In the beginning several live in the same cabin, but as they grow older these cabins are transformed into individual dwelling places. By and by, the younger boys go to join their seniors in the new village. While awaiting marriage, each boy works for his parents and continues to eat in the parents' house. Economically, the young man belongs to the old village; socially, to the new one. When the older boys get to be between sixteen and eighteen years old, they begin to resent the coming of young boys to join them, and the latter in turn start a new village of their own.[12] We are here faced with an extreme case where the division according to age leads to a social and spatial segregation.

Quite different in character is the boys' dormitory among the Ngoni of Nyasaland [now Malawi]. Such dormitories are found within the village community, but they remove the boys from the influence of women, starting at the second dentition.[13] The transition is abrupt, comparable to that of weaning, and often brings about a considerable loss of weight. All those of the same age are mixed and made equal, whatever their social origin. Age and power are the only criteria allowing a ringleader to impose his authority over his companions. Collective life must teach the boys how to conduct themselves with their equals and superiors. The younger serve the older, and do chores for them such as collecting firewood and fetching water. They receive hard treatment and are threatened with blows if ever they reveal what goes on in the common shack. The taking of cold baths is assiduously practised. Food is brought to them from their parents' homes and left at the enclosure, just as for grown men. The youngest members have to be content with the food left over by their big brothers. Driven by hunger they drink the milk taken from the livestock, hunt birds and lizards, and go marauding in the village in search of maize or nuts, running the risk of being severely punished. This very spartan type of life was of military origin. Later, the common life came to be organized and perpetuated around the keeping of flocks. It constitutes an excellent factor for social equalization. There, the boys are expected to learn the art of commanding, and to acquire a sense of responsibility, and of respect for authority. The older boys are the heroes and guides of the younger ones, and seek to maintain their reputation by exploits at the dance or at stick battles. This sport helps to reveal the potential leader, and a Ngoni young man never parts with his stick even when going to school. It sometimes happens that small boys gang up in order to resist the exploitation and bullying of the older boys. To enter the communal hut, where the seating arrangements reflect social rank and the subjects of conversation are those of grown men, is for the Ngoni youth tantamount to entering the world of men.

The treatment of girls is quite different. While at the stage of second dentition the Ngoni boy leaves the family house to go to spend his nights in a common dormitory, the Ngoni girl goes to live with her grandmother or with a widowed aunt. However, she will continue to work and eat at her mother's house unless the latter has a reputation for being a bad housekeeper, or for having a bad character which might affect the bride price which the girl's marriage may fetch. During her late childhood her life is characterized by a greater responsibility and a more or less absolute separation from boys. She is confined to a world, an atmosphere and a set of tasks which are exclusively feminine. She is brought up under the constant gaze of her paternal grandmother while at the same time being chaperoned by a slightly older girl, specially chosen. [14]

It can be said generally that among pastoral and semi-pastoral people, an important part of education takes place during the keeping of flocks—customarily reserved for the young lads who are under the authority of older boys. This activity gives them a keen sense of accomplishment in the work of the group. The concrete task which falls to them is theirs exclusively, and custom does not allow any other person to discharge it; this task puts them in a world apart. It is on the grazing pastures that the boys feel at home in each other's company.

According to O. Raum, the society of children among the Chagga is basically perfectly 'democratic' in the sense that all enter it with an equal chance of becoming the leader. The status of the parents does not count, only the boy's personal qualities. The competitive games help leaders to reveal themselves. The latter will have considerable, but by no means final, power on the grazing fields. The struggles for influence among personalities are frequent and bitter.

Among the Bambara, the society of the uncircumcised has a strongly initiatory character. The children are gathered around common, ritually functional tasks, all within a strongly structured organization, with its own officers, emblems, feasts, collective fields, traditions, and internal hierarchies. [15] An analogous situation prevails in certain sections of the Fulani people. [16] Among the Dogon, too, there are common huts for the youth of the same village or quarter. [17] Among the Tonga and the Gikuyu—described by J. Junod and J. Kenyatta respectively—these huts serve as meeting places for the youth of both sexes, and for the development of their erotic life.

As for the Tallensi of Northern Ghana, the groups of children do not seem to have a permanent structure. Group formation, however, seems to be based on stable norms from the age of five or six, and they involve mostly brothers and half-brothers. One finds together children of six to nine years, then those of ten to eleven years, and finally those who are older than twelve. From the age of six, boys and girls separate completely; their occupations and interests differ, the former becoming young shepherds, the latter taking to household work. Children are seen quarrelling bitterly to determine who is the oldest, for the latter will be able to impose his authority firmly, if need be.[18]

In the same way, among the Gusii of Kenya who live in isolated dwellings, one finds only a few children's groups which are truly organized apart from brothers and sisters. Besides, the parents seek to minimize the power that the group could exercise, and maintain direct control over their children, especially by intervening in their quarrels. However, while out grazing, the boys succeed in organizing themselves in a more or less independent manner.[19]

At the level of children one does not find the subordination of one sex to the other. But sometimes one does encounter a deliberate segregation during late infancy and adolescence, as among the Ngoni. Quite often it is a question of *de facto* separation, of each sex following a mode of conduct which is different and complementary, adopting gestures and attitudes, especially the assumption of distinct jobs so that the meeting of the two sexes can only occur infrequently. When, among the Tonga, a child performs a task reserved for the other sex, one tends to ignore it so long as the child does not understand what he is doing. But if he continues to do the same thing even when he is older, he will be ridiculed. However, in the Katanga region there are games during which boys and girls build huts and live there as 'husband and wife', perfectly imitating adult behaviour.

It is amazing how traditional societies of children are able to reconcile two apparently contradictory characteristics in their organization. In the first place, a society of children functions practically without the intervention of the adults, and children are able to conduct in it a goodly part of their education. They make their own rules and traditions, and establish structures which are astonishing in terms of their stability and rigidity. Nothing is more conservative and ritualistic than such an environment; old customs and practices long since forgotten by grown-ups are perpetuated there fragmentarily by means of certain games; archaic formulas are kept alive by means of chants and jingles which are repeated with much seriousness even though nobody knows what they mean any more. But, on the other hand, children's organizations often exercise a genuine function within the global society, and are organically linked to the adult institutions. Children in these groups watch the older generations eagerly, and follow their activities at a distance by the games they play. These run parallel to the tasks and rituals of the adults, coming gradually, as if by osmosis, to join in them.

4 . SOCIETIES OF CHILDREN AND SEXUALITY

Sexuality has an important role to play in the life of children's and adolescents' societies. This role varies considerably according to cultures,
their hierarchy of values, their more or less permissive or restrictive
attitude in this respect; in short, according to the manner in which they
look upon the social relations between the sexes. This sexuality is, until the
time of marriage, of the type that R. Bastide has classified as libidinous,
freely obeying the pleasure principle and having no importance for the
group. This is in contrast to the socialized sexuality which later will be the
object of unremitting control.

With regard to the people of Rwanda and Burundi, Vincent describes the
following four stages of the evolution of infantile sexuality: (1) the mother
caresses the genital organs of the baby to pacify it; (2) when the child stops
sleeping in his parents' bed where he used to witness sexual intercourse,
he starts to engage in sexual games; (3) these games develop until they
simulate sexual relations among the young shepherds; (4) finally, one
notices among them an evolution towards masturbation and homosexuality
just before adolescence. Among the Tutsi, for example, homosexuality
among young warriors is considered a refined practice. The adults make
fun of these practices, but they certainly condone them. It has been noted:
'Parents will take pleasure in seeing their son engage in sexual games
with young girls, for that proves that he is normal, and that he will be
potent.'

Nobody worries about the sexual conduct of girls before puberty. But the
moment she can become pregnant she is no longer allowed to go out with
boys. With girls masturbation is almost obligatory; a girl who does not
masturbate becomes everybody's laughing-stock, and acquires the reputation of not being able to marry and to procreate. Stretching of the two labia
is considered necessary for increasing the sexual pleasure of the future
husband, for enlarging the vagina and thus facilitating delivery. Through
the imitation of older girls, a small girl begins very early, and enjoys
masturbation. Encouragement is usually given by grandmothers and
aunts.[20]

In the society of peers, everything is open, and nothing, no matter how
private, escapes the penetrating and inquisitive gaze of the age-mates.
J. van Wing relates how the pubescent discovers one day that he has
become a *mbuta*, an 'elder', a man capable of procreating. Far from being
upset, he is completely happy and proud. The following day all his companions will learn of the event. Even if he does not boast about it, they will
soon know of it, for they observe one another closely.[21]

Young people are often expected to learn about love without indulging in
complete sexual relations. Among certain Bantu groups, a girl would be
ridiculed if she did not have lovers, and she is taught how to avoid deflora-

tion. The girl's lover officially makes presents to her parents and goes to work for them side by side with the bride-to-be. Old women examine the girl periodically to ascertain whether she is till a virgin. If this is not so, public opinion is merciless and the lover must pay a heavy penalty. Among the Pondo, meetings take place in the girls' own houses. At the time of initiations, festivities are organized, and the hut of seclusion (in which a girl is kept for several months in order to make her fair-skinned and fatten her up) becomes a centre of attraction for the youths of both sexes who congregate there to sing, dance, and play erotic games.[22]

Among the Gikuyu of Kenya meetings take place in special houses.* Firstly, an evening party is held in which food is brought and eaten in common. Then couples participating in the love-play form in a very liberal and unselfish way. The young man takes off all his clothes while the girl keeps on only her lower garment, a kind of apron which she tucks in in such a way that she cannot be deflowered. Any young man who would try to take' off a girl's lower garment would be ostracized and find no other partner that night. The young people emphasize that this institution is designed to force young people to maintain control over themselves and their desires. It is the girl who chooses her partner, and she must be ready to change frequently, or she will be considered selfish and anti-social.[23]

During puberty among the Umbundu, the boys build themselves huts and there they practise trial marriage which, however, does not allow complete sexual intercourse, for virginity is very much valued. Among the Kissi, each boy has a *barafa* who renders him small services such as washing his linen. But, observes A. Schaeffner, they also spend the night 'under the same blanket', and any boy without a *barafa* is made fun of in the saying: 'Take a banana tree and sleep with it.'[24] The Bambara people have an institution called 'woman-friend' which, except by accident, does not go beyond the limits of comradeship: the boy pledges to watch attentively over his companion, and even feels responsible for safeguarding the virginity of the one he considers his sister. He regularly gives her gifts. Besides the small services she renders him in return, the young girl with her friends prepares the meals of the initiates during the feast of the *N'domo* society. These liaisons remain hidden from adults.[25]

Among Gikuyu youths, masturbation is considered a normal preparation for sexual life before initiation, but scoffed at thereafter. This practice takes place among competing boys outside the homestead, under a tree or bush where the boys are not visible to their elders. Girls are forbidden to masturbate. Homosexuality is said to be unknown among the Gikuyu.[26]

The young Gusii begin sexual activity at the age of fourteen or fifteen, but they very much fear being discovered by their parents. As interfemoral

*These houses are called *mathingira ma anake* which means 'young men's huts'.— Transl.

or partial coitus is not practised, the girls fear getting pregnant with all the implications that that entails. Even after marriage the girls put up a resistance—real or feigned.* Masturbation appears rare, and homosexuality non-existent, but bestiality is quite frequent and generally unchecked. One often changes partners, and in principle, young men do not like having sexual relations with the girls they are going to marry. In situations where boys are found together, homosexual practices are viewed with leniency. Among the Nyakyusa they become frequent during the herding period and continue until marriage.

In matters of juvenile sexuality the Ngoni are restrictive. The most stern prohibitions regarding children are those concerning all forms of sexual games among boys and girls. In order to avoid the probability of meeting, the formation of different play groups according to sex is encouraged. It is only during his military service that a young Ngoni is able to establish intimate relations with a girl who is not necessarily his fiancée: but he must not cause her to lose her virginity or, worse, impregnate her.[27]

It is therefore frequent that young people, even children, have early sexual experiences; this explains the low incidence of perversions. These juvenile sentimental adventures and romantic loves are, however, independent of marriage and only rarely lead to it. They find their place in the group life of the young and sometimes take the appearance of real institutions.

5. FORMS OF SOCIALIZATION

The education given within the age-group differs from that given in other educative environments in that children are not constrained to enter into set forms of life and social interactions. But, to a certain extent, the cells of community life create themselves and take consistency with the collaboration of and under the responsibility of the children themselves. [28] One can discern in these fraternities a nascent social order. This is a very different phenomenon from the European or African urban street gang, which also has laws and discipline, often quite Draconian. The traditional age fraternity is a completely *official* school of social life entirely integrated into the global structure. It does not present an asocial or marginal characteristic; quite the opposite, it is the very expression of the society and of its educative function.

In the ordinary activities, work or games, herding flocks, and even in initiation 'schools', the most strict control a child can undergo is that of older children. He must submit to their ragging, respect their authority and privileges, and in certain cases discharge for them the hardest and the most disagreeable tasks in order to allow them to play games whenever they

*For more about this see S. Monyenye, 'The indigenous education of the Abagusii people', thesis, University of Nairobi, 1979.—Transl.

like. The adults have hardly to interfere in order to impose on the young a discipline which is already quite heavy. Rather, it is in order to lighten that burden that one sometimes sees grown-ups intercede with older children on behalf of younger ones.[29] Where necessary, only the older children are punished by adults who know full well that the punishment will pass downwards and hierarchically, becoming more severe at each step. We have there, says Jensen-Krige in connection with the Lovedu, a principle of education which is of considerable importance: children learn more easily and more willingly from their peers than from adults. Each one of them knows that he too will enjoy the privilege which seniority confers—and will thus enjoy uncontested authority over the younger children.[30]

The functions which the dormitories of the young fulfil are related to those of initiation camps. This amounts to separating the boys from the family—and especially from the mother—and subjecting them to a purely male authority, bringing them to identify themselves with the horizontal group whose sympathy they must cultivate by fulfilling its duties and defending its rights. Adopting the ways of the age-group and thus showing that he belongs to it is accompanied by a feeling of pride. Once the boy becomes a member of the peer group—especially after the second dentition—he becomes in all his doings much less dependent on his parents than his European counterpart. The nicknames, which are an affair of the age-set and of the reciprocity between individuals of the same generation, create a kind of social personage proper to being with contemporaries, and which the individual generally abandons when he reorients himself to the vertical axis. One is not considered to be quite the same person in the two situations.

The Nyakyusa society with its system of age-groups which enjoy a certain independence within their own villages, puts at the summit of its system of values sociability, bonds of sympathy and mutual aid born of friendship. These manifest themselves particularly in the pleasure of eating, drinking, and chatting together. The conversations and discussions among equals are considered the principal forms of education. The youths teach one another and ceaselessly confront one another and compare themselves with someone else. One who lives alone cannot develop his eloquence nor acquire wisdom. But discussions are only thinkable among equals; they cannot take place between people of different generations or sexes. Hence the need for people of the same age to live together. Eating with one's father is absolutely incompatible with the respect that one owes him. From the age of six, when the boy begins to look after the animals, he is encouraged to invite the largest number of friends to the house for meals, and to go to eat at his friends' places. This custom is going to be followed throughout life. As for women, they either eat alone or with the younger children.

Already, during childhood, the choice of an intimate friend is of great importance in certain societies. One should recall in this respect that among adults extraordinarily close bonds of fraternity, often sealed with blood, can exist.[31] The young Ngoni chooses himself a companion with whom he is going to conclude a true pact of friendship. The young girl will also have a friend—a confidant with whom she will make bracelets or go to bathe.[32] In the initiation camp two young Chaggas can enter into a life-long friendship, after agreement between their respective fathers, by receiving together, without touching it, their food from the camp-tutor. He addresses them, saying:

> Now you must abandon your childhood . . . You must show that you are men and adopt in everything correct conduct. Remain together as perfect companions, as a man and his brother born of the same mother. You must not separate, but help and care mutually for one another as one does with his brother.

Three times a day they receive a few light blows with a thorny stick.[33]

6. AGE FRATERNITIES AND INITIATION

As educative environments, societies of children are intimately connected to initiations and rites. According to Senghor:

> Like any other social group in Black Africa, the age fraternity is first of all a religious order. One enters it as a novice and begins by submitting oneself to the initiation ceremonies. The latter, with their suggestive symbolism, have as their aim to make of the ignorant a man who knows; to turn infantile anarchy into organized freedom; death of childishness into birth of life.[34]

Initiation is a rite before being an instruction. In the passage to the state of social puberty it is more a question of incorporation or integration than of introduction into esoteric knowledge. More than to religious truths which will be revealed to them only slowly, it is to new social structures that the initiates have access.[35] Being born together into the adult condition is, for the members of the same 'brood', the supreme act by which their fraternity is consecrated, by which they will be 'twins' all their life. In these intensive stages an education of the vertical type that the adults exercise on the young intersects with the horizontal one that the young exercise on each other as a kind of final synthesis before acceding to the status which consecrates them as substantive persons. For men, in certain societies, this stage used to be extended by a period of military life. While awaiting marriage the young men and girls are going to participate in the life and activities proper to their age-group. This will enable them to transcend the narrow confines of the village group, and to widen their horizons to regional, tribal, ethnic, and even national dimensions.

Within the society of children there often develops a deep-rooted initiation spirit which in every respect resembles that which animates the corresponding adult institutions. It is expressed in rites and through secrets proper to the world of children. It is in this way that in the *N'domo* of the Bambara there exist five classes, each with its particular emblem, and the passage from one to the other takes place according to an initiation rite: faced with a sound coming from a mysterious-looking instrument the novice recognizes his ignorance; then, the secret connected with it is revealed to him. Each instrument is an emblem proper to the class which the novice will enter, and it is also related to the animal which represents the class.[36] One then proceeds to a certain number of symbolic gestures, pronouncing curses of death should the secret be revealed. All this is performed by children without any participation on the part of adults. Among the Bwa neither the parents nor the young people taken individually may decide when it is time for initiation and entry into adult life, but only those involved; in so far as they live in organized groups where common games, life and work are practised: that is what decides their readiness to live in society. The age-groups, says J. Capron, are the catalysts of the community life of the initiated, and the whole 'fraternal' existence takes place there. The mask of the Do people can only be prepared and used collectively.[37]

Generally speaking the male rite is more constraining and more collective than the female rite. In virilocal regimes, it is important that the solidarity which unites all the male individuals of the same class destined to live together the rest of their life should be affirmed, consolidated, and deeply felt by all at the moment of acceding to a new social status. 'The members of the same age-grade owe one another reciprocal loyalty and devotion; men circumcised at the same time are united to one another by bonds almost as strong as those of blood.'[38] Any strong emotion lived collectively hastens the process of socialization and establishes a new fraternity—that of a shared experience, and above all that of common suffering which will unite all those who have undergone and accepted it as if by the most solemn oath. One thus witnesses the dramatization of the solidarity of the masculine members of the group. The young men are put at the centre of attention of the group of men, and they are allowed to identify themselves with the group. From now on, the boys will not be found at the side of men, but among them. On the other hand, marriage will disperse the girls according to the exchanges entered into by families, and there will be nothing in their future life to unite them in a particular way. Their initiation will have a much more individualistic and private character. However, it does happen that rites unite both sexes. Among the Bwa, young boys and girls are united by initiation, and a complicated system of exchanging gifts and services takes place among those initiated together. The rite of passage reifies a whole age-set; it makes of it a 'thing' to be purified and transformed; it seeks to raise it to the level of a common destiny.

7. DOUBLE INTEGRATION INTO THE GROUP OF BROTHERS AND SISTERS

As in all relationships, those between brothers and their sisters are governed by rules from a very early age. The integration realized by the group of siblings is at the point of intersection between horizontal and vertical axes, which explains its unusual importance in traditional environments. Within the same family, one finds oneself among individuals of the same generation—and therefore among equals—and distinct from those of the preceding and succeeding generations. But, on the other hand, the principle of seniority is fully operative. In this connection, the linguistic usage is revealing: where the European child says: 'This is my brother or sister', the African will say: 'This is my junior and senior', without specifying the sex of the sibling in question. [39]

The vocabularies proper to the classificatory systems of parentage must not lead us to think that these extremely extensive designations exclude nuances. Very early on the siblings make the distinction between those born of the same mother and those who are not. Among the former, there exists a bond of intimacy and a unique solidarity. It is said among the Gikuyu that having slept in the same womb and suckled the same breasts, 'they are of the same flesh and blood, and must therefore be one in all things'.[40] Children of the same father but of different mothers among the Tonga will scarcely feel united even if they have been brought up together. On the other hand, those of the same mother experience a great attachment for one another, even if they have different fathers and have been raised separately.[41] It is not therefore surprising to find strong rivalries between children of different wives in a polygamous family. They take on the jealousies and quarrels of their respective mothers. But towards the father or towards any outsider this group of brothers and half-brothers rediscovers its unity and harmony..

Sometimes even before weaning, but especially after this decisive turning-point which brings the early childhood to a close, the bonds between brothers and sisters take on a new significance. The habit of leaving a child with a sibling while the mother is busy confers on the older children a keen sense of responsibility in the education of their younger brothers and sisters, marking the start of a relationship of great affective intensity which will last throughout life. Carrying a baby is a favourite chore among the Rwandese boys and girls of five to seven years. The pride and joy entailed more than compensates for the fatigue involved.[42]

Read observes that among the Ngoni there hardly exists any rivalry among siblings. The child always finds someone to cajole him, and he has no need to assert himself vis-à-vis his brothers and sisters. When, after weaning, he comes back to his mother from whom he has been separated, the latter gives him her time and attention. His affective needs are therefore satisfied, and between the older and younger children there generally exists a true climate of affection and a feeling of collective responsibility.[43]

Popular psychology has nevertheless revealed feelings of jealousy which, in spite of favourable conditions, often develop in the older child at the birth of another child. Different means have been used to contain them.[44] The Tonga think that the relations between successive siblings, whatever their sex, are marked by a certain hostility 'due to blood', i.e. to the frustrations of weaning. However, clearly positive bonds of affection will develop between the first and the third child of the same mother, and between the second and the fourth, etc., for the older child is mature enough to take care of the younger ones all day long.[45] Fraternal relations thus contain elements of tension which are going to keep on increasing as the children grow. The habitual preference of the father for the oldest child and of the mother for the youngest only accentuate the latent reciprocal jealousies and rivalries which could burst forth later on the occasion of a succession or inheritance.[46] In general, the relations between older girls and younger ones seem less ambiguous, and the dependence is more easily accepted, for the same interests are not at stake.[47]

. . . .

Many researchers have noticed that after marriage the verbal exchange between a man and his sister prevails over that between spouses. This tendency is more prevalent in matrilineal societies, for the privileged relationship which develops between brother and sister becomes the pivot of this system. It happens that the sister wields real authority in her brother's house by dint of her role of guardian and priestess. She is, say the Bushoong, just like the mother, 'the woman that God has given us'. As Richards notes, the Bemba adopt a particularly sentimental tone when speaking about these relations, a frequent theme in their folklore.[48]

Speaking generally, it appears that in the Black African system of relationship, the brother-brother axis is almost as important as the father-son or mother-son axis, and clearly more important than the husband-wife axis. This is shown by the rules of succession in the majority of socio-political functions.[49] The individual is seen as ontologically dependent on those who precede him in the lineage, but socially he feels affinity with his peers. Horizontally, men of the same generation enjoy great autonomy in their actions. Hence the importance of the associations which unite them, their meeting places and their common life, the work done collectively, group dances, and a reduced emphasis on the intimacy of private life, but also the rivalries and the spirit of competition engendered everywhere that individuals feel there is some kind of equality among them. The 'brothers' of one generation do not seek the company of those of another. On the contrary, it is sentiments of fear, distrust, and hostility which oppose fathers to sons, uncles to nephews, etc. The importance of the brother-brother axis brings about a discontinuity between generations and contributes to concentrating social life on the present.[50]

Myths refer to incestuous unions which took place long ago among the founders and ancestors of the group, as if the original concept of marriage was marked with the seal of brotherhood. It is the union of the gemellary couple which constitutes the most intimate form of endogamy. In the kinship nomenclature the confusion between the terms designating sister and wife is not infrequent.[51] L. de Heusch has shown how the affective power of the fraternal bond used to burst forth in many a ritual. In the Rwandese marriage the brother follows his sister up to the nuptial bed; it is he who must give permission before the couple can sleep together. That shows how difficult it is to resolve the infantile complex which joined him to her. In certain other societies the brother-sister pair is substituted for the conjugal couple in important social functions.

But above all it is in the opposition between patrilineal and matrilineal structures and their corresponding types of marriage that the great value of the fraternal bond is manifested. In a patrilineal system the sister becomes more integrated into her husband's group, and thus more remote from her brothers. In a matrilineal system, on the other hand, it is the group of brothers which remains dominant after marriage, since it retains 'property' rights and control over the sisters and their children even in the families of their husbands. This family structure 'accepts and uses ambiguous relationships for the construction of a kinship group, appealing to the man's deepest attachment, but devoid of erotic content'. Any such construction rests on the brother-sister link as a transposition of the maternal bond, and the dependence of the nephew on the uncle, which objectifies the intimacy between the brother and sister. In a patriliny, on the other hand, one accepts the risk of totally surrendering one's sisters to another and confiding the survival of one's lineage to strangers. This amounts to a definite break with the infantile model of security. The refusal of this more risky conception of exchange makes the matrilineal society a more hesitant one, prepared only to lend its women but not to give them away. This puts a stake on the emotional security which is conferred by confidence among siblings, the definitive attachment to the mother through the authority conceded to the brothers, and the firmer consolidation of affective situations. Thus, a matrilinear society seems to be founded on symbolic incestuous situations.[52]

6

Social Integration and Personality

The number and intensity of social bonds entailed by belonging to a lineage, family, fraternity, age-group; the way in which one is initiated into social life and is progressively integrated into a particular collectivity—all these have determinant effects on the personality of the child, which are implicitly sought after. To these we now turn our attention.

1. THE FORMATION OF THE SOCIAL EGO

As we have previously seen, the person is plunged into a group which at one and the same time is extended and closed, which is founded on the interplay of consanguinity and marriage, and within which there cannot exist an intermediate state between insiders and outsiders. The sentiments and attitudes towards those inside and those outside are clear-cut, and in this sense there cannot be any neutral relationships. Life, even in the hereafter, flows in a series of social formations outside of which it does not have meaning, and within which one can only live with the other, through the other, for the other, and in constant reference to the other. The whole of education aims at making an individual participate in the life of his group, and it is not conceivable that he should take his own destiny in hand. It suggests to him an ideal of conformity, interdependence and submission to the common will. A culture erected on the pre-eminence of collective life is naturally going to favour those aspects of education which are a preparation for, or are consequences of, it. Where the life of the group in its totality is seen as the provider of the security necessary to life and leaves but little room for an internalized and conscious personal life, or for the intimacy of the couple, the child enters into a world where it will be difficult for him to regard the other as an autonomous person. In the modern Western family the child finds himself in a close relationship with a restricted number of persons and directs at them all his impulses of love and hate, of dependence and rivalry; his feelings, positive or negative, are commonly very intensive. Confrontations take place at critical periods, and identification with a particular adult whom the young individual wants to resemble and dreams of replacing seems to be one of the indispensable mechanisms in his development. In the traditional African family, however, the child establishes relationships with a distinctly larger number of persons, but by the same token the relationships and feelings they engender are more diluted, less consistent, more relaxed and more diffuse.

The climate of instability in which the child's life often passes, the casualness with which the child is separated from its mother at weaning— these constitute very clear indices of a kind of emotional neutrality and a levelling. If the conflictual relations are diluted and drowned in the crowd, the same is true of the positive and structuring relations. Inasmuch as communication and interpretation are intense at the social level, so are they poor and superficial at the affective level. The relations with the other tend to be more functional than personal. It is inevitable that sentiments have only a weak tonality where the quantitative composition of the group goes beyond a certain threshold and where the psychological distance between different members becomes too great to allow a sustained exchange between persons and a differentiated perception of one another. But within the mode of socialization we are studying here, this affective neutrality is not without functions: it leads the child to feel that it is with his lineage in its totality that he must identify himself, and hasten his participation in this collective being. The group is no longer perceived as an entity composed of individuals; it overwhelms them and takes precedence. Different psychological mechanisms concur to bring about this result.

Where the emotional attachments with the other are relatively weak, but where the relations with the group appear very demanding, the child acquires the feeling that he has no right to live for himself, that in order to be loved and accepted, he must conform to what others expect of him. According to the terminology of William James, the 'real ego', with its will, desires, feelings, its personal values, its capacity of judging itself, does not develop at the same rhythm as the 'social ego' which is essentially constituted of the recognition and esteem that one obtains from one's peers. Social integration, therefore, takes precedence over personal integration.

Genetically, weaning appears as a decisive turning-point in the emergence of the social ego. In the maternal sphere, the child was accustomed to a parasitic relationship, exclusive and all-embracing, in which his need for security obtained an optimum satisfaction. But once weaned, no other figure in his entourage will allow the perpetuation of similar relations, and the brusqueness with which this change is effected leads to rather regressive attitudes. Normally, there develops a deep nostalgia for the maternal, universe, i.e. one which is closed and protective. This quest can find no other adequate object than the extended family in which the young person perceives quite quickly the possibilities which it offers him to develop the sentiments of belonging and security, thanks to the interdependence of all the members. No longer able to press physically against his mother's body, he now attaches himself psychologically to the great social matrix which is the lineage. But as soon as he feels cut off from it and comes face to face with himself, he will be bombarded with sentiments of insecurity, abandonment, and depression. In their study of the Dogon, Parin and Morgenthaler have shown that, once separated from the mother, the child goes to join the group of his playmates and identifies himself with it. The sentiments which are born out of the contact with the mother are transferred to the group. This happens all the more easily as the child has had several 'mothers' to take care of him.[1]

Traditional education shapes a personality which has need of the group, one which cannot exist by itself and stand the test of solitude. From her clinical studies, M.C. Ortigues has concluded that solitude is only rarely experienced as a time of peace and relaxation because it favours the emergence of aggressive fantasies, thereby causing an immediate depressive reaction. Unless they are looking for solitude to protect themselves against contacts which produce too much anxiety, young people all describe how they are irresistibly drawn to go with friends, how for them to 'feel good' is to be a part of a group or crowd. It usually matters little whether it is a sports meeting, dancing, or just chatting. The presence of others is necessary and reassuring, and it defuses onto the background any latent aggressive fantasies. Elsewhere it is said: 'The best thing in life is to be with friends. Their presence and approval are necessary for the feeling of being oneself and of doing well. You seek yourself in the image that others have of you.'[2]

Because it hems the individual in to rigid categories according to his position in society and his degree of maturity, because it relies by this very fact on the great moments of transition when the child passes from one category to another: weaning, second dentition, and puberty, traditional education subjects an individual to a treatment which, in certain respects, astonishes by its discontinuity. It is regulated by the law of all or nothing. For example, a child is treated like a baby who ought to receive everything until the moment when, suddenly and without warning, the totality of behaviour towards him takes quite another turn. This is because it is recognized, by certain signs, that he is about to enter another age category. In his study of the Ga people, M.J. Field insists much on the change of attitude which operates during the second infancy: children are treated with indulgence and affection; then, suddenly, they become the object of a kind of scorn and severity which is quite capricious. They are made to leave home in order to go to live with other members of the family where they are forced to do hard work and to eat food of bad quality. According to a current proverb, it is annoying to be a child.[3] These facts indicate that the child is perceived, identified, treated, and thought about less as an individual than a member of a social group.

2. THE OEDIPAL SITUATION

After having described the family context where the parental images are considerably multiplied and where one is more a child of a lineage than of a couple, we cannot pass in silence the problem of the Oedipus complex.

Certain myths describe this conflict with particular vividness. It is thus that among the Dogon, Yourougou, the Pale Fox, is the first being to appear in the world from the original placenta without the permission of Amma, his divine father. He takes with him a piece of this mother-placenta, which becomes the earth, and commits incest with it. He represents, in this revolt, the dark side of man, man a prey to his destructive instincts, a fallen humanity returned to animality through its own fault. As M.C. Ortigues writes: 'The Oedipus complex is universal in humanity since it defines the minimal conditions of human structure short of which there is only madness.'[4] In the study of any problem regarding depth psychology, one must take into account the two levels suggested by G. Roheim, that first, the child reacts to what his parents do—and here we touch on that aspect of education which is determined by culture, but, second, he reacts still more profoundly to his parents' unconscious, to which no culture can dictate its orders.[5]

A small child—regardless of sex—begins by first belonging to the feminine world: small girls and boys occupy with regard to the mother an identical position—at least until weaning. Then, very slowly, they are going to be led to situate themselves differently with regard to femininity. While the girls are called upon to grow up inside the world of women, the boys are expected to make a gradual transition to the world of men. In this connection we notice three great moments: (1) weaning, when the child is taken from its mother; (2) second dentition, which for the boy ushers in the learning of and participation in, masculine tasks, sometimes including going to live in common dormitories; (3) social puberty, especially where it is related to the rites of initiation which effect a radical separation from the world of women and being taken firmly in hand by the men. The boy becomes a man only by cutting himself off from his mother, by becoming a new being which no longer remembers its infantile state. On the other hand, the accession to femininity does not imply a similar detachment or reconversion.

It seems possible to make a comparison between the experience of weaning in an African child and the Oedipal situation as found in a European child. Both have to do with a critical moment in which the bond between the child and the mother is called upon to restructure itself, but the ways in which this takes place differ profoundly. The situation may be shown as follows:

Oedipal situation (Europe)	*Weaning experience (Black Africa)*
1. The child, who up till then has evolved in the maternal sphere within the house (symbol of	1. Until then, the child has evolved in a particularly protective maternal sphere. The father is a

security), feels attracted, as he progresses in his maturation, by the world of the father, outside the home, and a symbol of risk and adventure. Having reached this decisive turning-point, he hesitates in his choices. Then, normally—and whatever his sex—the scale tips to the parental side.

2. Thus, very gradually, the child takes his distance with respect to his mother in order to adopt the paternal universe and its values.

3. The active movement through which the maternal universe is transcended follows a predominantly sexual symbolism. He has either to opt for masculinity or femininity.

4. Once transcended, the Oedipal situation thrusts the child forward; it stimulates his impulses; the passage takes place in the manner of a conquest. The child seems like a hero ready to 'kill'.

5. This movement corresponds to a progress in the direction of personal autonomy, and therefore of a determinant value for Western man. Without this progress, all social adaptation is compromised.

distant personage who, for that very reason, cannot attract the child strongly. For external reasons which have no relation to the spontaneous psychological maturation of the child, the environment decides that it is now time to detach the child from its mother.

2. The child. living until then in a symbiotic relationship with the mother, suddenly finds himself thrown into a relational void, a .lonely, cold, empty world where no single figure attracts him decisively. The first attraction will not come from his father—who is still at the frontier of his field of perception—but from his mates and 'brothers'.

3. The movement (endured passively) through which the child finds himself cast outside the maternal universe, follows a predominantly oral symbolism: separation from the mother takes the form of food interdiction.

4. Weaning—this brutal and unprepared frustration—tends to immobilize the child in a regressive attitude of nostalgia with respect to what was for him a period of oral happiness. The child seems like a victim who is afraid to die.

5. This regression has the effect of thrusting the child into a sentiment of dependence which alone enables the traditional family system to survive 'and perpetuate itself.

On examining the orientation of the feelings of hostility in different cultural traditions, one notices that they are sometimes directed against the paternal figure, and sometimes against that of the sibling. The mother-child cohabitation, reinforced by the post-natal sexual interdiction, seems to intensify the Oedipus conflict by attaching the child very intimately to the mother. It is understandable that the child may perceive the father as a rival and that the father can, in an extreme situation, consider the child also as a rival.[6] The fear of castration seems to refer preferentially to the mother, and manifests itself by a deep fear of desertion. The resentment of the child against the father is directed at him, not as a progenitor, but as the holder of a role which frustrates him and takes him away from his mother.

M.J. Herskovits observes that in the Dahomean mythology, the theme of the son who kills his father is not explicit.[7] But, invariably, it is the father who starts the hostilities. It is the fear of being replaced by a descendant—a sentiment often springing from a supernatural revelation—which drives the father to expose or suppress his son. Similarly, the theme of fraternal rivalry abounds in Dahomean myths. The author relates this fact to the normal experience of the child who lives in a close relationship with his mother until the moment she knows she is pregnant again. His being made to play second fiddle is felt as a rejection and creates sentiments of hostility towards the younger child. When the boy himself grows up and becomes a father, he might manifest towards his son this fraternal rivalry in the form of jealousy. The childhood competition for the possession of the mother will be rekindled and transposed in terms of possession of the woman. The mythological themes of fathers killing their sons in order to avoid being replaced by them is thus explicable in terms of a competition between generations which is rooted in a childhood experience.[8]

But in this question one must go deeper still. Family authority in whatever form it exists, and whatever its power—that of the father or uncle, that of the leader of the lineage—is never more than derived authority, overflowing from all parts of the person of its carrier. The latter is no more than a point of insertion in the present world of a power which is located elsewhere. In Black African metaphysics, paternity is not reducible to a transitory act of procreation. The father is the channel through which the vital force which is the source of all things reaches the son; he is the intermediary between the child and God. He himself is endowed with vital force because he is closer to the source of life. To be father is not only to beget, but to continue to vivify, to fertilize, to lead towards plenitude; it is to transmit existence in a permanent way. To be son is to remain in a state of ontological dependence not only with regard to God, but also with regard to all the intermediaries through which life is communicated from Him to men. Paternity is extended in a sort of 'paternization' of continued incubation of the father's vital force over that of the son in order to maintain it actively in existence, to protect it, to defend it against nefarious influences, to make it prosperous. But the father depends on his ancestor as the son depends on him. The descendants of the same mythical ancestor function as so many condensers on the same energy circuit. But, exceptionally, they can also play the role of switch and cut off the current. This is what happens in the case of cursing.

Thus it is explained how an individual can never make himself autonomous with respect to his ancestors, that he ought to fear more than anything else rejection on the part of one of his parents. The latter is supposed not only to evict him from the social sphere but also to cut off the umbilical cord uniting him to his group and to the life of his lineage. Without this bond, without this participation, he can only waste away on the level of being itself, fall into nothingness, being of no account to anybody. This also explains why the most dreaded type of sorcery is the one which operates within the clan itself, among the people who are vitally united with one another. P. Tempels writes about Bantu philosophy that:

> Creatures keep a link among themselves, an intimate ontological relation, comparable to the link of causality which unites the creature to the Creator. The child, even the adult, will always remain for the Bantus a man, a force, a dependence, an ontological subordination to forces which are his father and mother. The 'elder' force always determines the 'younger' force; it continues to exercise its vital force on it.[9]

It is this force on the level of being which explains the extreme psychological importance of the person and of the image of the father as described by M.C. Ortigues in connection with the inhabitants of Dakar: 'In all the observed cases, even when it was a question of children raised by their maternal uncles, and even if the child had not known his father, in all cases, the reference to the father asserted itself in an explicit, central, and incontestable manner.'[10]

One can therefore say that on the one hand the paternal function is assumed by a whole lot of classificatory fathers and that, on the other hand, the image of earthly fathers whose life can be participated in hardly differs from that of the fathers of the other world who are united to them by the same current of vital force, and whose immanence, efficacious presence, and fertility are referable to the immediate evidence of the lived. As O. Mannoni writes, 'The European child knows that he replaces his father and that he will inherit all power. The Malagasy boy knows that this will never happen to him. The source of paternal power is lost in the night of time, without becoming weak with distance, but rather the contrary.'[11]

Given the condensation of the image of the father with that of the ancestors who represent authority and the social law; given that the visible father always refers to the invisible father, all rivalry with him is radically excluded and becomes impossible. The more the image of the father is compounded with that of the ancestors, the more intense appears the repression of aggressiveness in his regard. One does not fight with the dead. Mannoni compares the situation of the young Malagasy to that of an imaginary child who is supposed to live in a family where all money and all authority are supposed to belong to a grandfather stricken with paralysis, and unable to leave his bed. From what he hears, the child becomes aware of the respect and the importance given to this invisible paralytic, or at least one whom he can see only on solemn occasions.

Through twinklings of the eye difficult to interpret, the latter succeeds in making his desires known, desires which are executed punctually on pain of seeing the family go to ruin. The child is convinced that this situation will never end, and he sees all round him analogous situations such that in his eyes things cannot be otherwise. 'In such an environment, the child will have no desire nor any means of competing with such authority. It is not enough to say: "He will never succeed in forming the idea that he can one day have a will of his own and which is found only in him."'[12]

It is with the help of clinical studies in Senegal that M.C. Ortigues has been able to show how the image of the father as legislator and rival tends to be confused with the image of collective or ancestral authority, that it tends to be absorbed into that of the assembly of men seated under a tree, discussing village affairs, the symbol of the social law par excellence, of the cohesion and fecundity of the group. At the fantasy level, the Oedipal rivalry can certainly be directed towards the father, but everything happens as if a direct confrontation with this figure were impossible or pointless. The symbolic function of the father remains intimately connected with that of the ancestor; one can never consider oneself as being equal or superior to an ancestor.[13] On the other hand, sexuality and fecundity being more an affair of the group than of the individual, the right of accession to them does not imply that of being equal to the father. In the European context, the conflict between children and parents fulfils a function in the development of the person towards his autonomy. The individual becomes autonomous only when he is ready to take upon himself the 'death of the father'. In the African context there is no such thing. However, the sentiments and circumstances favourable to the bursting forth of the conflict are overwhelmingly present. M. Fortes has shown that among the Tallensi the status of the son is completely wrapped up in that of the father so long as the latter is alive, and that his effective death—and not simply the symbolic one—consitutes an important stage in the development of the young man by allowing him to exercise his juridical and ritual rights.

If the confrontation with the father is impossible and unthinkable, how will the individual find his place as a man in society? The research of M.C. Ortigues leads her to answer this question in the following manner:

The pattern that one seems generally able to discern is this: to the extent that the paternal figure is not open to rivalry, it is the brothers who become rivals. A quite distinct general tendency stands out: as one gets closer to the traditional environments, the father-son confrontation tends not to be expressed directly, but to be horizontally displaced onto the 'brothers' at the same time that the figure of the father tends to melt into that of the ancestors. The child must find his place in the hierarchy of brotherhoods and age-groups.[14]

The central point inherent in the family system and the metaphysics which supports it seems to be that identification with the group of brothers has the function of neutralizing the father-son conflict. Instead of impelling one towards affirming one's individual autonomy, the Oedipal situation resolves itself, on the one hand, through the cult of the ancestors, and on the other, through integration into the brotherhood and through initiations in which the solidarity of the brothers is confirmed.[15]

If the reference to the ancestor defuses the rivalry and aggressiveness of the son vis-a-vis the father, the opposite is also true since, in an ideological context where the ideas of reincarnation predominate, the father must, in a sense, respect in his child the resurgence of his grandfather. This reference represents what we have previously called the vertical axis which situates man in time not only with respect to those who have preceded him but also with respect to those who are going to follow him. One might therefore compare this reference to the force of tension which unites each element of a spiral spring with the point of suspension which supports the whole. But because this point represents an absolute—which is somehow outside the system—each ring of the spring, i.e., each generation, enjoys considerable autonomy. What counts for the child is the father, not as an individual, but as a depository of vital forces transmitted by the founding ancestor. But because this force is an absolute which cannot be localized, but gives meaning to the whole, an individual cannot orient himself with respect to it. In order to situate himself with respect to his neighbour, an individual has no other possibility but to have recourse to the horizontal axis. One is thus led to conclude that the vertical axis has an ontological significance while the horizontal one has an essentially social importance. The study of the Dogon people, for example, shows that incest represents a confusion of generations: there is a breakdown in the moral order when, instead of presenting themselves successively, generations become contemporary, encroach on one another and become mixed. Such seems to be the meaning of the myth of the Pale Fox.[16]

3. THE PERSON AND HIS IDENTITY

Socialization and the Oedipal situation lead us inexorably to a psychology of identity. A Swiss medical team using the 'psychoanalytic approach' to the study of Dogon personalities has revealed its full importance.[17] According to these authors the processes of identification provide the people concerned with more libidinal satisfaction than the aspirations turned towards object relations. They constitute for them the most certain protection against external and internal dangers and the conflicts arising therefrom. The 'social' ego of the Dogon is structured in orality; it displays astonishing qualities of flexibility and elasticity which appear in different social relations across a very wide range of modalities of identification. On the other hand, it is characterized by an autonomy of an oral type which only allows him to function in a state of affective relaxation. Now, in order to insure this relaxation in the object relation, the individual must remain constantly dependent on his entourage. At the most primitive level, F. Morgenthaler and P. Parin insist especially on the identification by incorporation. Among the different types of identification which they list, these authors first distinguish those with 'fathers and brothers', that is to say, incorporation into a hierarchical order.

> The individual will always be dependent at the same on a 'bigger' brother who protects him and to whom he is subjected; and on a 'smaller' brother who requires his protection and is dominated . . . In this paternal-fraternal line, no individual is equal to the other. Given that the fear of castration is displaced very early onto the mother, the people of authority among the Dogon are not seen as menacing fathers and castraters.[18]

The identification with companions of the same sex and age-group is of a different nature, for at this level there is equality. It is the class as a whole which plays the role of mother; within it the individual objects of identification are interchangeable, and it is the success of the group as a whole which determines the amount of satisfaction gained. The unstable character of the attachment of the individuals to one another eliminates the fear of losing the object and constitutes thereby a bulwark against the fear of separation inherited from weaning. The two forms of identification thus described are themselves interchangeable, so that the individual easily transforms a relation of equality into a different relationship, taking his peer as an 'older brother' or 'younger brother'.[19]

But beyond these psycho-social mechanisms it appears that at the very basis of education as conceived by the traditional society, one finds a process of identification. In a culture where the same personalities and names are expected to reappear from one generation to another, each new-born child must first be correctly identified. Afterwards, one has to see to it that he becomes, at the social and visible level, what he already is

in the intimacy of his being. The sentiment of identity which always constitutes the internal core of the person, and determines in it the perception of
the ego by providing it with some sort of self-definition, becomes intensified
even more where the individual is called upon to model himself on the
mythic figures who are nonetheless familiar to the group. In the final
analysis, one can say that education is only possible because, on entering
into the world, the individual encounters an environment which is already
familiar and where his place awaits him: all he has to do is recognize it and
get used to it again.

It is the same cultural model which leads the group to identify the
individual and which in turn impels the individual to identify himself
strongly with the group. When a collectivity forms a quasi-organic unity,
the person appears as a node of relationships, and his ego essentially
coincides with the bonds which unite him to the group. Where Western man
asks: 'Who am I?' and 'Who is so-and-so in his own eyes?' the traditional
African will ask: 'Who are the others?', 'Who am I in their eyes?' This
explains the great importance accorded to the social character and the
exterior signs which allow a man to situate himself and to be situated by
others, among others, and for others.

By all the elements which determine his identity—not only socially but
also ontologically—the person situates himself from birth to death in a
precise and differentiated manner within that network of relations which
unite him to the others—both visible and invisible. The problem of identity
and the crisis of personality as they manifest themselves in the form of
frantic outbursts are, by their frequency and nature, characteristic of
African psychopathology.

The biography of a man can itself be regarded as a series of changes of
identity, a sequence of social statuses, responsibilties, and rules which
modify at each instant the image that one has of oneself and of others.
H. Collomb writes:

> Within rigid statuses the society offers also an uninterrupted sequence
> of partial statuses all through life: the status of a boy of seven who is
> supposed to court a girl of five, the status of the wrestler, of the host, of
> the circumcised . . . The importance of status is reflected in an indirect
> way in the long and formalized greetings. These latter have the aim of
> situating the other in time and space, in the social and family system,
> and of giving him an identity by an alternating repetition of names which
> often runs on for several minutes.[20]

But these successive definitions of the individual by these social co-
ordinates can only lead to an integrated personality to the extent that the
self is founded on a sentiment of identity with itself all through life. If taken
in all its Platonic literalness, 'Become what you are' could be adopted as

the motto of African traditional education. It also approaches the opinion expressed by Einstein: 'I don't believe in education. Your only model must be yourself, no matter how frightening it may be.'

7

Learning of Facts and Skills*

The mistletoe of the cotton-tree
From one of the small cotton-trees
Which grows along the path of teaching
When you are ready to go for instruction
Say to your mother, say to your father
'It is difficult to bear a child
But to instruct him is even more difficult.'

—A Bambara circumcision song [1]

After having described how a child integrates himself into traditional society, we must now examine how he assimilates the knowledge and skills which are indispensable to him if he is to participate meaningfully in the tasks, in the preoccupations and in the satisfactions which it offers him. We shall see in succession how he situates himself with respect to his material and human environment, how he enters into the world of tools and of techniques, into that of custom and know-how, and, finally, into that immense and vast world of the spoken word and meaning.

1. MODES OF THE ACQUISITION OF KNOWLEDGE

In traditional environments, knowledge is considered as a specific entity, enjoying its own existence and endowed with a formidable power. 'The one who knows' always inspires fear, whatever the domain in which he exercises his knowledge.

Knowledge manifests itself in two principal forms. First, there is a type of knowledge open to all, and which is the object of an obligatory transmission. This insures that everyone participates in the general knowledge of society. Second, there are other forms of knowledge which are restricted to specialized circles. These may be professional as in the case of 'drug' preparation or connected with secrets of manufacture, or they may be connected with initiations as in the case of esoteric knowledge. The teaching given there is highly selective, and it is only communicated to individuals with the right qualities and in a particular social or family context. Everybody is not subjected to the same teaching; on the contrary, the instruction is highly individualized. But the common oral mode of trans-

*This material is from Chapter Eight, the original Chapter Seven having been omitted.—Transl.

81

mission from one person to another gives an authentically popular character to knowledge which does not require the medium of writing.

Among the people of the Niger Valley one finds—in a very elaborate form—a classification of knowledge. The Dogon, for example, speak of a 'front', a 'side', and a 'back' of a word.[2] Knowledge is thought of in terms of the binary categories of dark and bright, of heavy and light, of masculine and feminine. Like any other object—human or cosmic—it is subjected to a sexual dichotomy: when a Dogon man comes across women talking among themselves while spinning cotton, they immediately become silent. One can never quite understand either the nature or especially the extent of the knowledge which those of the other sex possess. Moreover, any knowledge which is outside of the common domain is automatically stamped with a secret character whether it is part of the religious domain or simply of that of science and technology. Since its mode of transmission necessarily becomes that of initiation, it is only communicated to those who seek it patiently. The holder of knowledge must hide it, publicly assert his ignorance, and preserve it from all undue exposure. In myths, knowledge is often represented as constituting an object of theft or of forced removal.

It is always important to examine how the acquisition of knowledge becomes integrated in the *curriculum vitae* of an individual. Among the Paranilotic (or 'Nilohamitic') Didingas, a boy is removed from the maternal influence at the age of eight in order to go and join a group which transcends clan divisions. There, he learns the dances, how to handle the spear, good manners, obedience to the elders, animal husbandry, knowledge of plants, of rituals and of beliefs. At thirteen, he receives from his elders an intensive education in agriculture, hunting, astronomy, and magic. When eighteen years old, he learns beekeeping, and he is also introduced in a deeper way into tribal law, especially in its bearing on sexual matters. Then before marriage and prior to being able to fully enjoy all his civic rights, the young man at one time owed a period of military service for about ten years in order to become proficient in the handling of arms.[3] Knowledge is acquired in stages, and these are connected with the important turning-points in the child's life.

Related more or less to the pedagogy of initiation, one sometimes would find modes of instruction which could go on for months, even years. In these cases it is possible to speak of true 'schools'. The content of this education varied considerably. But as a minimum it contained a set of rules for governing collective life, sexual life, and relations with the elders; it was also capable of conveying a literary, juridical, gnomic, esoteric, and oracular patrimony which gave life and charm to the tradition, a set of extremely coherent and diversified religious, cosmological, and moral speculations. On a properly religious level, the stages in the 'convents' of the Gulf of Benin are doubtless the most permanent institutions. For, in these sanctuaries, not only does the transmission of sacerdotal or divine knowledge take place, but also the most extraordinary transformation of the person.

Even if they are only of short durations, the inititations of the young may generally be compared to schools as true pedagogical institutions. They have a public character and take place according to a regular calendar. In them one witnesses the emergence of specialized educative functions whose holders are chosen outside of family and kinship considerations, and there is a codification of method and knowledge. The whole content of education previously acquired through various means is now confirmed, completed, and in some way standardized into a coherent system. What until now was only an object of occasional teaching, without any rigid rules, is explained and communicated in a solemn manner. At the time of circumcision, declares J. Kenyatta, children somehow learn the theoretical principles which they have been applying in their daily life.[4]

If forms of knowledge whose nature requires secrecy are transmitted in a closed circle through initiation, those which belong to the common domain are communicated through participation. In this second case, one can discern, with M. Fortes, three major processes of learning: imitation, identification, and co-operation.[5] H. Hedenus cites a proverb of the Twi people which says: 'Nobody shows the son of a blacksmith how to forge iron; if he knows how to forge, it is God who has taught him.' The Twi themselves interpret this proverb thus: If you are working and let your son watch you, he will learn quickly. It is God who has given the child the aptitude to observe and to imitate. If your son seems to learn by himself what he often sees practised, in reality it is God who teaches him.[6] Thus, imitation is considered as a mediating element between what is given by God and what is invented by man, between instinct and intelligence; it is the foundation of any subsequent personal creation.

The child is therefore implicitly asked to observe, then to imitate, to practise, to try by himself. In the domain of skill, the educative role of the adult can be summed up by saying that he lives and works in front of the young. Occasionally, he completes what is thus taught informally by means of an instruction given in more or less concise formulas. In many kinds of teaching, the verbalized aspect seems reduced. One points at an object, indicating its name and function, but without insisting on explicit explanations. In certain languages the terms 'learn' and 'imitate' are synonymous. Young people are not encouraged to ask questions of their elders, and it is considered better for them to watch others and listen to them.[7] For the Tallensi, ability consists of 'having good eyes' for imitating and copying. When something takes place, children are there listening and watching attentively, and registering what they observe. Afterwards they will be able to reproduce faithfully through gestures, mimicry, and word, with extraordinary detail and accomplished art, all that they have seen.

The great interest in the activities of the older people very early finds a place in the spontaneous frolics of the young. A greater part of teaching in whatever domain, takes part through play. Play is not, for the African child, relaxation, amusement, recreation, anarchic and tumultuous rambling to calm his nerves, as it is tending to become more and more for the Western child. In traditional civilizations, one can still observe playful conduct in a more or less pure state. It is characterized by an active, creative, and serious attitude; by the observance of precise rules, a relish for making an effort and the pleasure found therein. The world of games is one of extreme variety in Black Africa, as researches in this domain show.[8] The child enjoys an amazing amount of freedom: he can stray far from the village or remain outside to play in the moonlight while his parents are already sleeping.

Imitation of adult occupations in all its forms predominates in children's games: they play at mother and baby, at marriage, at public discussions or the tribunal, at caring for the sick, at performing the rites, sacrifices, initiations, burials, farm and domestic work, at mimicking the white man, etc. They hunt small animals, build miniature huts and villages, dolls, tools, and musical instruments. Children do not only imitate the things provided by tradition, but all the new things they see around them. It is only in matters that would offend modesty and good taste, religious sentiments or reverence that adults would try to check the imitative activities of children. Given the unity of the social sphere, the playful activity of children very early emerges into a serious and utilitarian activity; the two are going to intertwine and coexist in such a way that nobody can dissociate them. According to J. Kenyatta, 'games are, in fact, nothing more or less than a rehearsal prior to the performance of the activities which are the serious business of all the members of the Gikuyu tribe.'[9] They thus facilitate the passage from the period of liberty and indulgence towards that when restraint begins to be applied. This osmosis between play and work, this progressive transition, this relative indistinction—all these have led some observers to say that the African child used not to play or did not know how to play.[10] But E. Franke is no doubt closer to the truth when he says that play is, to a large extent, the form of activity through which African youths educate themselves.[11]

Leaning towards his integration in the adult world, the child seems eager to assume its tasks and responsibilities. He is not purely a passive receiver, but participates in an eminently active way in the education given him. He learns by doing—even by teaching—for he himself is constantly invested with the role of educator with respect to the younger children. A learning situation is always more significant, and consequently an object of more intense motivations, where it is connected with, and integrated into, life.

D. Kidd has summarized quite well the mechanisms of the transmission of knowledge as it occurs in South Africa: 'When children are very small, they learn from their mother; when they get their permanent teeth, they question the older children; the older children go and seek answers from young people; and the latter go to question old people. In this way, knowledge and information descend step by step down the age-scale.'[12]

Generally speaking, traditional knowledge is not transmitted by means of a set of carefully defined concepts, or by means of precisely formulated rules and norms. The child is instructed through images, narratives and symbolic actions whose content infinitely surpasses in meaning what he can grasp of it at the time. But with this treasury of images, knowledge is deposited in him. Little by little, this knowledge is going to become explicit while remaining inexhaustible. From an early age the child is acquainted with the great themes which will form the content of his thought for the rest of his life. But they are presented to him in an easily accessible mode; one does not seek to explain them but simply to make them be lived. The child easily absorbs these elements of knowledge, even though in his eyes they appear as enigmas, allegories, parables, the meaning of which he must wait to have fully revealed to him. The individual bathes in an atmosphere filled with feats, initiations, religious rites, sacrifices, possessions, prayers, proclaimed myths, benedictions, conspiracies, and gestures aiming to scrutinize the future in a handful of scattered shells or in the marks left by an animal. Now this universe which always refers to something else, and where significant actions and gestures prevail over the expressions of conceptualized thought, does not act on the child by bringing him from the very first a ready-made ideology, but by fashioning and ordering a complex of images charged with emotion, which will later take on an archetypal value.

Under whatever form and at whatever level it is administered, education always emphasizes behaviour which is practical in a given circumstance. To learn is to adapt oneself to the necessities of a real situation, to seek to fulfil the expectations of others, to identify oneself with models before one's eyes, to engage in vital tasks. If the child participates as early, as completely, and as intensely as possible in adult life, a kind of equivalence between education and life itself is established. The content of the education is the whole of the culture, with its usages, the attitudes which it demands, its heritage of know-how, manners, ways of speaking, and above all, of being. As M. Childs writes: 'The school is the society, and the society is the school.'[13] For his part, J. Kenyatta has the following to say:

In all tribal education the emphasis lies on a particular act of behaviour in a concrete situation. While the emphasis lies in the sphere of behaviour, it is none the less true that the growing child is acquiring a mass of knowledge all the time. The very freedom which marks the period of childhood gives unrivalled opportunity for picking up all sorts of information about the environment; the child is not handicapped by attending school and listening to formal instruction which is for the most part unrelated to his interests and needs.[14]

Elsewhere, Kenyatta is more specific:

> The first and most obvious principle . . . of the Gikuyu system of education is that instruction is always applied to an individual concrete situation; behaviour is taught in relation to some particular person. Whereas in Europe and America schools provide courses in moral instruction or citizenship, the African is taught how to behave to father or mother, grandparents, and to other members of the kinship group, paternal and maternal. Whereas European schools in Africa provide training in nature study, woodwork, animal husbandry, much of which is taught by general class instruction, the tribal method is to teach the names of particular plants, the use of different trees, or the management of a particular herd of sheep or goats or cattle. After this the child is left free to develop his own initiative by experiments and through trial and error to acquire proficiency.[15]

As can be seen, traditional pedagogy never separates education from instruction or teaching. The strength of its efficacy consists in the constant relation which it maintains with the lived experience. Participation in social acts and relations is both its object and content. According to M. Griaule:

> The Dogon child, as many other native children, is plunged directly into life. He enjoys the invaluable advantage over European children of not having in front of him the monstrous screen which our system of training and instructing erects between them and reality. For his training he does not have the coalition of specialized adults, i.e. the school, and he is placed in a very different family climate . . . He has his own refuges, his own games, into which the adult does not enter or which he has forgotten. Through games he prepares himself in his own way for the struggle which awaits him. He directs his own education and does not neglect any of the institutions, feelings, or practices which he will encounter in his later life.[16]

This education necessarily presents a very diverse character, embracing all the dimensions of personality, and seeking to develop all the aptitudes which have a functional value in a given society. It is not enough to say that one educates *for* life and *by* life, but that education *is* life.

The emotional nature of relationships which prevail during teaching is not an easy one to define. We find an authoritarian aspect during initiations; this has its precedents in the teaching administered by the older children and the family as a whole. But much more important is the eminently permissive atmosphere thanks to which the child imitates, learns by trial and error, is inspired by what he sees and hears, and stores the knowledge which is communicated to him only fortuitously and incidentally. The teaching given by older children has at least the same importance as that given by adults to children even though in their aims they are not rivals but complementary. Within the children's groups there takes place a truly reciprocal education. Among the Tallensi, observes M. Fortes, each pupil becomes a teacher in certain cases, and one finds among children the same attitude to education as among adults.[17]

The African culture is thus assimilated in an organic and global way. The models of conduct are not built up bit by bit by a kind of addition which will last for a lifetime. They are present from the very beginning in a very simplified form, especially as a postural type, and little by little, the accumulated experience deepens them, refines them, adopts them, and allows them to be exercised with a greater discrimination. Among the Tallensi, M. Fortes notes, the general pattern of the dance movements is present from the age of three, and continues to be perfected up to adulthood. It is a question of going from the global, more general situations to a progressive differentiation.

On her part, M.C. Ortigues notes:

If writing has permitted the development of what we call ideas, the peoples of oral tradition have elaborated in the whole tissue of social life a way of signifying them, and from that very fact they have derived an ethic. More than the recounted myths and legends, it is its allusive element which characterizes the traditional teaching, the non-thematic way of transmitting things somehow laterally, by conduct which leads from one thing to the other. The word punctuates sensory experiences in which things are taken as witnesses of what is lived as inter-human relations. The fine fabric of traditional society, like the 'discussion tree', manifests that which does not belong to any one, but which seals the union of all.[18]

In this type of intellectual and practical learning, it is not sufficient to consider the content of education, but it is also necessary to take into account the way in which this 'tradition' operates, the tonal quality of the phenomena of communication involved, the affective value of the relations which underlie it. The different cultural traits only take on their full significance through the human atmosphere which permeates them. It is this human atmosphere which is the determinant factor in the formation and orientation of the personality, and it is through it that what may be called cultural impregnation is effected—a sort of learning through absorption, contagion, and osmosis which is of even greater importance where the modes of conscious transmission are meagre.

Now, we shall consider successively in greater detail how the exploration of the environment, the entry into the world of resourcefulness, of custom and of speech takes place, by way of preparation for bringing out in a more synthetic way the chief traits of intellectual and practical learning.

2. THE ENVIRONMENT AND ITS EXPLORATION

a. A poor environment?

In order to understand the mentality of traditional man, it is necessary to start with his ecological environment and to see how he lives; how he shelters, clothes, and feeds himself; his mode of transport; the land he cultivates; the animals he keeps; which goods he has in abundance and which he lacks. All these facts form the background to which one must refer in order to proceed to the analysis of what could be the human condition in such a region. In this connection, it is interesting to note that many observers—especially those with a psychological orientation—have dwelt on the poverty of the material environment in which the African child moves and the dearth of intellectual stimulation which he can draw from it.

Speaking of the young Muganda in the period immediately after weaning, M. Géber writes: 'The discoveries likely to stimulate his interest are minimal. All he has for a toy is what he himself can collect in his surroundings. Without any *joie de vivre*, he learns how to play with twigs, soil, grass, and banana leaves which he uses to make dolls as well as guns.[19] Likewise, M. Knapen notes that 'the daily environment of the Congolese child is striking in its dearth of intellectual stimuli.'[20] This way of looking at things finds its most systematic expression in the writings of R. Maistriaux:

> The Black child has no toys. He does not find around him any occasion to arouse his intellect. What he sees happen in front of his rustic eyes is not of a nature to excite his mind . . . The early childhood of the Black always takes place in an environment intellectually *inferior to any imaginable in Europe*. In the bush, we have said, there *literally* exists *no* element of intellectual education. The Black child remains inactive for long hours. He thus undergoes a terrifying head-shrinking from which it is virtually impossible to recover. The neural centres of his cortex, which should normally be used for the exercise, do not receive the necessary stimuli for their development.[21]

Along the same lines, much has been made of the passivity of the African child, deriving from that of his milieu towards him, from the atmosphere of boredom and inactivity which is said to smother him in an environment lacking any salient stimuli. These attitudes are said to be typical even of early childhood, especially in the area of grasping and holding objects. [22] Later, the child is said to grow up in an environment which is not only affectively but also intellectually neutral, where the adult speaks rarely to him, takes care of him rarely, and does not take advantage of circumstances to teach him things, an environment where the outside world seems to have no appeal for him.

According to H. Ashton, Basuto children give an impression of placidity by their slow gestures, haggard eyes, and vacant expressions. They do not show any spirit of enterprise even in their games, nor do they try to play tricks on one another, to show independence or to put up resistance. An intolerable or naughty child is rare. The author attributes all this to the educative methods in use, to malnutrition, a lack of sleep, the poverty of the environment, and the infrequency of external stimuli. The observations on which these judgements are based are fully valid for the ethnic groups concerned. For our part, we were likewise struck by the conduct of the Brazzaville mothers towards their children while in hospital: of a characteristic passivity and an apparent indifference. One sees a mother sleeping beside a whining child, or smoking her pipe or cigarette with an air of indifference. She makes no attempt to distract the child or to show attentive love. She is, however, very intimately concerned about the state of her child; but that does not lead her to an active attitude in his regard. Evidently, such behaviour is characteristic of the reactions of the populations observed in certain precise cases; but to generalize them at this stage of research—as very often happens in the psychological literature devoted to the Black child—leads to a way of viewing things which seems to us unilateral and devoid of nuances.

Judgements regarding the traditional environment are generally unfavourable if one adopts a comparative point of view. Its poverty is brought out vis-à-vis the richness of elements described as 'educative' which the European child enjoys. For example, R. Maistriaux writes that there is neither radio, cinema, advertisements, nor the illustrated press to familiarize the child with the life of the mind. [23] The absence of toys made by adults specifically for children is roughly accurate, although it needs to be qualified. But in the final analysis, everything depends on the perspective that one adopts. If the concern is to show how the child is prepared to enter the iconic, geometric or mechanical world of modern civilization, one will unquestionably find that the elements at his disposal are poor and inadequate. On the other hand, if it is a question of seeing how the child is introduced into the culture to which his birth destines him, one is struck by the coherent character of the contributions furnished to him by the environment.

b. From the material to the human environment

The attitudes of the African child with respect to the universe of things are determined in many ways. The fact that he grows up in a simple environment in which precious or dangerous objects which he could break or with which he could hurt himself are rare, where in general he does not wear any clothes which he can soil or tear, explains to a certain extent the laissez-faire attitude of the adults and the child's lack of worry. More fundamentally, the way in which, during early childhood, the individual is made to enter into a relationship with the surrounding reality, explains more deeply certain of his attitudes. One might recapitulate the whole period before weaning by saying that during this time the maternal figure represents, in the eyes of the child, a central object which serves as a privileged avenue for the perception of the external world. During this period, body contact is of first importance as a way of learning. This proximity, this contiguity, this body-to-body contact with the mother makes it unnecessary and impossible to set up an intermediary space filled with objects highly invested with infantile affectivity, and functioning to make the distancing of the maternal figure bearable. As M. Knapen has written: 'One may suppose that where the mother is the principal element in the satisfaction of needs, the other stimuli of the external world can only have a reduced affective importance in the development of psychism. They do not belong to this complex phenomenon which is the response to a need, and do not acquire the sense of 'signs' in its satisfaction.'[24] Thus, if the initial relationship tends to take on an immediate, exclusive, and totalitarian character, the world of familiar objects is not called upon to play a mediating role which would endow these objects with a symbolic value in the eyes of the child. In a word, the child, in becoming used to manipulating and dominating this animate object which is the mother, has less occasion to experience the resistance of an inert object. He becomes more adept at handling living persons than things. He moves in an 'animistic' universe.

The atmosphere of gratifying and all-embracing dependence in which the nutritional and affective needs of the child are satisfied is a fundamental given, but one which must be completed by other data. It is the vertical position of the child on the mother's back which makes possible the visual exploration of the environment, as well as an early participation in the totality of human relationships centred around the mother—things which are missed by a child lying in his cradle. The social stimulation which the African child receives in many environments seems particularly abundant; the child becomes the focus of the people around him; he is taken in the arms of any person who visits or meets him. On the other hand, the mother is not the only person who looks after the baby. Very often, the little 'nurse' who is in charge of him will adopt a clearly more active attitude towards him. According to M. Read, the Ngoni suppose that children are happier with their nurses than with their mothers. But above all—as we saw earlier—children are called upon very early to enter into the group of equals, and it is here, with slightly older children, that the greater part of their learning—both social and intellectual—is going to take place. A European observer, used as he is only to the vertical transmission of knowledge is liable to ignore this primordial aspect of reality. Obviously, where weaning is traumatic and in addition is compounded by serious nutritional problems, the child can become lethargic and passive, which will retard his participation in the peer group.

It is undeniable that traditional peasant culture is minimal with respect to dwelling, furniture, clothing, and tool-making. But this 'poverty, is quite relative. The environment Laye Camara describes in *The African Child*, where the child finds himself at his father's forge, on his uncle's farm, and with his grandparents is remarkably dense, rich, and varied, and the child has access to it at a very early age. There are many objects within his reach, and familiar animals never cease to move around. He sees adults engage in common tasks, and notices the older children use such simple materials as twigs, leaves, straw, clay, the millet stalk and its pith in order to make many marvellous objects which require a great deal of patience and attentiveness in handicraft. But above all, behind that which in the eyes of a Westerner appears as impoverishment, one must not forget the richness of meanings associated with the humblest object. This always increases as one advances in the symbolic perception of the familiar universe. The most ordinary objects—a hoe, a stool, a basket, a millet granary, the various household objects—all can become, at one and the same time, a subject and an instrument of speculation going from the simplest to the most difficult, and extending to infinity. This sort of disproportion which exists between the meaning and its referent is doubtless one of the most striking traits of traditional cultures.

Teaching in a Mossi rural school, it dawned on us what a profound knowledge the children had of the environment; there is hardly any grass or beast—no matter how small—that they cannot name and describe. And what evocative names are furnished by their language! These names help them to grasp in each thing the outstanding trait in an admirably imaginative way, orienting both their observation and reflection towards the place that such and such an element is supposed to occupy in the cosmos. According to M. Griaule's account, the Dogon child gathers insects, learns to observe them, take them apart, and string them. As for the plants, he asks his parents for the necessary explanations, and before long he is able to name several hundreds of them. He learns the broad categories which serve to classify them along with the connections which a thought system based on analogy has established between them. The manipulation and utilization of insects does not, for the Dogon child, simply constitute an amusing game. It leads him to observe places, materials, agents, times, natural phenomena, and rites. They lead to knowledge, and often to its specification and development.[25]

This familiarity of the child with nature is certainly due to the fact that his environment lends itself to this, but also because his culture impels him to it and considers it essential. The adults take care to control the child's spirit of observation and his acquisition of knowledge by tests, questions, and, sometimes, tricks. He is questioned about embarrassing points, and is given paradoxes to solve. In order to test the memory and the faculty of observation of a young Gikuyu, two or three animal herds are mixed, and he is asked to separate his own animals, or they are hidden, and he must track them. If the child makes a mistake, he is not scolded, but only asked to start over.[26] As F. Ngoma reports:

> Feigning complete ignorance, a Mukongo father will invite a child to solve an apparently simple problem, but the solution of which requires the experience of the father. According to whether he succeeds or fails the child will either receive a pleasing or a disagreeable nickname. The successful child will also be preferred to his peers in executing certain missions or in accompanying the grown-ups on their journeys.[27]

But much more than the exploration of material environment, it is the observation of the human environment which, in the traditional context, attracts the child. The world of artefacts, of vegetables, animals, minerals —the cosmos in its entirety—is, in a certain sense, only an extension of the human world, the threads and fringes of a spider's web of which man occupies the centre, the walls of a building of which he is the cornerstone. Cosmic beings have significance only with respect to man. It is he who gives them a name and a meaning, and thereby has a hold on them by the magic of his speech. The universe explored by the child is essentially anthropocentric. Even its wild, non-domesticated part is seen in reference to social reality. This profound humanization of the world's image takes root genetically in the quasi-exclusiveness which unites the child to its mother during a very long period; later on, it is kept up by the total ascendency of the family, the lineage, the clan over the totality of life and its cosmological props which are the earth, what it contains, and what it produces. It appears that the interest and the sharpness of observation of which the child gives evidence are even more developed in the case of human realities where he shows a remarkable gift of foresight, intuition, empathy, and imitation. Every European who has had any dealings with young Africans can verify how quickly and correctly he was judged by them. The nicknames that they give one another throw into relief, sometimes with a cruel aptness, the characteristic element of each personality.

It is through the 'prism' or through the 'spectacles' which a particular culture gives him that the individual gets to know the external world as he becomes socialized. The special interest that the child takes in a given domain rather than in another, the reactions and attitudes that he adopts vis-à-vis reality, are among the most refined manifestations and expressions of his culture. The passivity which is correctly noted both on the part of the child and on the part of those who surround him belongs to a general scheme of laissez-faire and non-intervention whose roots are in the traditional society's very conception of the person. Both these observations about passivity must be counterbalanced by a series of others which show that once he has traversed the period of perplexity which follows upon weaning, the child finds fairly quickly new vigour, thanks to which he soon embarks on the conquest of his universe. Passivity? A tribal teaching of the Chagga asks the future husband to insist that his wife be always busy, for in this way she arouses in the children the desire to participate, and they will thus tend to ask her how she goes about it.[28]

The same Mukongo child that M. Knapen has described as passive, has been given a totally different image by J. van Wing:

> Once weaned, the boy becomes a small man. Ordinarily, he is very keen and observant. If his sense of touch has lost its delicacy due to the rough gymnastics he has endured on the back of his mother during the first two or three months of his life, and due to the hard earthen floor he sleeps on, he has a pair of eyes from which no movement of any living thing can escape; he possesses a pair of ears which are very sensitive to every human word, to every animal cry, to every sound of nature, which the development of his vocal organs will enable him to imitate faithfully. At four . . . he begins to go his own way. He already knows how to make fire, and at his own hearth he roasts palm nuts and edible caterpillars and crickets. At six he leaves the maternal hut for good, taking with him a knowledge of the mysteries of life which would make a young European blush. From then on he accompanies his father when he goes hunting, fishing, or to the market, and to public discussions.[29]

The environment perceived by the child according to this description is perhaps one-sidedly rich, but certainly not poor.

3. THE WORLD OF TOOLS AND OF SKILLS

Whatever may be the situation of man within a given culture, he must necessarily submit to a deliberate training in several areas. The higher the technological civilization, the more specialized and diversified become the skills, requiring an evolution from collective modes of acquisition to more individualized ones. The technical training that the young African receives aims at passing on to him a know-how, a totality of skills, coming from an age-old experience, as well as the effective means of mastering an often difficult, if not hostile, nature. Training in craft, agricultural, pastoral, household, and artistic work takes place either at the side of the adult, often on a one-to-one basis, or within a group of children instructed by the older ones among them.

a. The child at the side of the adult

Generally speaking, during early childhood, there is no deliberate training to facilitate psychomotor development. Affectionately attentive to the performances of the child, the mother does not seek to provoke or to hasten them by stimulation. When a Dogon child makes an attempt to walk, the older children help him momentarily, although this help is not the result of a deliberate design.[30] It is the period of getting permanent teeth which marks a turning-point in learning. Until then, the child has been participating in work in a purely occasional and playful manner. From now on he is asked to contribute in a more systematic and effective way. The masculine and feminine tasks become diversified. Everywhere one notices that the adult makes only reasonable demands on the child, leaving him to work at his own rhythm, not forcing him to surpass his abilities.

The transition to real tasks is far from abrupt. The child learns to contribute to them naturally and progressively as his interests and abilities develop. The essential thing is that he learns very early to help all the people around him according to the rule of reciprocity. However, even if their contribution is negligible, the participation of children in the work in no way amounts to a mere pretence. As soon as they are able to accomplish a task or to fulfil a function, they are expected to do so. Quite naturally, their contribution and co-operation are recognized without, however, making too much of them. Due to this progressive habituation, by the time they are six or seven years old, the children are initiated into the most effective and realistic tasks and responsibilities. One notices that they set about their work with a lot of good will, joy, and a concern for doing well. The adult has hardly any need to make his authority felt. The children are left with complete liberty to amuse themselves on condition that the duty is accomplished. Thus, at this age, socialization is realized in two ways: on the one hand, the society comes to the child through the obligation to work and, on the other hand, the child comes to the society through the collective and imitative game. He gets the feeling that he is indispensable, and that his effective contribution to the domestic economy is taken into account. Any separation from real life is thus avoided.[31]

For the boy, there takes place at the 'age of reason', the first passage from a predominantly female universe to another where the masculine adult figures—those of the father or 'fathers'—become more and more real by dint of the roles they are led to play in the training to which he must from now on submit. From the age of about five, the young Mukongo begins to learn from his father the duties of a man. He accompanies him to the plantation, and during the journey, all the important details are noted: the boundaries, the sites marked by specific events, the names of edible as well as poisonous plants, dangerous animals and their habits, the prohibitions to be observed. He is shown how to make tools for hunting and farming; the use of baits and traps, the care of domestic animals. In the field, the father gets the child to weed beside him with a miniature hoe especially made for him.

M. Fortes notes that among the Tallensi, the teaching of manual skills follows a different method from the teaching of social skills. In fact, children are eager to learn but are not ashamed to admit their ignorance or lack of skill. They will laugh heartily when others do not know something, but never make fun of them in this regard. The weapon of mockery is reserved for bad manners. Among these people, adults as well as children are very sensitive to ridicule where it concerns moral or behavioural matters, but they are insensitive to it with respect to dexterity and ability. Concerning the former, the right conduct can only be known through the reactions of others; and there is no mean between success and failure: here, learning operates on the law of all or nothing. As regards the latter, one can judge oneself, so that the expectation of others is taken less seriously, and the acquisition of techniques can take place progressively.[32]

Work and education are thus a unitary whole; work becomes education when its gestures become more conscious due to the need to transmit them to others. It is around concrete tasks that the pedagogic consciousness takes shape and that knowledge is organized. The adult shows the child things, encourages him to imitate, and offers him help when he does not succeed in his task, but without doing it for him. The miniature tools that he will eventually give him are not toys, but real tools.

b. Learning within the children's group

Many different ways of learning take place within the same children's group, but many of the technical skills thus acquired will not survive to puberty. The sling made of rubber has become an indispensable instrument to the youth, replacing other forms of projectile. In small bands, the children go out to hunt small animals, sometimes setting the bush on fire. D. Kidd makes the point that the power of imagination among Black children does not develop in a void. As soon as it is able to make use of even the simplest and crudest raw materials, it sets itself in motion. The young Bantus very carefully mould wet clay and make bulls with spread-out legs and long horns. Kidd writes in addition: 'One is surprised by the sharpness of observation of which the young modellers give evidence. A sheep made of clay is distinguished from a dog by a very simple but, nevertheless, inimitable feature. Nobody can see these children work in clay without being convinced how desirable it would be if this skill were developed in school.'[33] Many other observers note how, in the most diverse regions, children are very fond of these same activities of modelling—giving evidence of a real skill. The creations thus obtained aim at capturing the principal and characteristic trait of the object. Pottery—which is more or less reserved for women—aside, the work in clay is often reserved for the domain of children; a tradition thus develops within their society without any inspiration from adult models.

What is true of clay can be extended to other materials. Children know how to shape interlaced shoots of grass into all sorts of animals, and they pass the model from one to another. In the Sudan, children can perform wonders with the pith of millet stalks which for them constitutes the equivalent of a 'meccano'. In addition, they use wicker, wood, pieces of calabash, wires, and canning tins for making different toys, figurines, weapons, traps, bracelets, baskets, hats, musical instruments and, today—cars, aeroplanes, trains, cranes, bulldozers, and contrivances with steering systems which are sometimes highly perfected. The child is forever researching as to how the different materials offered to him by the environment can be put to the service of the imagination. The swiftness with which new elements are utilized, and new models furnished by the mechanical world are integrated, indicates that the children do not simply stick to a servile imitation, but give evidence of a remarkable creativity.

The African child works with materials and not with ready-made toys. With them he can make what he wants, whereas toys made by the adult are just what they are. He thus commands a great deal of freedom in the use of the imagination. He acquires a remarkable power of self-reliance, which will stand him in good stead in crucial situations.

When the Nyakyusa boys set up their own village, they do all the construction work themselves. Instead of going to work individually with their fathers, they go in a group to work for the parents of one or another among them. Children not only work for the family and domestic needs, but very early on take their place in the production of goods for sale. In a very independent way, boys and girls will engage in artistic or agricultural activities and go to the market to sell their product—baskets, wooden objects, embroidered articles, fritters—or even water. To be able to tap palm wine, an activity requiring a lot of dexterity, constitutes, among the Bayombe, a real test of maturity. Generally speaking, the child is given the right to use or own certain objects which he has acquired: a knife, a chicken, a goat that his uncle has given him, a piece of land which he workd himself, and whose produce he is allowed to sell at his own profit. Grouped into age-sets, the young people sometimes also assume certain tasks communally, either because custom assigns them, as in the case of a field they hold collectively, or even in hiring out their labour collectively to an individual for payment, as is done in Bambara country when the society of the uncircumcised needs to refill its coffers. Everywhere in Africa a certain joy is felt in working as a group, aided by the rhythm of songs and drums, whereas work done singly is seen as empty and tedious.

In pastoral populations, the keeping of flocks is usually the main work of boys during their late childhood. Observers are unanimous in recognizing that the keeping of animals constitutes an important avenue of education. It gives an opportunity to the boys to organize themselves and to take on responsibilities, while remaining under the direction and distant supervision of adults; it also promotes resourcefulness, a sense of observation, and empirical knowledge.

For the young Bantus of South Africa, it is the onset of the second dentition which announces their readiness to herd the flocks. At first they are entrusted with small animals—calves, goats, and sheep; afterwards, when they are about ten, they are collectively given charge of the bulls. They receive precise orders from adults concerning the places of pasture and the treatment of the animals. But once alone, they do what they please. They like to meet other young shepherds from neighbouring villages to organize calf races. The winners will have the right to milk the goats and ride on the bulls of the losers. They use their own wits in training the animals and making them obey different whistling sounds. They steal animals from adjacent villages, which gives rise to Homeric battles away from the eyes of adults. On the game-boards used by young Rwandans, the counters represent cows which are to be stolen from one's opponent.

c. Specialized learning

People with a warrior tradition and aristocratic status attach very great importance to physical exercise in order to give the body suppleness, strength, endurance, and harmony. Among peasant populations the concern for regular training is less great, but even there one finds athletic contests and jousts, the practice of such sports as wrestling, competitions organized on a large scale, acrobatics and, obviously, dancing. With singing, dancing forms the background of African life. It is all-pervasive: in work, games, recreation, and feasts. Writes M. Griaule: 'If one can speculate that no pregnancy will stop a woman from expressing her mourning, then one can say that a Dogon dances from conception to death.'[34] The Ngoni boys practise in the evening before dark, at the very place where they milk the cows, at the gate of the kraal, in preparation for the festivities to take place after the harvest. The adults sit around, criticize, and give demonstrations. The young girls form several groups for this exercise while the boys compose only one.[35] The learning of these representative dances of an athletic tradition, imprint, in a way, at the somatic level, the idea of tribal solidarity, and thus constitute a decisive factor in the maintenance of an *esprit de corps*.

African art is not something added to life as an embellishment. It is present everywhere—in funeral masks, in small statues representing a dead twin child, in baskets used for carrying yams. The child thus acquires a very keen aesthetic sense in the exercise of techniques traditionally practised by his ethnic group.

Generally speaking, the feminine jobs in which the young girl is initiated follow a shorter time schedule than those of men and are less subject to changes and seasonal fluctuations. By that very fact, they are more monotonous. They tie her more closely to the house, to the yard and to its immediate environs. They make her become productive earlier, and in a more regular and time-consuming way than in the case of boys. A great deal of her day is taken up with the preparation of meals, the fetching of water and firewood, the care of younger children, the chores of cleanliness and of maintenance. The young girl is generally considered as a wife, and is integrated in the family group of her husband in terms of success in three types of activity: the procreation of children and the aptitude to care for them, farm work, and the preparation of meals. It is essentially in these three areas that the ambitions of the young girl and the educative stimulus that she receives are found. Allusions are constantly made in front of her regarding her future status as wife.

It is also in a global manner that certain forms of intellectual skill become developed. In is in this way that numerical problems, presented in the form of games, are put before the child from an early age. The young Bambara is only admitted into the *N'domo* society if he can count up to twenty—the figure which represents the sum of the fingers and toes of a human being, and consequently symbolizes the person in his totality. The simplest arithmetical game among Yoruba children consists in seeing who can count cowries the fastest. To say to someone: 'You do not know how much is nine times nine', is considered an insult. Among the Bororo Fulani and the Hausa, the following game is played: A cross is traced on the ground; at each of the right angles, three holes are dug around the centre, and three pebbles are inserted in each hold. Turning in such a way as not to see the figure, a player must indicate how the thirty-six pebbles must be shifted around. As soon as he makes a mistake by, for example, asking that a stone be removed from a hole which does not contain any, he loses the game.[36] Rapidity of mental calculation and memory are thus carefully cultivated.

Technical education is not absent from inititation schools. Sometimes it occupies an important part of the time, especially where the time spent in the bush lasts for months. The courses given there are a sort of recapitulation of the knowledge already acquired during childhood and a period of intensive training. The 'thondo' of the Vendas is one of the rare traditional institutions resembling school in the European sense of the term, where boys between the age of eight and the onset of puberty are kept. In the evening, after having tended the flocks, they engage in military training and artistic work in an atmosphere of strict discipline. [37] The technical activity, as well as hunting and fishing, in which the novices must train themselves in the initiation camp have, generally speaking, a symbolic significance in addition to their purely practical interest.

Depending on the political, religious, or professional status of the clan or of the parents, children are instructed in a specific sphere of knowledge. In his description of the life of a young Mandinka, Laye Camara brings out the difference between the experience of a child of a smith-jeweller and that of a griot. The two do not have equal opportunities to attend divination sessions, or ritual acts, commercial transactions, court cases, judgements, or of being dispatched with messages. Our own experience in a small primary school in a small locality, has shown us how much the professional status of parents as merchants, farmers, chiefs, butchers, craftsmen, civil servants, etc., determined the character and manner of their children's school attendance. This is because it oriented the whole extra-curricular activity, conferring on the children a specialized knowledge which enabled them automatically to play the role of leader in certain things, and fill precise functions for which others were not prepared. Even in the most apparently homogeneous society one must—in order to understand the life of the child—take into consideration all the possible differences. An individual is never put into contact, uniformly, with the whole of culture, but only with privileged aspects of it which are related to his belonging and to his status.

Very specialized professions are generally transmitted within the same lineage; their holders belong to a true caste of craftsmen, sometimes despised and sometimes respected, but always feared because of its mysterious knowledge and contact with such and such an element or material. It is for this reason that the blacksmith always holds a special place within the society. Such specializations as medicine or divination often rest on a secret body of knowledge and on formulae which constitute the family wealth, a patrimony transmitted through heritage. Learning in this case is based on the same principle as in the case of the other techniques: the child acquaints himself as early as possible with his future trade through his active presence and participation.

But whenever certain types of knowledge must be protected against wider disclosure, one observes a true initiation, a transmission which takes place between the master and the pupil in secret, and for which the beneficiary must sometimes wait a long time and pay dearly either in kind or in service. Children are often placed in apprenticeships with craftsmen in return for a certain fee.

It is the blacksmith who transforms the ore into pure metal, gives form to a mass which does not have it, handles what is malleable, and assists actively in the transformation of 'soft' to 'hard'. In many ethnic groups his wife is a potter, and her role vis-à-vis matter is analogous to his.[38] Their function is to 'shape', and it is not therefore surprising to find them both there where a human being is given a new direction, is educated, less in the psychological than in the ontological sense. In very many cases, it is the blacksmith and the potter who are the agents of the rites of circumcision and excision, and the corresponding initiations.[39]

If we reconsider R. Cousinet's analysis of the pedagogical processes of learning,[40] we find that the stages elaborated among Europeans are also found among Africans, but with a different emphasis: the older person—be he child or adult—first lets the younger watch, then invites him to imitate, and shows him how to accomplish such and such a task by doing it in front of him in such a way that the sequence of events is made evident to the learner. Finally, he gives him explanations in order to transform something done automatically into a reasoned action. It is at the level of the third step that the African teacher is the most simple. He avoids giving an answer before the child's question has crystallized, and he does not communicate knowledge ahead of experience. The child learns to do by doing. But at the same time he is given time to discover what he does not yet know. By giving him few explanations, he is encouraged to become more mature and formulate his questions clearly. First, he is led to imitate, to experiment, to acquire knowledge of an operational type. The learning of everyday techniques at this level takes place without their being further conceptualized or verbalized.

4. THE WORLD OF CUSTOM AND OF GOOD BREEDING

By *doghem-mikri*—to be born and to see, to enter the world and to notice what is done—the Mossi mean the set of customs, the rules of good breeding and of courtesy controlling social life. Custom precedes man; it is a pre-established order from which it is impossible to break loose. To conform to it is to make oneself acceptable to the community at every level, and to benefit from its favours; to turn away from the established order is almost to exclude oneself, to excommunicate oneself. With its many provisions, custom is not a simple incidental habit, a simple social contract appearing under a given form that could just as well be otherwise; it is the very basis of existence, the rich soil in which the roots of life are immersed; it is custom which, in the strongest sense of that term, *makes life possible*.

Through birth, man is destined to a particular group and to a particular lineage, and thus, to a particular cultural milieu to which he is vitally and ontologically bound.

a. Kinship as the object of knowledge

Learning the kinship system surely is the centrepiece of initiation into the customs, for it constitutes the special setting of traditional life. Because of its vastness, the family group can even screen other aspects of social life from the child. Once the individual understands clearly the complex hierarchy of his own lineage, he must extend his knowledge to neighbouring clans, especially if they are traditional allies or enemies, to all those who are linked with his family, for example, as slaves or as 'jesting' relatives. Kinship also provides the basis and framework of economic activity. Work is a service rendered and exchanged according to a precise scale, and the network of obligations it creates is an integral part of family relationships.

The respective position of different relatives emerges from the way cooked food is distributed. Without anything being explained to him, the child senses and lives the social structure long before he is able to understand it through precise concepts. Among the Southern Bantus, the cutting up and distribution of game follow minute rules, and must take place publicly; each piece is destined to a particular person according to his status. Those who eat and those who do not must be seen by all. The reason given for that is mainly of a pedagogical nature: since in such a distribution the social obligations which derive from the system of parentage are fulfilled, the distribution helps to instruct the children who attend it. When, among the Chagga, an animal is killed, the children are asked to invite their half-brothers and the sons of the paternal uncles (and not the other cousins) to participate ritually in the eating of the parts of the animal reserved for children.*

The importance of this silent instruction as it is given by the arrangement of meals and the sharing of cooked food cannot be overestimated. As L. and R. Makarius observe, the bonds of consanguinity fall outside the conscious experience of descendants and must therefore be explained by the elders, whereas the actions of eating are renewed several times a day,

---

*Among the Gikuyu, meat distribution followed a pattern whose criteria were dictated by a person's age and status. According to this pattern, the elders and heads of households ate what were considered the choicest pieces: the head, the thick fat meat on the back of a ram's neck (*ngata*), and the meat from a ram's or a he-goat's sides minus the ribs (*ikengeto*); on the other hand, uncircumcised boys were given what were thought to be the worst pieces: the neck from which most of the meat had been taken away, the lungs, and the thin parts of the legs. The other members, circumcised boys and women, were allotted pieces to match their intermediate status. As for the children, they were fed meat indiscriminately. —Transl.

and are self-evident. 'Genealogical consanguinity is therefore a theoretical, abstract notion, whilst consanguinity through eating a common food is a social, concrete, and practical expression thereof.'[41]

b. Greetings and invectives

In the domain of those interpersonal relations to which great importance is attached, greetings obviously occupy a privileged position. They follow minute rules, a kind of ritual, by means of which the respective position of the two interlocutors is expressed. To know how to greet correctly is to place the persons that one addresses in a multidimensional framework: often the time of day is mentioned and the place where the meeting takes place, as are the state and occupations of the speakers as well as their social status. All this is done according to well-established but stereotyped categories, gestures, and vocabulary, taking into consideration rules of priority, age, rank, distance, or familiarity. The manner of greetings that one expects from a child varies according to his age, and this becomes more complex as his understanding of relationships refines itself, and as he succeeds in operating in his human environment these subtle classifications which are required to give the correct salutation. Obviously, there is in this type of learning some voluntary explanation given by the adult according to circumstances. But, here too, what is essential is realized through imitation and transposition: when a child hears his father address another person as 'my son', he knows that he ought to refer to that person as 'my brother'. The Chagga child learns during the first two or three years of his life the terms with which he must address all the members of the family group—a learning which is strictly controlled by his father. Politeness and good manners are learnt between the ages of three and six years. From simple terms of address he passes on to phrases. [42]

Among people who are constantly intermixing, it is necessary to establish a certain distance. Couples follow precise rules in addressing one another and may do the same when they address their children. An older brother is in principle deserving of respect from his younger brothers. A whole phenomenological analysis would be required to show, for example, how certain gestures express distrust, the desire to sound out the other and to neutralize the virtual menace that his presence entails. Given that a greeting, in addition to gestures, involves vocal intonations and mimicry— which are sometimes very affected—it becomes a part of one's physical responses and thus leaves a particularly deep mark on the individual. Each ethnic group distinguishes itself by a certain style, in the way it presents itself, and by the way in which it confronts the other groups, erect, proud, even brutal, or bent, bowed, and obsequious. Even a traveller who is not forewarned can easily tell when he is passing from one population to another simply by observing the deportment of those around him.

Opposed to the greeting is the mocking or insulting invective. By learning to react to different forms of insult which, by the way, are very common among young people, the child absorbs numerous intellectual and ethical categories. First of all, he learns how to put them in a hierarchy, to classify them according to their degree of seriousness, and this without any direct teaching from anybody. An insult aimed at a physical defect will be felt less strongly than one concerning a moral imperfection; and an individual will react even more violently if the insulter minimizes his social value or that of his family. The height of abuse is reached when the expression used is directed at the genital organs of the individual or of his parents, especially those of his mother and, if he is married, of his in-laws; for this is to touch the very roots of life and that which is eminently sacred and respectable in it, the very foundation of society. The child must also learn to discern the source of the insult, for among certain relatives some of the coarsest forms of abuse are not only permissible but almost compulsory.

As in rural Europe, the inhabitants of different villages or even of different districts—especially if they are of the same age-group—exchange jokes in standardized forms in which they ridicule the pronunciation, accent, and the vocabulary peculiar to a group, the proverbial defects of its members and of its history. G. Calame-Griaule has indicated the educative importance among the Dogon of these completely official lampoons. In fact, the child must learn to observe his interlocutor in order to rapidly identify a detail of language, custom, or usage which will help him to launch the first blow of mockery, failing which he must learn to give tit for tat. He is thus led to affirm himself as an element of a group, of a linguistic and cultural community, and he learns that diversity is not a source of annoyance but of equilibrium.[43]

c. Precepts and rules of conduct

. . . .

The knowledge of customary law is transmitted to the young people through the rules which adults mention from time to time concerning respect, propriety, or sexual conduct. As soon as he is judged capable, the youth attends men's meetings where controversial and litigious matters are debated in order to resolve them in the light of tradition. He is supposed to question his elders on all points which appear obscure. It is in this way that a Mukongo boy starts to attend public discussions and judgements very early, and learns to play-act court hearings with his companions. From a mere spectator he very quickly, depending on the course the debates take, becomes a messenger, then, gradually, he ventures to intervene.

'With precautions of usage (learnt, by the way, through the code of propriety), he will give his opinion regarding the direction he deems traditional or reasonable. It is through his cautious interventions that he reveals himself.'[44]

The instructions which in certain cases are given to the young people more or less systematically also transmit numerous elements which perfect their aptitudes for finding their way in the complexity of arrangements, norms, and customary rules.

There exists a hierarchy among the various precepts and it is necessary to learn how to sort them out and replace them in their order in a total context. Anyone who wants to take part in a discussion must learn to distinguish between a divine precept, an ancestral prescription, civil law, established custom, or simply local usage, and to know the degree of culpability associated with each of these.

In cultures where there is a central authority and where society is divided into well-defined classes, young men from the ruling and aristocratic circles used to be sent for a stay in the courts of kings, chiefs, or in the environment of capitals to improve their education in good manners and custom. Among the Southern Bantus one used to find a kind of military and labour service keeping the youths in the chief's entourage for a shorter or longer period after initiation. In Rwanda, the young people from upperclass families used to go to court in order to become acquainted with the political, administrative, juridical, literary, and artistic customs under the direction of the hereditary trustees of the royal traditions and secrets whose teaching seems to have been largely esoteric.

It is above all through active participation in ritual ceremonies that the individual is led to feel what is valuable in the eyes of the society. He acquires the correct affective attitude towards the livestock or towards cereal grains less through an explicit teaching than through being present at rites where these elements are used. He learns there that success in any domain whatsoever does not only depend on knowledge but also on the correct handling of the ceremonies, on prohibitions and customs, failing which, for example, the rain will be late in coming and the crop will be spoiled. What a man knows, it is thought, is less important than what he does, the way in which he lives, acts, and uses the ritual means at his disposal. Success and well-being are closely related to morality.

The study of the way in which the child penetrates into the world of custom and good breeding is manifestly very closely related on the one hand, to that of the word, and on the other, to that of ethical values—subjects to which we now turn.

8

Entry into the Universe of the Word*

'The verb is African; everything happens as if the wind of
words were indispensable to the movement of life.'
—R. Jaulin [1]

In essentially oral cultures, one must not be astonished by the importance
bestowed on the word in pedagogy.

To the Dogon, tradition appears as the 'ancient word'. Essentially it
embraces, in their eyes, the mythical accounts of the whole set of ideas and
interpretations inherited from the ancestors concerning the mysteries of
the world and of existence. The wise man is the one who 'knows the word',
who is able to transmit it, and to coin it in the concrete circumstances of life
by giving useful advice.

With respect to the peoples of the Niger bend, a physiology and a
psychology of the production and reception of the word has been described
corresponding to the total image that they have of man's spiritual organism. [2] These often complex elaborations justify to the peoples in question
certain provisions of a pedagogical nature having as their aim to give to the
word its complete scope and its full informative and formative power.
Language is itself a divine gift, full of symbolic meanings, and it must be
decoded in the same way as an immense field of signs, exactly like the
material universe. One must not be surprised to find in traditional Africa
a veritable theory of speech, its nature, its birth, its life and death, as well
as a reflection on language, comparing similar words, looking for their
etymology, engaging in the play of assonances and homophonies. [3] Traditional man is aware that he can find in his language a reflection of his
culture, and he is happy to draw from it justifications for his ideas.

1. LANGUAGE AND LANGUAGE LEARNING

The mother tongue constitutes the most powerful bond between people of
the same group, creating among them an intellectual as well as an affective
bond. From an analysis of the principal characteristics of African languages,
one can see many indications regarding the systems of representation, of
the thought and values of which they serve as instruments. The richness of

*Section two of this chapter has been omitted, and section five transferred to
Chapter Ten where it really belongs. Thus the chapter now has four sections
instead of the original six. These have been renumbered consecutively.—Transl.

105

the vocabulary, the use of different words to designate an object according to its position in time and space, its form and function, the abundance of onomatopoeias, the way in which abstract ideas are rendered—all guide the exercise of thought in very definite directions.

It seems that children learn to speak correctly very quickly. Speaking of the young Mukongo, J. van Wing writes—not without some exaggeration—that 'at four years old he speaks his beautiful Kikongo better than a twelve-year-old European speaks his language.'[4] How does this learning take place?

Most observers remark that adults do not use any special language with the child, and that conversation between the two takes place in a normal fashion. There exists, however, a 'baby talk' which undoubtedly takes on less importance than in Europe where the distance between the domain of children and adults is greater. On the other hand, the tone in which one addresses a child is never quite identical with that used among grown-ups. It does not appear that the latter are in the habit of systematically correcting children in their speech except when they make a mistake or use wrong formulas in addressing people. Kind encouragement always prevails over direct and explicit intervention.

The Dogon child learns from his mother, in her own dialect, the first elementary vocabulary concerning the things of the house. After the child is weaned, the father gradually assumes the linguistic education of the boy but never that of the little girl. Taking the children out, the parents teach them the vocabulary concerning the bush, animals, plants, tools, and agricultural techniques. This transmission takes place almost exclusively from father to son and from mother to daughter respectively. In man, therefore, language acquisition revolves around a male-female opposition and complementarity. After weaning, only the paternal dialect is used. Later, an important part of the vocabulary is acquired through contact with other children, brothers and sisters first, then companions who introduce the child to language proper to games, bring in dialectal differences, indulge in 'village mockeries', and reprimand by laughter and mockery all faulty expressions and slips of the tongue, and thus lead the child to speak correctly.[5] It can be affirmed in a general way that for learning and amusement, the African child depends more on the universe of interpersonal relations than on that of objects.

Of the various types of learning, that of speech is one of those manifestly most important, and does not take place without symbolic actions. Among the people of the Valley of the Niger, there is a true 'eugenics' of speech; in order to give it more lustre, they resort to filing the teeth. In order to help a young girl master speech more easily, her gums are stained blue, a particularly painful operation.[6] The Dogon put small rings on the lips and at the edge of the earlobe; the holes thus made at three and six years of age are aimed at facilitating the entry of good words. As G. Calame-Griaule writes: 'When a girl of ten or twelve goes on making mistakes in grammar and pronunciation, the grown-ups laugh and say she needs to have her nose pierced. In effect the time has come to complete her symbolic learning of speech: piercing her nose will complete its regularization.'[7] When the Bambara child is late in speaking or mispronounces, they put into its mouth two halves of the nest of the 'mocking bird', for they believe that the first prattlings reproduce the language of birds. [8]

Everywhere eloquence and speech arts have a fundamental importance. They help to give weight to a man in public meetings and assemblies. One admires a person who can speak clearly, convince others with the proofs he adduces, and intersperse his speech with feelings and maxims. Speaking constitutes one of the privileged occasions where free expression and creativity are made possible—not in a disorderly manner—but within the limits of a tradition which imposes on the speaker, orator, or story-teller the necessity of operating within a rather rigid framework, while providing him with a rich linguistic instrument, a stock of images and phrases making possible a very precise rendering of thought. When a young Ngoni girl gathers around her other younger girls to tell them stories, the adults listen with attention and admiration to this 'eloquence coming from the heart'.[9] In children one can always see remarkable gifts of improvisation.

But the word has value only when it is mastered, dominated. In the same way that secrecy gives value to knowledge, silence gives value to speech. The implied, euphemism, allegory, and the reluctance to reveal what one knows are among the most common techniques of oral expression and they are all found in the children's subculture. 'Among the Bambara,' explains D. Zahan, 'the word constitutes a kind of sonorous mask behind which is hidden thought whose true countenance the listener is invited to detect.'[10] The use of an artificial language (a 'pig-Latin') by children has a triple aim: firstly, to afford them a sort of escape from the habitual system of communication into another one of which they have the impression (or illusion) of being the creators and masters; second, to acquaint them consciously with the manipulation of secrets and of the knowledge reserved for those who hold the key to the code which controls its communication; finally, to stimulate intelligence through oral gymnastics which serves as an introduction to the exercise of thought and confers upon it a greater mobility.[11] The use of a true secret language acquires its *raison d'être* in connection with initiation teaching, for it imparts to those who receive it the feeling of forming a closed, interdependent, and superior group. Very often initiators repeat in front of the novices formulas of an increasing complexity, which become engraved in their memory, and whose archaic and indeed incomprehensible character enhances even more the respect which they elicit.*

*A parallel case is the Mass said in Latin—a dead language. When with the Second

Just as a particular language or dialect constitutes a link for a community and a powerful means of identification for its members, such a secret language enables a group of initiates to assert themselves vis-à-vis the others.

Let us follow the thought of young Camara as he watches his father make a piece of golden jewelry:

It occurred to me that my father could have confided all this work of fusion to one of his helpers, all of them very experienced. A hundred times they had attended these same preparations, and could no doubt have carried the smelting to a successful conclusion. But I said: My father moved his lips! The words we did not hear, those secret words, those incantations which he used to address to something we could neither see nor hear, that was the essential thing. The adjuration of the spirits of fire, wine, and gold, and the conjuration of evil spirits—my father alone had this science, and that is why, alone, he carried out the whole procedure.[12]

Language learning accomplishes in a privileged way the most profound aspect of socialization, namely cultural impregnation. Not only does language serve as a tool for the totality of other acquisitions, but in itself it constitutes the principal means of interchange and communication. Without his realizing it, those around him are forever sanctioning, punishing, rewarding, approving or disapproving the child even if it is only by their tone of voice. The adult changes his way of speaking according to the status of his interlocutor. In this way, the child who is listening is enabled to make an implicit but rigorous social classification. With regard to those outside, who speak differently, language enables the child to identify himself with his own group and to affirm his feelings of belonging.

Behaviour and attitudes, ways of judging and feeling, are only weakly communicated by formal teaching, but they are inextricably bound up with the life of the community as a whole. According to Jensen-Krige, values flow quite naturally from situations, and are indissolubly bound up with language. He continues:

A group of young girls was playing at keeping house in the sand with twigs, pebbles, and small clay pots. 'What have you put in these pots?' we asked. 'Vyalva, some beer,' was the reply. But the intonation, the meaning they gave to the word, their facial expression while pronouncing it—all referred to a social situation. It was clear that to them, despite

---

Vatican Council the Mass was 'vernacularized', some people—especially the older ones—had a great difficulty in adjusting. In their eyes, the Mass said in a living language was 'plain' and seemed divested of its mysterious and sacred character. It did not have any meaning for them.—Transl.

their youth, the word 'beer' did not signify for them such food as porridge, but something quite precious, a source of pleasure and joy, a very important element in life. In a word, their attitude towards beer was that of a Lovedu, an attitude which does not have an equivalent in European society. A European child could not have put so much meaning into this one word as they did.[13]

Modern linguistics confirms the fact that man always thinks in terms of a universe which his language has first fashioned. As E. Beneviste writes, 'We see that the mental categories and the laws of thought do no more than reflect, to a large measure, the organization and distribution of linguistic categories. The varieties of philosophical and spiritual experience are unconsciously dependent on a classification which language brings about by the very fact that it is language and that it symbolizes.'[14]   For A. Martinet, 'each language is an instrument of communication according to which human experience is analysed differently in each community.'[15] Each linguistic system is a prism through which one sees things, and by means of which one classifies and interprets external reality, a means both of analysis and synthesis, and by this fact it directs one's mind towards a certain conception of the world. By assimilating his mother tongue, by making it his own while surrendering to it, the child locates himself culturally and becomes imbued with a particular tradition. By teaching him how to speak, those around him determine and shape to a large extent his thought, sensibility, and perception of the universe, as well as the attitude which he will adopt in regard to it.

2. POPULAR NARRATIVES AND THEIR EDUCATIONAL SIGNIFICANCE

It is through oral transmission of the literary heritage that an essential part of education, both intellectual and ethical, is carried out. By their beautiful language and their art of handling the word, the story-tellers familiarize the youth with a vocabulary, grammatical forms, and an elegant intonation uncommon in ordinary conversation. Children take particular pleasure in listening again to their favourite stories presented in the same terms, with the same gestures and modulations of voice. A good narrator uses onomatopoeia, a vivid and clear style; he is able to come to the end of the story in one stretch without error. Intervening as soon as the child is awake to the life of the mind, creating in him a sort of familiarity with the world—even with a kinship—and the things in it, these occasions are an absolutely decisive factor in steeping the person in his culture.

There is a variety of literary genres. First of all, there are fables and stories. Among the Dogon, one can distinguish in this category between narratives portraying animals, those depicting persons, and finally astronomical and cosmic tales where the sun and moon are actors. Generally speaking, the Dogon classify riddles, proverbs, fables, and portents, which need to be explained in order to be understood, in the category of 'weaving words'. Indeed, the pulley of the loom, by its regular squeaking, never stops speaking, but no one understands it: its language is 'secret', full of mystery, like that of the water-sprite, the first revelation of the word at the beginning of time, which men did not understand.[16] As for the mythical narratives, a few of which resemble fables but from which they are carefully distinguished by these people, they belong to the category of serious speech, an object of belief and initiation. They form the background of their traditional thought and world view. According to A. Rattray, the myths are the 'Old Testament' of the Africans. They transmit the principles which underlie the social order, referring them to the action and will of the gods and founders whose memory is honoured, and they thus contribute to society's cohesion and preservation. They appear as a summary of the system of values on which society rests—not in the form of a theory, but of narratives which are indissolubly linked to action, and whose object is the justification of existence.

Without neglecting the faculty of improvisation, oral transmission, as it ordinarily occurs with respect to these performances, is based on the use of memory and rhythm, its effect being to develop the power of retention. The sequences heard must be reproduced as faithfully as possible. The Dogon even consider stories and fables as 'ancient', and if anyone were to invent new ones, he would be called a 'liar'.[17] A fortiori, the sacred texts and myths require, for religious reasons, an absolutely faithful and integral tradition, not only as regards content, but also with respect to tone, mimicry, and the gestures which must accompany their proclamation. Among the Dogon, they are transmitted either through a rhythmical recitation during ritual ceremonies and feasts, or during initiation either individually from father to son or collectively within the men's society. Fantasy, imagination, and emotion evidently have their place in all the extremely diverse performances, but they are, at the same time, channelled, hemmed in, and confined in the culturally rigid, static, and stereotyped moulds which enclose an individual in a universe of symbols, relatively closed in on itself.

Among people with a strong political organization, traditional history occupies an important place in the fostering of ethnic and national consciousness. The Mossi children are accustomed to hearing the old people constantly refer to the origins of the dynasties of the Ouagadougou emperors 'in the time of Naba Oubri'. In villages where important chiefs live, one notices everywhere in Africa demonstrations intended to make the past come alive, especially through the recitations of griots. In everyday conversation and in songs, great past events having an exemplary value are invoked. A Ngoni father, while assembling children, says, 'Listen! Do you hear? What I am going to say concerns the origins of our people. Understand it well and do not forget. The Ngoni cannot forget their past.'[18]

The literature of fables and stories that the child starts to absorb from the early years when he is still living within maternal intimacy comes to him from various sources due to which the literature is constantly enriched. The Dogon mother tells a child stories when he is very small, to make him go to sleep, so that such stories are systematically associated with mother's milk. J. Kenyatta also mentioned songs and lullabies that the mother improvises for the most part but which, nevertheless, impart a true education concerning, for example, the history of the family. The questions which children are asked as soon as they are able to talk check, in a physical manner, on the knowledge thus assimilated.[19] When the young Ngoni leave the paternal house at the age of four or five in order to go and stay with their grandmother, they learn from her a lot of traditional stories. The mothers, like the popular story-tellers of which the Grimm brothers* speak, watch over the accuracy of the tales. They intervene in order to correct the mistakes the children make in their narration. Around the age of ten, the young Dogon come together in order to teach one another what they have learnt in their respective homes.

Among these same people who live around the cliffs of Bandiagara, the father in turn communicates his knowledge of oral literature to his sons when they go with him to the fields. In the whole of Africa, the nocturnal conversations in which all the members of the family or the settlement participate without any age distinction, where all manner of subjects are broached, are decisive not only for the transmission of the literary, juridical, or religious heritage, but also for the transmission of a particular frame of mind and a form of sensibility. In connection with the Kongo tales, Struyf notes:

> These tales are transmitted from one generation to another almost word for word. Since childhood, everyone has come to learn several hundreds of them. The whole village, young and old, has the habit of gathering together in the evening around the intimacy of the fireplace. One of the elders takes the floor and tells stories for hours on end. All listen with great attention to his words and repeat, as a refrain, the last words of the most striking lines.[20]

In certain regions, professional story-tellers go from village to village. Because of their buffoonery and adeptness in manipulating words, they are

---

*They are, respectively, Jacob Ludwig (1785-1863), and Wilhelm Karl (1786-1859), and were born in Hanau, Germany. Philologists, they published in 1812-1813 their collection of folk-tales which have become common knowledge throughout the world.—Transl.

looked upon as incarnations of wisdom. The grandparents—privileged holders and conveyors of oral literature and the teaching inspired by it—are also seen as the primary agents of education in areas other than physical exercise and productive activity. On certain occasions, their function as story-tellers assumes a quasi-ritual and institutional character when it comes to the transmission of maxims, genealogies, and historical, legendary, and mythical accounts. The very intense pleasure that one experiences in hearing these narratives is not due to novelty—since they are known by all—but to hearing them recounted in a faithful, expressive, and elegant manner.

The fables which are transmitted by the oral tradition are one of the privileged ways of introducing the young to the 'light', exoteric knowledge open to all, then later[21] —if they show themselves capable—to the 'heavy', esoteric knowledge reserved only for the initiated. By its enigmatic character, the fable is susceptible of receiving multiple interpretations, existing at different levels. G. Calame-Griaule distinguishes three of these: at the level of individual psychology and of social morality, value judgements are made on the conduct narrated and advice applicable to the life of the listeners is deduced from it; at the natural level attention is drawn to the behaviour and habits of animals; finally, at the level of mythical symbolism, young men who show the right frame of mind can have access to the interpretations which introduce a synthetic vision where all the other levels converge.[22]

A remarkable relationship between the story and the myth exists. If, as this author thinks, the myth is a deliberate moralization of the master ideas which cannot be put at the disposal of anyone at any time, the story is apparently a moralization at a higher level, and this even less transparent. Only the initiated can detect, under its disguise, the vicissitudes and characters that the myth shows clearly. The dualism between the water-sprite and the incestuous fox reappears, for example, in contrasting but complementary animal couples. The apparent immorality which is prevalent in stories, explained at the social level as a type of conduct to be avoided becomes—at the level of esoteric symbolism—the victory of the forces of life over those of death. From this it is easy to see that stories, too, can become the object of belief; in a sense, they are doubly esoteric. Hence, their metaphysical and social significance which is perceptible beyond their literary simplicity. Their recitation contributes to the progress of the world and to the unleashing of the great powers of creation; this recitation is therefore highly beneficial. At the pedagogical level it constitutes a first stage of learning, presenting to the young in an amusing and colourful form, easy to retain, the dramas of creation and the knowledge that they must acquire at different levels of their initiation. Later these essential truths will be differentiated, little by little, from childish imagery. It will suffice to transpose them in order to catch a glimpse of the cosmic mechanism.[23]

The Bambara stories and fables, observes D. Zahan, are an excellent means of acquiring a knowledge of social life and the institutions which. govern it, and of becoming familiar with the ideas which are the very basis of knowledge. These tales, he says,

> constitute an integral teaching accessible to all, requiring no prior initiation . . . Through the exploitation of the innumerable materials at their disposal—thanks to clever and original settings—the stories and fables reimmerse concepts in the matrix which has engendered them. They aim at unfolding, in an allegorical form, and in time and space, the conceptual content of thought. They are a symbolic projection of abstract ideas in the objective universe.[24]

In contrast to stories, myths transmit more general truths. But they also manipulate them according to the modalities of sensory perception, and transpose them onto a concrete plane. In this sense they appear as pedagogical instruments similar to the other narratives. But as far as the education of the child is concerned, the influence of myth is less direct.

These literary productions seem, therefore, to assume a double function: on the one hand, they bring facts to light and, on the other, they contribute to the creation of ideals. They serve as important material for formal education through the moral precepts and rules of conduct which they convey, often in an explicit manner; but often they leave it up to the listeners to extract the implicit content themselves or they steep them in it without their being aware of it. The stories are the tiny seed that is placed in the child's soul and which, little by little, sprouts and grows to become a pervasive undergrowth. In some ways they act as a model for the ordinary communication of thought. In fact, says L.S. Senghor, any language which is not 'fabulation' either bores or is not understood. For G. Calame-Griaule, 'fables are a sort of special mould in which are fused all the elements of culture'.[25]

The chiefly narrative content of the cultural patrimony and its exclusively oral transmission preserve its living character, enable it to be relived at each generation, and to charm, in the strongest sense of the term, to spellbind in some way, those who receive it. L. Frobenius has emphasized the 'demoniac' world which the popular tale creates when passed on in the traditional way, from mouth to ear with every gesture and intonation faithfully reproduced. This world disappears completely when the same stories are read and thus intellectualized.[26]

It is of the nature of esoteric teaching to use enigmas and to avoid direct revelation in clear language. In order to determine, with respect to a certain individual, how far one can go in the communication of knowledge, it is important to test his intelligence and curiosity continually, to see whether he reacts by asking pertinent questions or whether he remains passive. A certain use of fables is therefore necessary, for it is a question of at one and the same time revealing and hiding, of disclosing and disguising, of enticing the spirit and then leaving it unsatisfied. Those not posessing the necessary frame of mind to have access to complete knowledge, must content themselves with hearing without understanding. Confronted with inexhaustible knowledge, the art of the initiator is never to let the pupil satiate himself, but always to sharpen his appetite anew in order to lead him to a deeper search.

3. PROVERBS, MAXIMS, RIDDLES, AND SONGS

'A clever child is told proverbs, not fables,' say the Twi of Ghana. Proverbs require a lively mind to discern, in their condensed form, all the observation, experience, humour and good judgement they contain, and to decide how the general verities they express may be applied to particular cases, for they do not take on their full meaning outside the speech which includes them. Maxims are both a prop and a stop-cock for one's thought. They make the argument flow into a tradition, into something ready-made, and thus strengthen, control, and direct it. Brought in at just the right moment, they are unanswerable and accepted by all. Still, the maxim always has its antidote, which rectifies it, neutralizes it in part, bends it, by expressing another aspect of what society regards as the truth. It is not the isolated maxim, then, which accounts for the ways of the group, but the complex of complementary and opposing proverbs which serve as boundary markers for the movement of thought and shut it within an abundantly fertile, but nevertheless closed, field.

The young Bambara is first acquainted with words by listening to the songs of birds and the interpretation which people around give to them. According to these people's myths, 'it was a bird which first provided the model for the first man's attempt at organized language. The lessons of the "master" have an advantage over those of men in being simple, often full of humour and gaiety, enabling the child's intelligence to develop while his knowledge increases without fatigue.'[27] In this ethnic group they distinguish between maxims and proverbs. The former (*foliw*) express, in condensed form, facts about ordinary life—the fruit of experience and good common sense, and possess by that very fact, a normative character and authority. As for proverbs (*n'dale*), they express in an irrefutable manner an observation which applies analogically to a reality different from that expressed by the statement. Given the facts which they invoke, they need to be transposed to another plane. Whilst maxims can be cited at any time, the proverbs—because of their 'obscurity'—are reserved for the night-time. A good story-teller knows how to compare different proverbs, to link them together and thus provide a thorough teaching.[28]

The riddle, with its striking images which are baffling in their conciseness and unexpected comparisons, can also take its origin from a real situation and lead into a universe of symbols, and thus constitute the point of departure for a true form of teaching.[29] Like the fable and the proverb, its recitation is closely related to certain conditions of place and time, and of the people present. Among the Dogon, it can only be recited at night and during the slack season. Riddles are forbidden between father and daughter, mother and son, a man and his in-laws, and between brother and sister of marriageable age. Among the Ngoni, this 'obscure' thing called a riddle is allergic to the light of day; furthermore, it cannot be engaged in by those between the ages of seven and fourteen.

Let us look at some examples of riddles among the Dogon:

The riddle 'I have tied my father's horse to the house, its tail is outside,' with its reply 'smoke', introduces an explanation of the cycle of rain, the clouds being symbolized by the smoke, the sun by the fire inside the house, the idea of water being suggested by the horse according to Dogon mythology, and that of rain by the horse's tail. Starting from this image the child will be told that it is the sun which heats the earth to form the clouds which fall as rain. A similar lesson is provided by 'My big red hen licks the bottom of my big black hen.' Here the emphasis is on the earth (the black canary), and on the sun (the red fire). A third element which is implied is the water in the earthenware pot, which the fire turns to steam. 'My mother has given birth, and I have not seen the end', with its reply 'the earth' is used to make children understand the continuous rebirth of vegetation and the nourishing role of the earth.

According to F. Dufay, in Rwanda a riddle is not a problem to be solved from the elements given by the statement. There is indeed nothing to guess: one must *know* the answer. The trick in riddles consists in flinging question after question at the one being queried, and thus affording him as little time as possible for listening and understanding.[30] Among the Gikuyu, there are a series of questions to which one must give an instant answer or other questions. But question and answer are learnt by heart and must follow each other rapidly.[31] Thus, thinking or reflection plays but little part in this competition involving mental alertness, quick reaction, memory, and rivalry in the art of speech. Among the Ngoni, slow or inadequate answers are laughed at but quick and right ones applauded.[32] Those able to give the answers experience a feeling of complicity and joyous satisfaction.

Among the Bambara, this game of hide and seek, the riddle, is played preferably between grandchildren and grandparents—a fact which is helpful in understanding one of its most profound aspects. According to these people, a man who has several grandsons is like a tree full of mistletoe; he knows that he is condemned to die soon. In an unavowed and unconscious way, he tries to avoid meeting his grandsons, for the Bambara say:

> The riddle renders in an exact way the flight of the grandfather from his grandsons. The former hides in his questions while the latter tries to find him through his answers. A grandfather fears nothing more in these verbal matches than a young interlocutor who always finds answers to his riddles. At that moment he feels discovered and subjected to the control of the 'parasite' which will end up finishing him off. From this we see that even if riddles take on the appearance of a game, nevertheless, at bottom, they are the little episodes of drama hidden deep in the personality.[33]

In a general way it can be said that getting used to the enigmatic language of the riddle helps an individual to dissimulate his thought, to say delicate or dangerous things in a polished or beautiful language, without seeming to do so.

Alongside riddles, there exists a set of sleight-of-hand or conjuring tricks, which are meant to stimulate and exercise a child's intelligence, and to make him familiar with the images, objects, animals, and plants whose symbolism he will later understand through frequent observation.

Finally, music, song, and choreography are intimately related to oral literature. The song is the adornment of speech, and the dance is simply its unfolding in space. Animation by movement, translation by gesture and mimicry, are ways for the whole body to express itself. Through some of its aspects, it can be assimilated to enigmatic, even esoteric, speech—and thus represent superior, transcendental forms, using registers which are least easily comprehensible. During the dry season, the young Ngoni takes to singing without the help of any musical instruments, by simply harmonizing action and voice. One also finds among them histories and narratives which a song leader intones and which the others punctuate by refrains. Ritual songs accompany all the great moments of the cosmic and the human life cycle; jingles and dance steps animate children's games in the same way they do agricultural and household tasks. The nights of the full moon resound until dawn with the melodies and hand-clapping of the assembled youth. 'For the Bambara,' writes D. Zahan, 'speech is inconceivable apart from song and rhythm.'[34] The productions of oral literature can in no way be appreciated and judged independently of the sounds and gestures which give them their full aesthetic quality and put man in his totality in motion.

4. WORD AND THOUGHT

Those around him draw a child's attention to a particular reality and provide him with its interpretation. This interpretation can be explicit, but very often it remains implicit in the sense that one is content, through allusions which tend always in the same direction, to place a specific object in relationship with other elements. An individual gets used to a whole gamut of transitions which always recur under different forms. He learns to carry out certain special comparisons, to pick out one particular set of correspondences rather than another such, to organize his thought according to preferential axes, and finally to cast it into the rigid and highly structured categories which his culture offers him. One constantly pushes beyond the individual fact in order to integrate it into a framework having a larger meaning thanks to the use of analogy and allusion. One is more sensitive to the context and the halo of connotations which surround a word than to its strict meaning. 'The importance of a term stems from its power of evocation and the notions to which it can be related, and which help to clarify its significance.' While apparently remaining on a tangible plane and without transcending the concrete image, thought thereby succeeds in propelling itself to a higher plane of abstraction and generality.[35] African thought is like a hieroglyphic text, but a trained mind cannot err in deciphering it since the context clarifies the meaning of any image utilized, and helps one in choosing from among all the possible images furnished by the society. D. Zahan provides an illustration of this:

> The Bambara illustrate the most abstract themes by bringing in the medium of the elephant, hyena, hippopotamus, horse, donkey, dog, plants, spices, etc., selected according to the idea to be expressed. If he wants to speak of the 'delights' and 'savour' of knowledge, he will invoke salt, red pepper, ash, sauce. If he is trying to describe the immensity of knowledge, he will have recourse to the elephant, the largest animal he knows. The lion will incarnate the noblest aspect of education. The hyena will represent objective knowledge made accessible to man, etc. Each object, natural or manufactured, is, in teaching, a symbol which, however, should not be used haphazardly, since its value is a function of an analogy which may or may not be established between these abstract concepts and the real and intrinsic attributes of the referents of the symbols. To these materials borrowed from the external world, Bambara symbolism joins gestures and the bodily postures of the person himself. That is why every 'lesson' is mimicked, danced, and organized like a sacred drama.[36]

This essentially concrete mentality, observes R. Allier, does not shrink from abstraction 'provided that the latter is clothed in a garb which seems to divest it of its purely general character and makes of it something particular'.[37]

Speaking of the ordinary ways of reasoning among the people of the Niger Valley, D. Zahan said that if Bambara logic does not differ much from our own in its form, it nevertheless departs from it appreciably where it conerns its content, based as it is on the individual and the implication of facts rather than on the universal. He goes on to say: 'This observation enables one to understand why the intellectual training of children is carried out from a very early age, in the form of reasoning (which we could call *sorites*) destined to lead their minds towards the interior of things and prepare them for mysticism.'[38]

This form of reasoning can be described as being in a chain, where no terms are contained in others, but evoke each other. M. Griaule was the first to discover this type of reasoning in childrn's games and to dub it 'litanies'. D. Zahan has shown that among the Bambara this amounts to polysyllogism, where the predicate of the first proposition becomes the subject of the second, and so on*—a type of reasoning here restricted to children.[39]

With C. Lévi-Strauss, one can describe African thought as 'tinkering', meaning that it juxtaposes, amalgamates, and strings together words without binding them together, or by uniting them through analogy or some resemblance which to a Westerner is purely external. Often this thought has, at least in appearance, a rambling character. Hampaté Ba has expressed it well: 'The European is sytematic: if he speaks of the mines, he is speaking only of the mines; whereas we, while speaking of the pig, may very well be speaking of the ass, the elephant, or man.'[40]

But is it not the function of symbol to transform objects or actions into something else, and thus to reveal the fundamental unity of several levels of reality? By becoming a symbol, each thing annuls its concrete limits, ceases to be an isolated fragment in order to become integrated in a system. It unifies without confusing; it permits a transition from one level to another.[41] The processes of thought based on symbolization and the linking of ideas and images rests on a fundamental mobility—a kind of slippage which is essential to it—, and which leads to the limits of know-ledge through all the analogical relations. Meanings blend in such a way that the universe appears as a vast tissue where each element is joined by the threads of the woof and the warp to an infinity of other elements. An object can never be considered uniquely in itself, but it is like an avenue open to the world, making possible immense but not infinite perspectives. Within this superabundance and profusion of possible correspondences, thought needs—in order to maintain its rigour and to avoid fluctuation—these dikes, these boundary markers, these stop-cocks which, among

---

*This is in fact the meaning of 'sorites'.—Transl.

others, maxims and classifications provide. It is necessary to push to the limit the image of the fabric which is not only a criss-cross of bonds, but also an organization, a system, a rigorous chequerwork, resistant and tight.

9

Assimilation of Moral Values

> 'In Black Africa, ethics is active wisdom. It consists for the living man in recognizing the unity of the world and in working for its ordering. It is not a catechism which is recited: it is an ontology expressed in and through the society, and first of all in oneself.'
>
> —L. S. Senghor[1]

'A society,' wrote E. Durkheim, 'can neither create nor recreate itself without at the same time creating an ideal. This creation is not for it a kind of superfluous act through which it could complete itself once formed: it is the act through which it makes and remakes itself.'[2] What a society judges good or bad for its children depends on what it intends to make of them, and the model to which it wants them to conform. With moral education, one is dealing with the most synthetic aspect of socialization. The other aspects touching on the collective, intellectual, and practical life are raised to a much higher level of synthesis and consciousness by the ideals of life and the conduct that society recommends to its members.

Any moral habit that one inculcates in children proceeds, according to R. Hubert, from the principle that other people exist and that one must take their existence into account. In education envisaged as a guide to moral growth, one may distinguish three successive stages. First, the child is helped to come out of himself by adapting himself to the small groups inside which his childhood is evolved. Afterwards, the child is helped to enlarge his field of action by becoming aware of his obligations in wider circles. Finally, the child is helped to realize himself by becoming a member of a reasonable humanity and by entering into the world of spiritual values which support its life.[3]

Moral education seeks to lead a child from a simple conformity to rules, to feeling the attraction of values, and finally to hearing the call of the ideal; it intends to lead him from a simple adaptation to social constraints to the creation of his own norms; from a legalistic attitude to one which is the result of reflection; from an imposed obligation to one which is accepted and internalized.

1. CULTURAL ENVIRONMENT AND MORAL ATMOSPHERE

In leading the child to internalize the values and ideals of his society, the ever-present permeation by the environment, and the slow, imperceptible modelling of the personality according to the group's intrinsic norms are more decisive than any other mode of transmission.

The values which a group promotes are intimately related to its economic, social, and political structures. They form a system which embraces a structured set of concepts according to which, explicitly or implicitly, a society thinks the world and life ought to be governed and organized. A culture is always more than the sum of its parts; it is essentially a style of life, a way of feeling things, a search for the better. In spite of the inevitable gap—sometimes even the contradiction—which exists between the order of the ideal and that of the real, the two are equally important for the complete understanding of a civilization. In order to understand the moral training which a child receives in the traditional environment, one must take as a point of departure the values which justify life in a given society and which give meaning to the ideal personality which acts as a 'pattern' for the educational action which is exerted by the adult world in order to attain its ends and realize its goal in the upcoming generation.

With reference to the attempts at typology undertaken by G. Gurvitch,[4] one can say that the morality of the societies we are studying here unquestionably rests on the ascendancy of custom and tradition, a set of predominantly peasant and family values and ideal images, an assured regularity born of recurring processes. Here it is a question of traditional morality, a product more collective than personal, which is strongly normative, founded on rules, duty, and law, a social structure which, although not always appearing authoritarian, nevertheless exercises a considerable diffuse pressure, especially by surrounding itself with a supernatural halo. It is a morality in which personal conscience and its aspirations certainly have a place, though a relatively reduced one. Prestigious and yet familiar models play a vital role: values do not have a characteristically abstract existence, but assume concrete incarnation in the persons of ancestors, chiefs, elders, and sages; in seers who are interpreters of the invisible, in devoted older sons, in obedient younger sons.

The more precarious the material conditions in a given society, the more the survival of small groups requires that all the members pool their efforts. In this perspective, individual liberty is seen as a potential threat. It is the ideal of sociological interdependence which is going to prevail, expressing itself concretely through solidarity and a sense of responsibility towards one another. A fixed and intangible custom is seen as indispensable for mediating between individual wills. There is hardly any circumstance in which conduct is not controlled in advance by norms inherited from tradition, in such a way that each one knows how to act, and what others expect of him. C. Pairault notes that in the final analysis, traditional life is summed up in the maintenance of *decency*, whose principle and definition correspond to what is necessary for a stable and well ordered community. Personal attitudes and feelings become internalized within a group and receive from it their orientation. As C. Pairault writes:

It is not in front of himself but in front of his equals and through them that an individual knows how to judge good and evil. He has no other maxim execpt those of the tradition which hems him in. In other words, the ethical substance of the community overwhelms every individual and prevents the individual conscience from seeking the moral law in itself.[5]

In concrete terms, it is not the parents who, in everyday life represent absolute authority in the eyes of the child; he has a considerable margin of freedom from their control and many ways of escaping it. Authority appears mainly through a set of collective pressures. It is more diffuse and impersonal, and by that very fact more constraining than would normally be that of an individual of flesh and blood with whom one would have everyday relationships. Authority resides primarily in the lineage, with its exigencies, its customs, its threats.

It has often been remarked that there exists a kind of contradiction between the child's life of total freedom and the feeling of absolute dependence which finally dominates him with respect to the fundamentally ontological entity, the lineage. Outside this centre of vital forces, the individual is almost nothing: he no longer has the structure or the necessary internal backbone to sustain him.

As F. Ngoma has said: 'The clan being the sum total of the dead ancestors, the living members, and the members not yet born, its safeguard and its harmonious development must be at the basis of all education.'[6] The internal force of traditional society does not consist in amassing riches, but in assuring the continuity of generations. Individual happiness consists in finding a wife, having children, and in having the wherewithal to feed them. A. Richards shows how at the approach of puberty young people of both sexes aspire to being fathers and mothers, and are troubled by the thought that they might turn out to be impotent or sterile.[7] What is important is the survival of the group—its unity, prosperity, honour, and force. The individual is considered as a necessary cog for the good functioning of the whole, as a cell in an organism which transcends him. If, socially and ontologically, he can only exist when he is united to a lineage and a family group, his main fear will obviously be that of isolation.

But the group is not only of concern to the people here on earth. The Black African conception of parentage places the ancestors at the centre of the existence of those living. It is through their intervention that the present generations are joined to the source of all life. It is on them that the authority of the lineage is projected, for it must be given a name and a face. They represent the group, and at the same time personalize and humanize a little this 'thing' which is the clan-based society. It is they who have instituted custom and given today's society its face. Everything is explained through them, and ethnologists well know the answer given over and again to the questions they ask: 'It is the ancestors who have told us to do this.' By the fact that they are the founders, they are also the guardians of the group's norms, and remain attached to whatever has value for the living. They thus stand as a collective superego. There are only two attitudes possible in their regard: to obey them or to appease them. In any case one fears them and waits for the sign of their approval, for on this depends happiness or misfortune on earth. The family priests are closer to them because of their function and the elders because of their age: it is they who normally act as their intermediaries and channels of transmission. The ancestors are obviously always on the side of custom and established authority, of which they represent the most efficacious support. Man can revolt against a flesh-and-blood father, but not against invisible fathers who are omnipotent, omnipresent, and on whom one has no hold.

Groups founded on the bonds of kinship are essentially hierarchical social realities, which are structured according to the principles of seniority and primogeniture, the vital influx which sustains the individual in exist-ence being transmitted from parents to children, from older to younger children. A person's status is circumscribed by the interplay of forces having a pyramidal shape, with the ancestral founder representing the summit. People interact with one another on a truly ontological level. A father's anger or that of an older person is more formidable than that of an equal. The reason for this is that on the social level they have more authority, and control the means of getting their forebears to diminish or dry up the vital forces of their descendants, and this inevitably leads to bad luck, sickness, wasting away, and death.

The main directions of traditional ethics which are the logical conse-quences of the organization of the kinship family must not be allowed to obscure the differences which can exist. Moral values and rules of conduct not only differ from one ethnic group to another, but also according to such elements of social life as associations, classes, and castes. According to whether these entities oppose or complement one another within the more or less integrated whole which constitutes the community, the modes of behaviour and the norms which govern them will also conflict or be comple-mentary.

A child belongs to many social groups representing for him so many educational environments. Each group has its own normative structures and elaborates its own models of conduct. One does not behave in the same way within an age fraternity as in the parental group. One does not learn to observe the same rules within one group as within the other. It can also happen that there are contradictions between these groups, and that in this way a child confronts not one coherent morality but a plurality of moral codes.

But it can be affirmed that the internal life of all the different groups—extended family as well as associations of equals—is governed by a law of interdependence and solidarity which places the common good above all other considerations, and demands that all bear the consequences of the possibly untoward conduct of one of the members. In order to be socially integrated, one must agree to take upon oneself the burdens imposed by mutual support. Not to be in a position to help one's parents or sisters when circumstances demand it, or to intervene by paying back the bride-price should circumstances require, or to take charge of part of the family, or to offer customary gifts, or provide hospitality, not to share with others what one has or what others think one has is to expose oneself to shame, contempt, reprobation, and even to exclusion. The help given to others is always free in the sense that no one expects any remuneration, but it is based on the principle of reciprocity.

Families and associations are also governed by the law of sharing and equality which demands that no one should elevate himself above the average economic level of his status—on pain of becoming the object of envy and the target of evil practices. The one who has must make others share his wealth. Prestige is found not in amassing riches but in distributing them. C. Pairault notes that in Chad all goods are destined for sharing; no one is supposed to keep to himself more than he distributes to his family. Hospitality profits the one who gives it. The virtue of saving has no meaning in such a context. One would rather speak of it as a vice, for to keep things to oneself is to stop the flow of exchanges which is indispensable for the good functioning of the community. Avarice is equivalent to theft or a wicked act. The value of an individual is measured by his capacity to give his blood to a large number of descendants, food, lodging, and clothes to his neighbours and acquaintances, and to give gifts in return for those he has received.

Generosity in sharing is a value that is cultivated from an early age, especially where it concerns food. In principle, it is the old people who have the role of distribution. The Ngoni consider individualistic attachment to personal wealth as a major fault. Among the Tallensi, even a bird or lizard that one catches must be shared equally. For his part, J. Kenyatta writes that the notion of sharing is the basis of educational principles. As they grow, children find sharing quite natural as is said: to live with others is to love them and share everything with them; it is only wizards who live and eat alone.[8]

In a social system where the horizontal axis of equality between peers and the vertical axis of continuity and authority are always counterbalancing, the virtue of justice, through which an individual receives his due according to his worth, is central for guaranteeing equilibrium and peace. For instance, the importance that the distribution of food has—whether it is to co-wives or to children—sharpens very early this sense of fair distribution to all. Experience shows that the young African is extremely sensitive to any injustice because it is an insult to his status, touching not only his property but his very being.

In a very general way, it can be said that African societies have set up complex and meticulous institutions for maintaining the equality of all within the group, for counterbalancing powers, regularizing access to prestige, frustrating any attempts at individual autonomy, neutralizing acquired privileges, and for limiting influences which may be too powerful. Anything which makes an individual stand out undermines the foundations of the social order and must therefore be checked, if necessary by having recourse to occult intrigues.[9]

The fact that individual liberty is seen as a menace and therefore is suppressed does not prevent its existence and manifestation. Any form of individualism will appear intolerable and has therefore a negative value. In it one sees a will to power and destruction which must be controlled. Among the Dogon, it is expressed in terms of the myth of the Pale Fox in revolt against Amma-god, his father. But because it seeks to exercise control over everything within it, traditional society knows—with the characteristic realism of its world view—how to set up deviance, transgression, excess, and even orgy itself as counter-patterns, thus, once again, as rules. It operates safety-valves so that the hostility which is ordinarily repressed can have an institutional expression. In the final analysis, the evil which is the exercise of freedom is considered beneficial in its effects if it is properly channelled, for it sets things in motion, questions an always imperfect status quo and gives, through the dialectic which it introduces, a certain savour to existence.

Sorcery is considered as an extreme individualistic and antisocial activity. All researchers agree as to the mastery it has over minds. It appears as an extreme counter-value, and in this way dominates moral life, of which it constitutes a negative pole. The intrigues woven at night explain sterility, sickness, death, success, and failure. A man who rises too high in any sphere in society is considered to be a power in the occult universe. Sorcery is met with a counter-sorcery, which detects and neutralizes it, but is founded on the same principles. Thus distrust and envy become major feelings, and suspicion one of the most basic attitudes in interpersonal relationships.

An informant of R. Bureau has spoken the following words: 'When a White man sees his neighbour build a beautiful house he says to himself: I am going to build an even better one. In the same circumstances a Black man will say: I am going to destroy it. One needs a lot of courage to be the first to build a house with strong materials and to roof it with iron sheets.'[10]

In such a universe aggressiveness is everywhere latent, imprecise, enveloping. A question which is too direct or too personal, a compliment, a familiarity, an approach which is too brusque—all can be seen as agressive and as a sign of danger. One must constantly be on the lookout to dispel the danger as it comes, but also to reassure, and prove that one's intentions are good. This is the object of the long litanic questions which help people to 'feel' one another out, and to inspire confidence, of laughter and jokes, of words which express just the opposite of what is meant, of paraphrases and metaphorical language.

This aggressive feeling one experiences towards others can only with difficulty be assumed on the individual level. Generally it is inverted and projected onto the others, who are seen as aggressive and persecutors. We have had occasion to mention the paranoid component of the personality of young people in Brazzaville.[11] In Senegal, M. Ortigues notes that the mechanism of projection is preferred as a means of formulating the problem of evil, and that all interpersonal relationships are strongly tinged by the fact that everyone easily perceives himself as being persecuted. 'One might say that a large part of the energy which, in another context, would be used up actively, is here consumed in self-defence. In all circumstances it is appropriate to protect oneself against threatening intents.'[12]

The emotional and moral atmosphere in which traditional society is shaped is thus marked by a very strong ambiguity. A manifest action is only understandable through its motives and through its repercussions on the level of the invisible. Everything is an object of interpretation. The most tenuous clue must be taken into consideration. Human beings are not the only ones to be reckoned with. The other world is eminently close, and one can easily communicate with it. The powers which inhabit it—the deceased, the ancestors, the evil genies, the spirits and the gods—weigh heavily upon men's lives; they get involved in them and attempt to orient them. But this other world obviously represents an immense field for the projection of desires and fears, of individual and collective symbols and fantasies. The constraints which emanate from it are in fact constraints which are internal to man, and only represent a more subtle expression of the pressures that his culture exercises on him.

2. THE PRACTICE OF MORAL EDUCATION

a. Early childhood experiences

According to a Lari proverb, 'the education of a good man begins at the age when he has only a small scrap of material as a loin-cloth.' The sum total of the experiences that a child accumulates as he grows up and particularly during the first few months of his life, not only orients in a decisive manner his perception of the external world and of the other person, but also determines the manner in which he will assimilate and integrate the system of values that his society offers him. Between the culture which characterizes a community and the individual who must gradually make it his own, parents and the other near relations play an essential mediating role, and this right from birth and during the first stages of life because these are—for man as well as for other animals—the critical phases propitious for the fixation of affective reactions to certain types of objects.[13] The important thing, as R. Hubert says, is to mould the affective dispositions which will make the child an effectively social and moral being.[14]

From the very beginning, the child is used to being left by himself and to expressing his desires freely. As Jensen-Krige writes:

> Compared to the life of a European child who is always under the supervision of a parent or of other people charged with his care, and who is sorrounded with valuable and dangerous objects that he is not supposed to touch, wearing clothes that he is told to keep clean, subjected to a regular timetable, the life of a Bantu child appears astonishingly free and unconcerned in the midst of many companions.[15]

The way in which the child is taken away from the mother and made to enter the company of his equals, of his father, and of the extended group, puts him slowly but progressively under the influence of external models. The weaning situation—as we have seen—represents in a very general way a break with respect to the experiences of the preceding period. The frustration which results from it is felt as a disorder, a devaluation of the ego, a reversal of all the attitudes which have taken on vital importance in the eyes of the child. He is thus plunged into a perplexity and a distrust which are in obvious contrast to the quiet assurance of the preceding period. Clinical experience shows how propitious this moment can be for the emergence of a sort of preculpability,[16] which tends to become ingrained not in the form of conscious feelings but of behaviour. Its incidence in Black Africa is seen whenever one studies the theme of wrong-doing on the level of the total culture.[17]

Toilet-training—a very important stage in the internalization of certain values among European children—takes place in Africa without much insistence, and without the threat of punishment hanging over the child. In this area behaviour varies more from one group to another than is the case with feeding; the categories of clean and dirty do not have the same relevance and their projection onto the moral level does not take place in the same way. The simplicity of dress and of environment allow for more indulgence. The little child imitates the conduct of adults without being the object of constraint or pressure. But from the moment he is considered old enough to be clean, the initial laissez-faire can—at least in some cultures—

give way to more exacting attitudes not excluding punishment or public appeal to feelings of shame. The first ethical attitudes are inculcated in the family circle, especially in connection with food and the mastery over desires and gestures which is demanded of the child as soon as he is allowed to eat with others. He is asked not to be greedy, to eat slowly and according to the rules, not to serve himself without having been asked to do so, or ahead of older people.

In addition to the slow inculcation by the environment which no doubt fashions the personality at a most profound level, each cultural tradition also gives rise to a formal education which is more conscious of the values which it seeks to promote and the methods it intends to use. Obviously, it does so in terms of a particular concept of man. For centuries, moral pedagogy in the European tradition was founded on fear and coercion. It is a matter of inculcating the rules of conduct into the child and of correcting a nature gone astray if not basically perverse. An observer himself educated according to this scheme cannot but be perplexed by an education of another style, and it is in effect on this precise point that one notices among many European educators working in Black Africa the most profound astonishment and condemnation.

b. Rules, incentives, and constraints

It must be remembered that moral and social rules vary considerably from one ethnic group to another, even among neighbouring populations. Thus, the Rwandese and the Nuer encourage their children to fight among themselves, while the Gusii ask them to take their quarrels to an adult and to fight in front of him.[18] Two Bantu people—the Pedi and Lovedu—which are otherwise similar in many ways have, nevertheless, social norms, and consequently educational rules which are profoundly different, indeed quite opposed. The former aim at subjecting the child to the authority of the group; they inflict frequent and very severe corporal punishments on him and seek to make their boys aggressive and quarrelsome. The latter are more individualistic, and basically peaceful. They believe that corporal punishment does serious injury to the personality. A feudal and authoritarian political system cannot yield the same norms of organization as one which is purely clannish and strongly egalitarian. Such aristocratic societies as the Ngoni and the Tutsi develop in their members a lofty image of themselves, an ideal personality which is more exacting than elsewhere.

But even within the same tradition, affective and moral education contains also an indefinite number of variables. It is especially after early childhood that a diversity of educational behaviour is apparent, even to the point of an apparent total absence of norms and an oscillation between the extremes of severity and permissiveness. This phenomenon does not hold for complex and highly diversified societies. The fluctuating and only barely conscious character of the models appears when people generally do not know how to answer an outsider's questions about this area; the information gathered in this way is amazingly flat and uninteresting. The action exercised by the adult on the child either in the sense of repression or non-intervention nevertheless falls within certain precise limits set by the society. For example, how severely should a child be punished? In general, the European environment is less indulgent than the African one; Europeans would nevertheless disapprove of putting pepper in the eyes of a child to punish him: they would consider that as *going too far*. It is less the rules or types of behaviour which reveal in themselves the specificity of an educational system than the margin left to them to vary and the general tendency which unites them and makes them models.

Depending on the specific tradition, some societies lean more on the side of coercion exercised directly by adults or on that of the freedom exercised within the children's group but tempered and channelled by the severe requirements of this communal life. Where children have their own societies they develop particular rules of conduct which sometimes run counter to the general morality. These appear in the form of laws that the young impose on themselves just outside the adult world. Because they have fewer opportunities of coming together and organizing themselves, and also because their conduct at marriage must conform to precise norms, young girls are in general more strictly controlled and subjected to more standardized patterns of conduct.

Previously we have shown how the child is introduced to the knowledge of the mechanisms of traditional organization and to the rules of good manners which govern his integration. It appeared to us that the major part of the teaching which the child received either openly or under the cover of symbols had a very strong normative character. This is inevitable in a system of education where explanation is given only when questions are asked or when concrete problems arise, where all the forms of instruction are geared to the immediate reality, and where one always aims at transmitting to children the correct behaviour.

M. T. Knapen has shown that among the Kongo the use of self-respect and pride play a far less important role in child education than they do among Europeans. The mother does not make the child participate fictitiously in certain tasks with the intention of making him feel important. One would find this kind of encouragement and stimulation ridiculous and out of place. If she asks him to do something for her it is because she really needs it, and it is normal at his age to do it. These services are expected of him as soon as he is able to discharge them. The reward—even verbal—will be as rare as punishment and quite unnecessary, too. This is an essentially realistic attitude. At each stage the child is taken as he is; there is no desire to push him to high performances by using the motive of self-respect. It is less a question of making him adapt a personal ideal than of getting him used to a social role. Rather than develop his pride or his belief in his own value, one will attempt to adapt him to the demands of communal life. The individual is not made a star, and it is always towards the social group that all is directed. It is not individual accomplishment which is sought, but integration into the group, and this is best realized through participation in real tasks useful to all. Also at work is the mechanism mentioned by E. Durkheim: When the child notices 'that everyone around him always behaves in the same way in the same circumstances, he considers it impossible to behave otherwise'. [19]

With respect to the Chiga of East Africa, M. Edel notes that when several months old, the baby is considered as an individual with his own nature, character, desires, and aversions. They seriously consult a child of three years, and as soon as practicable, his behaviour is considered just as difficult to modify as that of an adult. Between the two there is no essential difference; only that the child is not expected to have knowledge of certain matters, and he is therefore not held responsible. The personality is taken as it is, and therefore no systematic attempt is made to correct or amend it. One will scold a child, to be sure, but without expecting a real change to take place in him. It is through chance or bad luck that one is as he is. Punishment is not aimed at discipline and it is not a part of a coherent educational goal. Rather, it appears as a vindictive or nervous relief. A child's whims and even insolence are accepted, and if he refuses to obey an order, one does not insist. [20] E. Mangin reports similar facts about the Mossi:

> On the pretext that the child does not know what he is doing, his parents let him act as he likes, let him satisfy all his whims without correcting him, let him hurl the grossest insult at his mother, and make a fist at her, without incurring any punishment. Witnesses content themselves by saying that the child will one day be a fighter.[21]

The Pondo say that a child is precious and to strike him is to corrupt him. In fact, they have recourse to punishment only in serious cases such as telling a lie or negligence in herding cattle to the point that crops are spoilt. [22] Among the Lovedu, Jensen-Krige observes that a child enjoys great indulgence, without, however, being spoiled. He is rarely with his parents who are busy elsewhere, but is with his companions, and it is from the older children that he learns what discipline is. The child's likes and dislikes are taken into account and his property is respected. Praise is not stinted, and if threats are frequent, actual punishment is rare.

As the child passes from one stage of maturity to another, the attitude of those who surround him becomes more and more severe. Weaning therefore signals everywhere a new stage in moral education. For instance, among the Basuto, as H. Ashton says, one reasons with the child, using force if necessary, for from now on he is considered big enough to understand and to carry out orders. Among the Ngoni when a child misbehaves, he may be punished, although he is not really held responsible: it is rather his mother or his nurse who is blamed. But with the second dentition, the boy is considered ready for a new type of life where he must no longer depend on the adult, and where he is outside women's jurisdiction. He is no longer protected or consoled during his quarrels. Social sanctions: reproaches, exclusions, jokes, reprimands administered by the peers begin to be fully applied in such a way that he becomes very sensitive to the opinion of others. From this moment the responsibility for his acts is imputed to him.[23]

The adult appears pedagogically most effective when he uses methods that are barely perceptible, which can hardly be distinguished in ordinary conversation, which mobilize the social sentiments of the child, stimulate his motivation to work and his desire to participate in communal tasks: exhortations, encouragements, tokens of recognition and approbation, recommendations, advice, references to models for imitation. Such are the usual methods, which are difficult to observe and analyse because they do not stand out. Since he practically addresses the child in the same way as he addresses his equals, the adult shows that he takes him seriously, thus fulfilling the child's greatest desire: having value in the eyes of the adults, being recognized by them as an active member of society, seeing his activities approved of and appreciated. In an environment where positive judgment and social valuation prevail, it is evident that reproach, scolding and insult, appeals to shame and ridicule, are very much felt, and for that reason reserved for serious matters.[24] According to F. Ngoma, encouragement in the form of material rewards is supposed to be common among the Kongo: giving a child clothes, food, money, a chicken to raise.[25] However, this observation should not be generalized.

The society acts as a vehicle for a large number of maxims, having as their principal aim that of keeping children within the bounds of propriety. If a South African Black child yawns too much he is told that he is going to break his jaw bones: to make fun of someone is to put oneself in danger of being bewitched; if one comes out of a hut backwards, one runs the risk of being transformed into a lizard; to pull off young shoots will cause a stormy summer.[26] Among the Dogon, as reports M. Griaule,

to change one's mind when one has decided to wash oneself, not to wash oneself completely, to walk with only one sandal, to help someone climb up and not help him climb down again, not to purify oneself after a fight, to forget to dance in one's mother's honour when one comes to a cross-road—all these are acts which imperil the lives of parents. A child, frightened at the thought of losing his mother, is soon going to acquire certain ideas of the consquences of his actions and learn to pay attention. He will eat his meals properly on pain of never satisfying his hunger or of seeing his fingers fall off. He will take good care of his clothes.[27]

With regard to the moral education of children, one can point to a whole pedagogy based on fear, appealing to frightening creatures taken from the folklore: bogeymen, sorcerers, spectres, ferocious animals, demons, and jinns. But the use of these threats will have a different effect according to whether the adult who uses them believes in them or not. Their fundamental ambiguity is seen in that the child is not to be indefinitely duped, but that he sees on the other hand that on certain occasions even the adult himself is frightened, and therefore takes seriously the existence of those evil creatures of which everybody has had an experience at one time or another. In modern Africa the White man, because his colour reminds one of ghosts, is used to frighten Black children.[28] White men eat Black children. In studying the words adults use especially to make the children afraid and thus keep them on the right path, it appeared to us that quite often they had a ring of oral menace, and that the themes of biting and devouring were predominant in them: 'the ghost is coming to eat you', 'the snake is coming to bite you', etc.[29] Jensen-Krige shows how much among the Lovedu grown-ups take pleasure in seeing children frightened by this kind of talk, even if they have not been bad.

Initiations exercise an educational and disciplinary function during the whole period of childhood, long before they take place. The child knows he will have to undergo them, and that at that time he must take his place in a definitive way with respect to the men's world and its authority. He is made to fear in advance. He is told that his outbursts will be revenged, and this is not an idle threat. Frightened on the one hand by what he perceives of this secret drama, and on the other hand eager to submit to it as soon as possible in order to have access to a higher status, the child perceives this institution which is always talked about in veiled terms as highly ambiguous. In certain cases the thrashings which take place during initiations are real punishments deferred until that moment. The absolutely general phenomenon of ragging appears every time that a group of elders and of young people come together on a continuous basis and share life together. A peculiar kind of hostility breaks out between the two groups, born of the feeling of superiority on the part of the elders who feel that they form a well knit group which is the repository of customs and traditions of which the young are ignorant.[30] Ragging is practised in good humour in children's societies, and during the initiation stages which prolong them. Even though these societies do not ordinarily sanction transgressions, they have an undeniable disciplinary function in that they allow the older children to establish their authority.[31]

There is also the threat of malediction which is very effective. It is doubt-less the most characteristic constraint of the Black African ontology. Being cursed by one's father, mother and—in a matrilineal society—by one's maternal uncle, is equivalent to being cut off from the lineage, to no longer being plugged into that current of life which flows from the ancestors, and which alone enables a person to maintain himself in existence. The individual is affected at the metaphysical level, and risks falling into not only social but existential nothingness. This absolute weapon also constitutes a very real threat. In order to make themselves obeyed and to stifle any inclination to freedom, the family authorities use this menace quite freely against those under them: many young Africans who say and believe that they are free from custom still live in constant dread of the curse. Intellectually they deny its power, but affectively they cannot throw it off. Unless one wants to seek reconciliation and thus to put oneself aright, being cursed is—in the short or long run—being condemned to death.

It must be kept in mind also that traditional man actually has but little occasion of punishing since, for the most part, the child lives away from him in his own organization, one in which his immediate seniors are in charge of his education. On the other hand, if physical sanctions are used reluctantly, it must be said that the word carries quite a different significance from that which it has among Europeans. A piece of advice, a reprimand, a verbal reproach, a threat, and especially a curse, are very efficacious. In an oral culture, the word has not lost its force, and is not employed uselessly. Whoever speaks gets a hearing. The word is like a seed that once deposited germinates, works, spreads, changes and converts. To be sure, a mother's words, because of their too frequent use, are not as effective as those of the father (or the maternal uncle) which are more distant, more reserved, more serious.[32] For our part, we noticed the great weight which the young Kongo attach to such sentences as: 'My father has advised me.'

Speaking of corporal punishment as it formerly existed in European schools, E. Durkheim has shown that as an organized system, it had its origin in the school and not in the home. When education is given exclusively within the family, corporal punishment exists only sporadically, and it is rather indulgence which prevails. As school life becomes more organized, its arsenal of punishment becomes richer, and its application increases. Eventually these disciplinary attitudes confaminate the home atmosphere. Durkheim thinks there is something in the very nature of schools which pushes them strongly toward this type of sanction. Instead of leaving the young to *teach themselves*, spontaneously, according to the instigations of life, *they are being taught*. The author goes on to say:

Now such an action necessarily has something coercive and laborious about it, for it forces the child to go beyond his own nature, to do violence to it since he is required to mature more rapidly than he is capable of, since from now on, instead of leaving his activity to drift freely depending on circumstances, the child must consciously and painfully concentrate it on subjects that are imposed on him. In a word, civilization has to some extent made the life of the child more gloomy. [33]

Even though the ethnographical data we have at present do not allow a detailed comparative study, it appears that traditional societies in those parts of Black Africa which have come under the influence of Islam and Koranic schools have elabocated much more systematic and also more violent systems of correction than the other societies. [34] The same can undoubtedly be said about the parts of Africa under Christian influence.[35]

One often hears it said among Africans that before colonization and the introduction of the modern school, people were more strict. Doubtless, in extreme cases they used to apply Draconian measures which have since disappeared. But it appears to us improbable that in the usual practice, one often had recourse to physical constraints. Comparing in this respect the rural and urban populations in the Congo-Brazzaville, it is undeniably among the latter population that one finds greater brutality in the treatment of children. Severity increases with Islamic and Christian influences, for a new, more pessimistic, concept of the person is in those cases substituted for the traditional view.

Among the Kongo, the mother punishes more often, but the father more effectively. With the mother, the child lives in constant familiarity, and this weakens her authority. The father is more distant and interferes only in serious cases. The mother often speaks to the child in the name of the father as if to compensate for her own weakness, for she knows that she is too indulgent. She threatens to report to the father the bad conduct of the little ones, but then does nothing about it. If the father punishes the child, the mother may rush to console him and show him tenderness. She may even get angry with the father for punishing the child. But quite often the mere presence of the father and the authority of his words are sufficiently imposing so that he does not have to punish.

The family system has repercussions on the way children are punished. In a patrilineal society, it will be bad for the mother to punish a child, and she can only do so if no one else is present. On the other hand, in the matrilineal system, it is the father's interference which can be considered abusive. We have noted a certain characteristic conduct among the Kongo: the mother will place herself between the father and the child, affirming her rights over the child; if matters get worse, she will send the children to her own family, especially to their uncles. Obviously, the child notices very early the weaknesses of the constraint mechanism weighing on him and he learns to take advantage of this fact. But such differences are not systematic. It is not rare to see maternal uncles urging the father to punish the child and to see them blaming him if he does not do it sufficiently.Everything depends on the type of relationship prevailing between the two family groups—on whether this relationship is cordial or is one of suspicion.[36]

The family system is involved from still another angle: a moral fault has consequences depending on whether it is committed within the clan or outside of it. R. Jaulin shows how among the Sara one is not treated severely in case of theft or even murder if it is committed within the lineage. Such conduct is seen as being so aberrant as to be due to chance. The injury that one perpetrates against someone in his own lineage is done against oneself, because the basic social unit is not the individual but the group, living in the same neighborhood. On the other hand, stealing from another lineage exposes one to being sold as a slave: one is then a real thief. Still other considerations come into play: transgressions committed outside the lineage implicate the group's reputation, and give rise to feuds, litigations, and collective payment of fines and damages.

We have seen these themes show up continually during our research at Brazzaville. A quarrel or some other minor offence had few repercussions for the child if it took place in a district where his family was not known. However, he was severely punished if neighbours were involved. A theft against a White man is not taken seriously, for the latter is outside the system governed by the usual rules.

3. TOWARDS AN IDEAL OF SELF-MASTERY AND WISDOM

After describing the social, intellectual, and moral aspects of entry into life, we must now seek to establish what, in the final analysis, is the supreme value which African society recommends to its members. Many observers, especially M. Griaule, believe to have discovered in the notion of 'sophia', of wisdom, the ultimate ideal towards which African humanism strives. To say wisdom is to say culture and knowledge also, but an integrated knowledge, a conception of the world which is expressed by a refinement of mind, an art of living, an aptitude for perceiving the taste, the zest, and the humour of things, a certain kinship with them. This wisdom is found more on the side of being than that of having,* but because it is a

---

*In this and the previous sentence, the author seems to be referring to the philosopher Gabriel Marcel who makes a distinction between 'being' and 'having'. Marcel transposes this distinction into one between 'mystery' and 'problem'. According to him, a problem is something which can be solved in an objective, analytical manner, where the subject and object are seen as separate. In a mystery, on the other hand, the subject and object constitute only one thing, thus implying

state of mind, it permeates life, mentality, and action in their totality. The pertinent question to ask is how concretely this ideal is developed and perceived in Black Africa.

Seeking to discover the ultimate motive force of traditional African ethics, D. Zahan has concluded that the African values above all the idea of the domination of man over himself, the ability to control his passions, his emotions, and his behaviour. He writes: 'Everywhere and at all times, a single rule governs the education of the human being: the stoical endurance of pain which is considered the best training in self-mastery', [37] and which thus becomes the basis for the human condition lived in its fullness.

It is especially during certain rites that young people are asked to master themselves through courage, to show themselves insensitive and indifferent to the pain occasioned, for instance, by placing rings in the nose, by filing the teeth, by bruising the gums, and above all, by sexual mutilations. To appear cowardly at circumcision is such an infamy for the Dogon that such conduct must be kept secret in the village. [38] In initiation schools, thrashing as a ritual ordeal is zealously practised. Well before circumcision, in order to train themselves to bear the pain, the Bambara youths flagellate themselves with lashing rods until they bleed. [39] At a given moment during the ceremony they demonstrate their indifference by insulting the blacksmith-circumciser, and by spitting the kola juice in his face. Among certain Fulani groups, youths are caned by an adversary without flinching and they will treat him in a similar manner on another occasion; young male children wait impatiently to wear their first shorts, which gives them the right to be thus tested. [40] When at the time of second dentition the ears of the young Ngoni are pierced, he must show courage by undergoing the ordeal with a stiff facial expression. [41] Any one who shows weakness on these occasions risks being reminded of it by an insulting nickname his whole life long.

One can see the imprint of the ideal of self-mastery during the whole period of the child's education. As early as the time of giving birth, the mother is sometimes asked to bear the birth pangs stoically so as to strengthen the character of the future man. With greater or lesser insistence—depending on the ethnic group—children are asked to contain their reactions in the face of painful situations, especially if these are purposely created by the group in order to test them and thus to assure their better integration. From the time they get their permanent teeth, the young Bantus of South Africa described by Kidd are required to master their feelings. The same observations are made apropos the Dogon: 'A child must not cry. When a baby moans, the mother rocks and suckles him.

---

synthesis and kinship. What Erny is saying here agrees very well with the distinction which L. S. Senghor sees between the African and European modes of thought.—Transl.

Later, when he does the same, he is either mildly scolded or calmed. But a child of five or six who cries because he has fallen and got scratched is given sharp orders to keep quiet.'[42] J. Kenyatta remarks that every Gikuyu young man 'has been taught from childhood to develop the technique of self-control in the matter of sex, which enables him to sleep in the same bed with a girl without necessarily having sexual intercourse.'[43]

A considerable number of cultural traits which we have noted previously can be considered from the point of view of self-mastery. The requirements of politeness, composure, impassivity, the conventional aspect of certain manners, inhibitions in the expression of sentiments and of affections— even between spouses and between parents and children—are all rooted in self-mastery.

The type of self-mastery most appreciated—that which makes a person be most esteemed—concerns the organ of speech. To know how to control one's words, to keep a secret, to speak or keep silence as the occasion demands—these are qualities about which one is very sensitive. The word assumes its full value only when surrounded by silence. As D. Zahan puts it:

> Silence has nothing in common with the other moral virtues unless it be that it constitutes at one and the same time their point of departure and their target. It is the virtue par excellence; it subsumes integrity, courage, strength of character, prudence, modesty, and temperance. Silence defines the man of character; it is the prerogative of the wise. Whoever knows how to keep silence possesses true happiness.[44]

Knowing how to contain his anger, his desire to speak ill of others and to spread rumours, a man will avoid quarrels and will be a peace-maker for those around him.[45] This mastery of the tongue, the inhabitants of the Niger Valley believe, is more difficult for a woman than for a man, and often requires on her part practices of a ritual order such as placing rings on the lips and tatooing the gums.

It is to the extent that a man succeeds in mastering his sensitiveness, his affectivity, his desire to show off, that he causes himself to be esteemed, accepted, integrated into his group. As D. Zahan observes about the Bambara:

> A true *homo socialis* is a person closed in on himself; he does not display his feelings. The 'virtue' to which he aspires—and which he must practise above all the others—makes of him a dispassionate being, not betraying any emotion, sentiment, or perturbation. The value of a human action is gauged according to its positive or negative charge as regards life. Only those procedures are good and worthy which tend to affirm the 'in-itself', those which lead a person towards his own being as if to allow him to affirm his perpetuity. The essence of the Bambara soul

is, in a way, meditation and intentness of mind, and nothing is more reprehensible among these Sudanic people than an individual who does not know how or is not able to internalize himself . . .But for them morality goes beyond the domain of human conduct. It is wisdom, it brings man closer to the divinity, for whoever succeeds in securing mastery over himself possesses inner peace, equilibrium, and stoical indifference. Unshakable even in the face of death, such a man has nothing for which to envy God.[46]

Since the individual expression is thus checked, channelled, and disciplined, it allows the collective emotion to manifest itself in a manner all the more powerful—but nevertheless regulated, controlled, and coherent—each time the society opens one of its safety valves to let it escape.

10

Initiation Pedagogy
and Spiritual Experience

Many observers, especially among the earliest, have created the impression that traditional African education can in fact be reduced to pubertal initiations. These rites of passage appeared to them not only as the apex of traditional education but also as the unique moment when the society seemed to explicitly foster in the rising generation a long and exacting educational scheme comparable to that of the European school. Starting out with a much wider conception of the educational process, we have found it to exist, at least in a diffuse manner, throughout the life of the child within his group. However, the fundamental importance that traditional society itself attaches to the rites obliges us to give them a special place in our treatment, if we are to respect the hierarchy of values characteristic of the societies studied.

Initiations are above all rites; they culminate in feasts during which the entire society takes cognizance of the force which animates it. When, under the force of an external influence an educational system disintegrates, initiation pedagogy is often the first victim. Because initiations address themselves to the child only at a late stage, at the precise moment when he is supposed to accede to the status of an adult man; and because they crown by a multifaceted and highly complex rite all previous education, because they are found at a high level of consciousness and are intimately related to collective symbolism, they are affected by the least change in the thought and life of a people. Other customary institutions, especially child care, continue unaffected by major social upheavals.

To be properly understood, initiations must be seen in a global context. They are an expression of a culture, having their place in a comprehensive pedagogical scheme; they stir up considerable emotional powers both at the level of the individual and of the group; they take place according to a symbolic ordering which touches man at the deepest level of his unconscious; they propose to guide him, by means of a particularly intense spiritual experience, to the threshold of mystical life. They are all these things at one and the same time, giving a glimpse of a richness that we must analyse point by point.

1. DIFFUSION AND TYPOLOGY

The rearing of children is incontestably homogeneous across Africa, and the education given during middle and later childhood also reveals remarkable constants, but initiation pedagogy at first sight appears so diverse as to make its study baffling.

All models are represented. There are societies without any institutions resembling initiation rites. Elsewhere they seem to be of recent introduction and one senses that they are poorly integrated into the total culture. Then, in other societies, one finds only a few elements of these rites and those in a degraded form, mere survivals, having no function and sometimes restricted to certain classes. Among certain ethnic groups only boys undergo initiation rites; among others, only girls. In some societies boys and girls are initiated together while in others, more numerous, they are initiated separately.

The rites themselves which mark accession to maturity are varied, and each ethnic tradition has a tendency to give more value to a particular function at the expense of the others. They may be practised immediately after the appearance of the physical signs of puberty, and given a role of purification, protection and the conjuration of dangers inherent in this change, especially the appearance of the menstrual flow. Elsewhere it is a question of confirming an individual in a sex which until then has remained undetermined, or of practising fertility rites connected with nubility, stressing the new power of procreation. In other cases, the sexual aspect is overlooked, and only the aspects of social maturity and accession to a higher status are stressed. Thus, the chronological coincidence with biological puberty is completely neglected in favour of what could be called social puberty, which allows the child to be no longer be at the side of the adults but among them. It even happens that tiny children undergo initiation, because they are rich, at the same time as poor adults who have not been able to pay previously: in these cases the ritual acts are devoid of educational elements, showing that the ritual itself is more important than the instruction given.

The emphasis may be on the transition itself, or on the life the child has just left behind, or, lastly, on the life ahead of him, with all the expectations that the whole group entertains with respect to him. The mutilation may be at the centre of the rite, but may also be practised apart from any ceremony; sometimes there is no evidence of them at all. A number of ethnic groups have traditionally practised circumcision or excision apart from any initiation context properly speaking. The same can be said about the seclusion to which young girls are subjected at the time of their first periods. In some places, initiation may only be a minor rite, full of indulgence, whereas elsewhere it may consist of months or even years of a Draconian training. Certain ethnic groups successively practise rituals which have different functions: a child may have to pass through several 'schools', each one preparing him for a new stage of development. In these cases puberty is only a stage among others, as among the Bambara, where the adult is destined to traverse a whole series of initiation societies which form a logical sequence.

Obviously, each of these particular institutions has a different social background and this must be taken into account. Each ethnic group will emphasize the aspect of life which appears to it the most important with respect to its own hierarchy of values: for some it will be war, for others, man's bonds with the soil, for others again procreation, knowledge, the relationship with the ancestors, the encounter with divine wrath, the revelation of the sacred, submission to authority or custom, or demonstration of the group's riches. Quite often, the various rites have an obvious multifunctional character.

Let us take two examples.

Among the Basuto, the initiation of boys, preceded by the piercing of the ear common to both sexes, was not supposed to produce an immediate change in life, but was meant simply to inaugurate it, and to make the individual take a more serious and worthy attitude towards life. There, characteristically war-like training predominated, fostering obedience and courage, while sexuality was of minor importance.[1]

Starting about the age of ten the young Efik and Ekoi girls used to be secluded for a period of two to seven years. During this time they were exempted from all regular work, had to eat and to become as fat as possible; they were massaged in order to make the muscles firm, and were instructed in sexual matters. The longer the seclusion, the greater the family's prestige, for this demonstrated in the eyes of all that they were well-to-do, since they could afford the luxury of leaving their daughters inactive for such a long period. It was hoped that the girls' skins would become lighter, a sign of beauty which would enhance their value at the time of marriage.[2]

The pubertal initiations which interest us are not the only forms of initiation that exist. It is necessary to distinguish them carefully from:

1. Rites through which one enters into a confraternity, a fraternity, one of those societies usually referred to as secret, but which should rather be called initiation societies;
2. Individual initiation into a social function or a particular profession (priest, diviner, healer, blacksmith, hunter)—the enthronement of a chief or a king generally takes the form of an initiation ritual;
3. Initiation into a particular cult. Thus along the coast of Benin there are sancturies in the form of 'convents' where neophytes receive very long initiations, and are trained in the technique of ecstasy connected with the cults of possession. A highly selective recruitment takes place there with the help of divination methods. Certain individuals, through their ability to

enter into a trance, reveal that they are destined to become 'sons' or 'daughters' of a particular god. The education given in these sanctuaries aims at imparting to those subjected to it a sort of double personality. This is one of the most expressive forms of African mysticism, for it is essentially a matter of entering into direct contact with the divinity, leaving it to act freely through the person initiated.

In spite of these distinctions, these different rites have many features in common, a true analogy of structure. Consequently one can speak of initiation in each case.[3] In a society where these practices are current at different levels, there develops a true initiation *spirit* which permeates in a diffuse way all of life, and constitutes its most important element. For transmitting a spiritual influence and linking it to the initiation chain, the rite appears as an essential element, for by its very stereotyped form, it guarantees permanence. 'Without rites there could be no initiation whatsoever'.[4]

2. EDUCATION AND INITIATION*

It is doubtless during initiations that the most profound knowledge is transmitted. Certain Kongo rites described by F. Ngoma appear to have the function of effecting a conscious synthesis of all the different types of knowledge and skills already acquired. Their 'role is to teach about the traditional techniques, the mysteries of life and the benevolent powers, about eloquence and secret language, about rituals, formulary protocol and the social hierarchy'. They teach 'love in all its aspects as well as clan solidarity, the values espoused by the group, political and individual rights'. The author gives the example of the *ndembo* rite whose teaching is, according to him, a total education: 'religious and civil, juridical and literary, economic and social, where the young people learn what they must know in order to participate actively in the life of the group. This instruction relates to the history of the tribe and the genealogy of its divisions, to land rights, to jurisprudence, to technology, and to sociology which is perhaps paradoxical for illiterates. But we must understand that it is the question of learning, by whatever method, the mechanisms and institutions of the group. This last point, incidentally, is related to the teaching of cosmology and etiology: it is necessary, for example, to explain the interactions of the cosmos and the origin of diseases. Other themes with which the teaching of the *ndembo* is concerned are societal values, the ideal wife and husband, which are stressed by stories and myths; also eloquence, a talent for which the Ndibu have no equal among the people of the lower Congo.'[5]

Certain extended initiations also include instructions at levels which

*This section is transposed from Chapter Nine of the original work, pp. 180-185. It replaces a similar but less detailed section in this chapter.—Transl.

pertain to technology, to crafts, to agriculture, etc. But one must be careful not to draw a wrong conclusion here. The child does not usually learn anything new; he is simply made to understand that the technical motions already familiar to him have still another dimension: they also put man in contact with the invisible, with the dead who live under the earth, and with the genies of the bush; they also enable one to act on hidden powers. The child will return to his old environment, and apparently nothing there will have changed. In reality all has changed, the previous environment has become different because the individual himself has undergone a change. As G. Lapassade writes, initiation changes the meaning of the world by changing the meaning of life. It is therefore necessary to learn everything again from a new angle in order to transform one's previous knowledge into a new wisdom. The motions are techniques only in appearance. Essentially, they are efficacious on the symbolic level. The breathless pursuit of game during a communal hunt could, for example, signify the way in which knowledge must be sought.

The instruction given at initiations is often a heterogeneous mixture of elements. In some cases it takes the form of a sort of catechism with questions and answers. More often it is a moral code or a law in its several different sections that the young must learn.[6] Among the Bira, traditional instruction during initiation takes place with the aid of drum language, whole phrases being drummed in long and short beats on a special gong, the meaning of which is understood only by the old initiates. When it is a question of making important truths sink in, a physical or emotional shock is used in order to impress the individual, and thus increase his receptivity.[7]

Most often the rites of passage do not, by themselves, impart any deep knowledge, but they make the person more disposed to receive such knowledge, and put him in a state to understand the significance of the passage from the profane world to that of the initiated.[8] The Bantu women who organize the *Chisungu* rite, as it is described by A. Richards, have three expressions for justifying their activity: 'We are making the girls grow, we are making them into women like ourselves, we are teaching them.' The stress is placed very strongly on the 'instruction' which is thus given, employing emphatically the same word used in speaking of modern schools. In fact, it does not seem that instruction in the proper sense of the term, instruction as we understand it, can take an important place in this kind of rite, even on subjects adapted to the circumstances such as sexuality, maternity, household tasks. It would be useless, to say the least, since from their earliest years, the initiates participate in all the occupations proper to women; moreover, well before puberty, the girls often start living with their husbands, and so have already experienced sexual relations.

In what respect then, can we speak about instruction? In the first place, the initiates learn secret and archaic terms and songs, an allusive way of speaking which help spouses to discuss among themselves matters of sexual intimacy which are jealously guarded. Secondly, the *Chisingu* does not really teach the techniques of performing specific domestic chores, but the attitude which a woman must henceforth adopt in carrying them out, the spirit in which she must accomplish them. This is the result, not of any explanations which are given, but of the songs, emblems, and figurines that are shown to her. It is also the result of symbolic acts that are imposed on her and of mimes that are performed in front of her. During the very rites which are supposed to 'instruct' them, it is not rare that the girls are absent or hidden under a blanket so that they cannot directly observe what is going on. More than the details, it is the general atmosphere which matters. We must not forget that we are dealing essentially with rites which contain within them their educational effectiveness. The year after, the women will be present at new ceremonies as helpers, and it is then that their knowledge is going to increase most. Those who are more alert seek explanations from competent matrons, and from year to year they penetrate deeper into the mystery of the symbols which are used; afterwards they can in their turn prepare themselves to become future matrons. Those who take no interest will never have more than a superficial knowledge of these rites. Among the Lovedu, a girl is not considered truly initiated until she has attended initiation ceremonies six times.

During the *Chisungu*, there is a constant use of emblems whose names and meanings are secret. Coloured terra cotta symbols represent familiar objects, animals, symbols of fertility or historical symbols, either in a realistic or purely conventional form; other clay figurines are left unbaked. On the inside walls of the initiation hut panels with geometric patterns are sketched. Finally, small bundles of common domestic objects complete the set which will serve as material for rites.[9] Different objects of this material act as memory-aids, thanks to which women remember the right song to intone at each stage as the ceremony unfolds.[10]

Behind its stereotyped form, each figure, each painting, each symbol used during initiations, possesses a multiple power of evocation eliciting the most unexpected allusions, associations, and explanations—sometimes most contradictory. But because these things form part of the structure of a system of organic and coherent thought, they are never arbitrary. The interpretation can vary according to the age, the degree of knowledge, the character and the concrete situation of each individual. As A. Richards says, 'What is essential to *mbusa*, the *Chisungu* emblems, is not their exact meaning, but the fact that they are what they are—objects received from tradition.'[11] For that reason, they must be reproduced with great precision. They are the sign that things are going to take place now as formerly, that the powers transmitted are identical to those of the past. But the permanence of the form does not prevent a multiplicity of meanings of which some are standardized while others depend on a purely personal interpretation.

It is in this way that the figurine of the tortoise whose head protrudes and then retracts, is meant, on the one hand, to teach the wife what she must do—to keep silence especially as concerns her relationship with her husband, and on the other what she must not do—to look with envy at the food in someone else's house or to refuse to look after her own guests. The emblem representing the caterpillar and the millipede and the corresponding song require the future mother to purify herself after the birth of twins, and also to refrain from too frequent sexual intercourse in order to avoid having as many births as the feet of the millipede. From the figurine of the hoe emerge the following ideas: the initiate will have to work hard with this instrument; she will have to learn how to handle it without injuring herself when she is pregnant; she will be 'tilled' by her husband as the earth is tilled with a hoe, and she must prepare herself for defloration which for her signifies fertility—here being compared to the fertility of the soil.[12] In the absence of a written literature, these symbols are preserved and perpetuated by the group of initiated individuals who enjoy considerable prestige because of this.

The example of the fertility dolls that certain Bantu women give to their young daughters constitutes another typical case of initiation taking place with the help of symbolic objects but within the family unit. When very young, the little girl plays with the red clay figurine which has obvious sexual characteristics, treating it as 'her child'. To this doll game is added at puberty a real teaching given by an old woman of the lineage who introduces the individual to 'the laws of her child'. At the time of marriage, the figurine brought into the conjugal house must be redeemed by the husband before the union can be consummated. P. and J. Roumeguère have shown in a particularly clear manner that these very modest objects serve as teaching aids, revealing an amazing intuition of depth psychology and of the possibility of catharsis and emotional discharge that these symbolic substitutes offer. Speaking to the subconscious in its own language, the effectiveness of their manipulation might be compared to that of a psychodrama which would enable the small girl and the young woman, from the time when she plays the games of childhood to that when her adolescent preoccupations take shape, from the wedding night until the birth of her first baby—to resolve in the dynamism of a unique symbol the two complexual tendencies: castration and the Oedipus complex. She finds inscribed in this doll the different roles of mediatrix which concretely determine all her life and all her development as a woman in her relationships with her mother, her lineage, her husband and his lineage, as well as with her own child.[13]

In order to facilitate access to knowledge—even at the highest esoteric level—one always uses as symbolic material some of these odd objects of simple appearance to which meaning is given in relation to the system of thought to be transmitted. A basket with a round opening and a square bottom was shown to M. Griaule by an informant as a means of making the Dogon cosmology intelligible. In the last Bambara initiation stage a long pole is used on which are hung more than two hundred objects representing' the totality of the things known in the universe. With his back turned, the master gives the name of each one of them and then explains what each item stands for. There is here a real lesson of things 'able to shape the mind until then accustomed to seeing only one aspect of the surrounding reality. The initiate learns to pass from one meaning to another, from the material to the spiritual.'[14] Even the children's games have—for him who knows how to place them in their larger symbolic context—an unsuspected range and meaning.[15]

We are here in the presence of a pedagogical constant: in this apparently poor and deprived enviroment, each object constitutes a well, an inexhaustible reservoir of hidden meanings which need only to be brought to the surface. Initiation seeks to make manifest and audible those symbols, for they furnish the key of knowledge and illumination, and make the invisible world visible.

3. ATMOSPHERE

A universal trait of the initiation societies of Africa is this: the mastery, the domination that man succeeds in exercising over physical suffering is the attribute par excellence of spiritual life. Nature flees from pain: to come to accept it silently, to assume it, to integrate it into oneself, to even look for it, is the sign that through the spirit one is overcoming nature, that one is refusing to accept it as a pure given in order to elevate it to the level of social creation. Suffering, writes G. Roheim, is an interference of law in desire. Ragging, it is well known even in Europe, produces an *esprit de corps*. It is a sign that the child is passing from a feminine domination to a masculine one. All these themes are closely linked.

Through the emotional intensity which it produces, initiation pedagogy seeks to realize a total subjection to the tribal tradition, a kind of standardization or reduction to a common denominator. The collective experience must be sufficiently strong so as to make an indelible mark on the mind. At this stage, education is not so much interested in the transmission of knowledge, but in the definitive and irreversible creation of a sensibility, for it too belongs to the cultural heritage. It is necessary to direct the personality in such a way that it can no longer conceive of life outside the framework of custom. Rites, therefore, pursue two ends which are contradictory only in appearance: on the one hand, to depersonalize, to cause the boundaries of individuality to disappear in order to dissolve them in the collectivity; and on the other hand, to strengthen character and to affirm the new personality born of the drama. To be able to evoke this experience, it is normal that the initiates make use of a special language.

The whole society takes part in these rites of accession to social maturity of a new age-group, since it is an event pregnant with meaning for its life. Among the Lovedu, the initiation of boys used to take place on a national level every twelve or fifteen years.[16] The ceremonies lasted four months, and during this time all social life came to a stand still. Among the Sara, it is not only the family of the initiate who live his drama intensely; the whole population is involved in a very onerous way: the chiefs confess their sins, the dignitaries let themselves be beaten, everybody engages in fasting and abstinence. The men are involved as godfathers and assistants. For a time, initiation becomes the unique preoccupation of all, conditioning in a homogeneous way the social-ritual calendar, making everyone vibrate in unison. 'It is the whole people', writes J. Hallaire, 'which participate in the birth pangs of a new generation of men. On this occasion, they experience their unity in an almost physical way.'[17] Anxiety and joy are overflowing in parents who see their first-born take leave of them, since for them, too, it means a passage to a higher status. Initiations are fertile, they cause the whole community to penetrate into the universe of symbols which serve as a fertile ground for its spiritual life. They regenerate the life of the group by a return to the mythical history and by a participation in the primordial archetypes.

The appeal of these rites is almost irresistible. O. Raum reports that, among the Chagga, children belonging to Christian families for three generations run away so as to be able to undergo them like the rest. Generally speaking, the non-initiated are made to understand that they are vile and ignorant beings, unimportant, despicable, unreliable, who can only become someone through ordeal. Uncircumcised boys are ridiculed on every occasion, for example while taking a bath, by those who have been initiated. It is therefore normal for the young people to aspire impatiently to these rites. But an atmosphere of mystery and dread is also maintained concerning them: they are associated with death; children are constantly threatened with the sanctions they will incur during the rites. As they face such an ambivalent institution, they are torn between desire and fear, but it is the desire to pass through this step which is the dominant feeling.

4. PASSAGE

The initiation of boys usually takes place in the bush, in a wild setting not tamed by man, and which represents for the village people a 'beyond' where one has contact with the invisible powers—with gods, genies, ancestors, and with 'demons' in the old sense of the term. The novices belong to the other world, that of the deceased and of individuals not yet born. They live in close proximity to them, for they too are 'dead', 'buried', 'devoured'. Their behaviour ought to be as far removed as possible from normal behaviour. They enjoy aberrant rights; for example, that of stealing. They dress in a special way, and their bodies are covered with white kaolin which makes them look like phantoms. As is supposed to be the case with the latter, they are sometimes obliged to seize their food with their teeth. In other words, they assume the condition of spirits, and in some way they identify themselves with the group's spirits. The appearance of masks represents without doubt the most poignant moment of this contact with the invisible world. In feminine rites also there is generally a moment when the young girl is considered dead, 'gone with the moon', as the Baluba say, enclosed in the house as in a tomb, where she must not do any work: she must not wash herself, must speak only in a low voice, and must come out only when it is dark; in a word, she must act as if she were no longer among the living.

In a second phase, the neophyte is treated like a new-born child, naked and mute, who knows nothing and is unable to do anything, who recognizes nobody, who is taught to eat and to drink, and to speak a secret language, who is given—as among the Yondo—a new name, and a new face by cuts which become facial scars. He has become a stranger to the reality of this world and must gradually reaccustom himself to it.

The initiation death makes a blank slate of the individual's personal past. By this very fact it does not constitute an end but a beginning. It appears, not as an annihilation, but rather as a regression to an embryonic stage, to the maternal womb, the necessary condition for rebirth. Often, moreover, this death is seen as a swallowing up, thus as a return to the original womb in an oral manner.

By using death symbolism, G. Lapassade writes, initiation does not present itself as an absolute and final passage: at the moment when it reveals to man the ultimate meaning of his existence, it also shows him his finiteness.

> [The rite] announces to man that not only is he becoming an adult, but also that he is mortal. It brings him 're-assurances' and underlines the difficulty of existence. Initiation shows that each step in life is an advance towards death, and that it is necessary not only to die to childhood but above all to assume death in order to accept life.[18]

Only initiation confers on death a positive function, observes M. Eliade.[19] Man learns how to die in order to know how to live truly and the ultimate mystery of existence is thus revealed to him. The ritual celebration of the drama of life and death assumes an almost sacramental value.[20] But, as R. Jaulin remarks, initiation appears also as a kind of death in reverse: in fact, physical death is a return to nature, and by that very fact a failure of culture, while initiation death is an entry into culture and consequently a failure of nature from which society takes over. 'To life and death which are given to them, people have added initiation through which they transcend the disorder of death. Initiation affirms culture where nature is judged guilty; it is understood that this guilt should be related to death.'[21]

Unless the grain dies it will not bear fruit. Between birth rites, death rites and initiation rites there are such close structural analogies that they cannot be studied separately. If to be born is to die to the 'beyond', and if to die is to be born in the 'beyond', being initiated is at the same time death and rebirth. Everything holds together; everything is inter-connected. In the background of this structure emerges the outline of the cosmology as it is handed down by myths. The different stages of Bambara circumcision retrace point by point the vicissitudes of birth. But these stages also help the novice to relive step by step the myths of creation of the world and of man. All the gestures of the blacksmith and of his acolytes, all the objects used during the operation and the subsequent seclusion period not only recall but also actualize the events of the beginning of the world. Children understand the social importance of these events but without as yet realizing their full extent and implications. The time of circumcision helps them to relive the genesis of the universe and to become the contemporaries of the birth of the world.[22]

5. DETACHMENT AND INTEGRATION

. . . .

The fact that pubertal initiation as an institution is linked to societies which seek to promote an ideal, not of personal autonomy, but of sociological interdependence, that it is also linked to an education whose mainstay is not the nuclear family but the extended group, is in itself significant. Initiation manipulates the relations of the child with the nuclear family and seeks to introduce into it an element of discontinuity.[23] Like some forms of weaning, it traumatizes, then forbids return to the proven sources of security, especially being swallowed up in the world of women. Through the violence of its interference, it does not allow an individual to emerge from dependence, but makes this dependence evolve towards new objects: the group, the fathers, the ancestors. It constitutes only one element among a whole set of devices which oblige the child to review from one stage to another the type of relations which he has with the parental couple.

But it is not simply a question here of detaching the young boy from the mother or from the other specific women within whose orbit he was living until then, but also of effecting separation from everything these women symbolize: the intimate life tied to the house, the yard, and the village, affective comfort and security, existence within groups founded on blood relationship. The masculine initiation societies, intimately linked to the institution of age-groups, are not opposed to the woman as such, but to the types of blood relations of which she is the basis. Moreover, the male child must be freed from all that which, in his own nature, may have a feminine valence. We have already noticed that in the Niger valley, one of the principal justifications for sexual mutilations is the androgyny which is attributed to the child. Among the Herero, the boys used to arrive for circumcision dressed in feminine clothes, finery, and jewels in order to show that they were still carriers of a partly feminine nature. After the operation they are referred to as 'those who are no longer girls'. [24] L. Frobenius, H. Schurtz, and E. Jensen-Krige have emphasized the fact that these rites are products of a masculine mind; they operate against the world of mothers and aim at liberating the boy from the 'stain' which is the result of being born of a woman. To this first birth which generates the ties of blood is juxtaposed the birth which creates the bonds with male society.

Through all these features, a boy's initiation appears as a conversion, a change of heart, where one burns that which until that time has been one's most cherished possession. The young man turns away from childish things to turn positively towards those matters which concern adults. The boy renounces those things in his life which used to belong to the feminine world in order to assume complete masculinity. The valley where circumcision takes place among the Lovedu is called 'the place where one forgets'. The whole system of relationships which united the person to the society, to himself, and to the universe will be restructured. The individual changes both his social condition and his ontological status.

6. PARTICULAR POINTS

a. Secrecy

There is no initiation without secrecy. Secrecy covers everything which takes place in the bush camp: the nature of masks and of rhombuses, the fact that initiation death is not, as outsiders are supposed to believe, a physical death. It is made concrete in formulas, in codes, in passwords, in names, and especially in a language learned during the probation.

Secrecy is essentially a discipline. It is this which constitutes its pedagogical value. It helps to establish a clear separation between the sacred and the profane spheres, between those who have 'graduated' and those who are still waiting, between the masculine and feminine worlds. Its imperative character helps both the individual and the society to keep constantly before them the distinctions which guarantee social stability.

b. Nudity

At all the great moments of life—birth, initiation, marriage, and death, man appears in his nakedness. Such an apparently simple matter carries multiple meanings and contributes by that very fact to their synthesis. The nudity of the young initiates essentially signifies that they are dead, are reborn, and are ready to marry.

The neophytes are naked like new-born babies, but also like the earliest men at the beginning of history. 'To be naked is to be speechless', said Ogotemmêli to M. Griaule. Through the leaves and fibres with which they often cover themselves later, they act out another stage in the evolution of primitive culture; at the same time this act signifies that they are children of a savage world, of the bush; in the final analysis, of the other world.

Ritual birth is not individual. Born collectively, the neophytes are all twin brothers; having emerged together from the womb of the ancestral earth, they are no longer children of a couple but of the whole clan and ethnic group. Nudity signifies the fraternity which must henceforth unite all those of the same age-group: in fact, their common nudity signifies that there is no longer any secret among them, and no shame, that nothing separates them, that they are ready to expose themselves and to deliver themselves without defence to the control of their companions, to do away between themselves with this barrier, this physical and social protection constituted by clothing. Nudity represents, at one and the same time, asexuality, child-like innocence, and the sexual life to which social maturity leads. The new clothing which initiates put on at the end of their retreat is a sign of their accession to a new social status.

c. Masks and rhombuses

Rhombuses and masks always represent the powers of the other world which erupt among men.

They sometimes make their appearance as early as the children's societies. During certain manifestations of the Bambara *N'domo*, it is a child who wears the masks of the society of uncircumcised while he dances in complete silence, thus symbolizing the being which is still enclosed within its own integrity and perfection as is the child at this stage of his social growth.

The disclosure of the true nature of rhombuses and masks often constitutes an important aspect of initiation. At a particular point during the rite, the Bwa children are lying on the ground, naked, when suddenly they find themselves in front of a mask which terrifies them. But they must make a stand in an attitude of combat. Then the mask crumbles, as if dead. They mourn for it; a priest revives it by blowing on it; he gets up, takes off his bonnet, and the child then recognizes someone from the village. The neophyte had until then more or less accepted the explanations given to him regarding the masks. The day he discovers their real nature, a reorganization of his emotional experience will ensue, which may be accompanied by violent affective reactions.[25] By encountering them he passes from the control of actual fathers to that of mythical fathers who are the only true initiators: he enters into contact with the numinous, the transpersonal, with the collective in its symbolic expression.

But it must be pointed out that this encounter takes place precisely in the form of a demystification, as if, in becoming reality, the myth did not any more have need of its veils. By discovering who is the real bearer of the mask or the manipulator of the rhombus, the child ceases to feel the domination of a world which is strange to him, but plunges right into it and enters into connivance with it. Indeed, the neophyte can himself become the mask for those outside, if only by putting on calabash spectacles or by smearing himself with white earth to assimilate into the world of the dead. He thus takes on this transpersonal reality, melts into it, and loses himself in the anonymous group.

d. The name

At the end of initiations, a new name is often given to those who have just been reborn. This signifies that they have changed their personality as do chiefs at their installation.

Obviously, this practice must be connected with the name-giving which normally takes place sometime after birth, and which effects a first integration into the social order by conferring on the new-born a status and an identity, by inscribing him in the 'mystic birth register' of the group—to use the expression of L. Lévy-Bruhl. Among the Bwa, this rite confers the right of being ritually interred in case of death, and rejoining of the ancestors. But this first entry into the community takes place in a passive manner. Initiation represents an active integration, for it is not simply received or granted, but also conquered, merited, and grasped as the result of a hard struggle.

In the final analysis, all depends on the onomastic system in force in a given ethnic group. Some confer on the person several names at birth. Among the Dogon, for example, one name is given by the patriarch of the paternal group, another one by the patriarch of the maternal group, and a third one by the 'totemic' priest. To all these names are added nicknames which are in use in the age-group. The names signify a certain belonging, and will all be retained throughout life without any new ones being added. In other societies, on the other hand, it is at each great moment of his social development that the person is given a new name. Instead of making a cross section, the onomastic system then slices layer by layer. In this case, initiation is one of those privileged moments in which mutation takes place.

Among the Goula Iro of Chad, the adolescent comes back from the bush camp bearing the name of an ancestor which his godfathers will have given to him. The first male child of the family will receive the name of the maternal grandfather. But in inheriting a name an individual also inherits, with respect to women and the non-initiated, the blood relationships implied in that name. The homonymy between the initiated youth and the ancestor determines *de jure* and *de facto* the identity of the deceased and of the living person. As C. Pairault writes: 'The deceased person seizes the living person and the living seizes the deceased. The elders survive in the family, and not just by being remembered. Beyond the individual deaths, the community keeps alive the name and rank of the deceased ancestors.' There is no real incarnation of the grandfather in the grandsons, but the homonymy certifies to the society the effective immortality of the dead. The conferring of the name of initiation has therefore a double role: negatively, it renders obsolete any nominal reference of the initiated to their contemporary surroundings, visible or invisible; positively, the new names restore the many bonds broken by time within the lineage. [26]

e. Food

In the perspective of oral symbolism, initiation is first of all a weaning. The novices are subjected to numerous food prohibitions, privations and fasts. They are given insufficient or unflavoured food or food of poor quality. They are forced to eat in a queer manner, for example to gulp food at a great speed, or to eat straight out of the plate without using hands, like women who have just given birth, in order to signify their marginal status. By being made to suffer hunger, the neophytes are being sensitized to the many symbolisms built around food. For those who will have suffered together in fasting, the common partaking of food will assume the dimension of an act of communion. Subjected to an unsavoury food, they crave salt, pepper and spices, but these ingredients symbolize precisely the durable and savoury knowledge that the neophytes must desire and pursue.

In certain circumstances the initiates are obliged to look for their food in the bush or to beg it from the village people. The point here is to teach them the importance of sharing food and that its acquisition is only possible through common effort: the individual alone will not succeed without the help of the group. When among the Yao a man refuses to share his feed, he is ridiculed by being called 'uninitiated'. [27]

Among the Bwa of Upper Volta, initiation is called 'an act of eating'. [28] In the Yondo of the Sara, involving no sexual mutilations, the most solemn moment consists in the eating of a ball of food. A. Richards says that among the southern Bantu, the absorption of food was the source of the most intense emotion, and provided the basis for the most abstract notions and metaphors of religious thought: it becomes a symbol not only of the social relationships but also of the most exalted spiritual experiences. [29] Together with sexuality it gives an account of the realities of mystical life.

f. Sex

Initiations are intimately related to sex first because it is often at this moment that the precise rules which govern its exercise are communicated to the young, but above all because sexuality is at the centre of the mysteries of life and of fertility which are celebrated and exalted in these circumstances. As J. Roumeguère-Eberhardt has noticed among the Venda:

> The dialectic association of a man and a woman as givers of life is always and everywhere present in the consciousness of every initiated person. The whole substance of the teaching that he has received at puberty . . . consists precisely in having given him the knowledge to manipulate these symbols and meanings, dialectically and linked in long series, in a moral atmosphere which has nothing to do with the awkwardness, the inhibitions, or the embarassed prudery which in Western societies characterize the approach of any subject relating to sex. In fact, in western societies sexual connotations have often lost the essence of their symbolic and religious content and implications, and have retained only the erotic or obscene ones. This is totally foreign to the Bantu language and sensitivity which put so much emphasis on the beauty and plenitude of everything that connotes procreation.[30]

The theme of sexuality is not without relation to that of knowledge. Does not the expression 'to know' a woman or man in the most diverse cultures signify a sexual relation? Does not orgasm lead to a kind of ecstasy? Is there not in the most diverse traditions the image of mystical experience, of intimate knowledge, of union with the Other, the delectable meeting with the Invisible? Does not the establishment of the sexual link lead one to desire, to remove veils, to denude, to penetrate, to enjoy the possession of the object, all metaphors which are applicable to the search for knowledge?

The theme of sexuality is also closely related to the theme of death.[31] By reaching sexuality, an individual has the very distinct feeling of having crossed a bridge, of having entered a new universe, of having relinquished something of himself in surrendering himself to the other. To the extent that he gives birth to life, the individual embarks on the road which leads to the ancestor state, and by the some token, he gets closer to death. He attunes himself to nature for it also renews itself in the stream of life which never ceases to traverse it, in an infinite cycle of deaths and rebirths.

7. FROM KNOWLEDGE TO WISDOM

In a vision of the world where man is at one and the same time centre and keystone, principle of intelligibility and of action, it is obviously self-knowledge, the Socratic 'know thyself', which is the basis of all wisdom as of all science. It leads man to humility within the universe, but at the same time it enables him to understand the eminent place which he occupies. Powerful in his knowledge and in his skill to use the many connections which govern his life, he experiences an exalting feeling of being its incontestable master. As Zahan writes:

> Man orders animals and plants, he exercises his authority on the march of time, he makes the clouds drop the rain, he summons thunder to go away. Through self-knowledge, man becomes a thaumaturge, or believes himself such, for, in knowing himself he knows the others who are joined to him through invisible links, and he can appreciate the value of all that surrounds him. Centre of the rational world, man becomes its sovereign.[32]

This wisdom through familiarity and connaturality with things can only be acquired with age. It is the object of a life-long education, and from the beginning the child knows that it is only when he has reached the state of an old man that he can hope to gain full mastery over his culture. Because they are closer to the other world, the child who is leaving it and the old man who is getting ready to return there are images par excellence of wisdom. The two live in a kind of innocence, a folding up upon their interior life that they do not succeed in expressing; the two recognize their ignorance. But in the one case it is through default, and in the other through plenitude. Both have attained supreme wisdom when spiritually they become children. The kingdom is revealed to them.

The traditional man knows that all knowledge of mastery or of efficiency, even all cultural knowledge, is incomplete if it does not open on to a liberating knowledge, an *Erlösungswissen*, as M. Scheler terms it. From that springs the relation which exists between wisdom and initiation knowledge under different forms. The science of the mysteries of symbols which the latter puts in motion is indispensable to the delightful perception of a universe loaded with infinite possibilities with which man is led to weave endless links. Ritual transformation is also necessary for creating this new being capable of such an apprehension of things, able to lift itself to the level of a total vision, to immerse itself in the life of the world. One is born to wisdom as to a second life.

11
Problems of Mental Structure

1. INTELLECTUAL ATTITUDES

Here we shall only touch upon the questions raised by the intellectual personality of the Black African in the traditional environment. They have been debated for more than a century in keeping with the predominant ideas of each period.

In early work such as that of R. Allier, many psychological notions are introduced which no longer correspond to our mode of seeing things. Thus, W. H. Bentley says that

> The African does not think, does not reflect, does not reason if he can help it. He has a prodigious memory. He has great talents for observation and imitation, a lot of verbal facility . . . But the faculties of reasoning and ingenuity are dormant in him. He apprehends the present circumstances, adapts himself to them and provides for them; but to elaborate a plan seriously, or to make a logical deduction, is beyond him.[1]

We hear the same thing echoed by H. Dieterlen:

> The Negro is content with vague ideas and is not perturbed by the flagrant contradictions between them. He does not specify, does not reason, has no logic, he does not look at things closely. . . . Besides, these Negroes have no theory. They do not even have convictions; they only have habits. If a thing is absurd, ridiculous, what is that to them? They do it, not by conviction, but instinctively, blindly, without reflection or reasoning . . . Our arguments cannot convince them because we appeal to a reasoning which in them exists only in a rudimentary state, and which they only use periodically and unskilfully at that.[2]

These words are characteristic of an age which had not disentangled the mechanisms of traditional thought.

L. Frobenius says that in this type of civilization, no dichotomy exists between a lived experience and knowledge, that knowledge is not able to go beyond the level of the Gemüt, the heart. This knowledge appears so self-evident that it remains unconscious, and does not manage to verbalize itself, to clothe itself in words. It remains hidden in customs lived by those concerned without their being able to report or explain these customs.[3] One thus sees the importance of what American anthropologists refer to as the 'covert culture'. All is *received* from a tradition which is often implicit, unexpressed. This explains why thought is much more influenced by sensuous factors: the proverb, for example, creates not only a logical conviction, but also an affective one. Because they curb conceptual elaboration and do not favour the process of explanation, these mental structures are not modifiable by a purely intellectual or moral teaching. But the day one element is tampered with the whole edifice risks collapsing. This dependence with respect to external stimuli and emotional factors confers on this kind of thought its explosive, concrete, momentary, primary, and often unstable character; it explains why it advances by leaps and starts. Linked with a keen sense of observation, it is also expressed by a remarkable sense of intuition and empathy which help it to appreciate quickly and rightly the character and desires of the other. There, synthetic perception precedes analysis.

Mental functioning is very closely related to the cultural background, and this sometimes varies considerably from one ethnic group to another. A differential study of the reactions of Yoruba and Nupe children undertaken by S. F. Nadel with the aid of figures to be described and stories to be reproduced, shows that the first insist on logical and rational aspects, go for the essential, are interested in overall motivations and neglect minor details, while the second faithfully list even the non-essential details, make a complete inventory without seeking to understand its purpose, remain very close to reality by noting the purely descriptive, dramatic, and circumstantial elements. Now, it is known that the Yoruba have a closely interconnected system of social structure, laws, and beliefs, and a figurative and symbolic art, while the mental universe of the Nupe is less hierarchical, simpler, and their art is more ornamental.[4]

Many observers have been struck by the difficulty people in traditional environments have in considering any fact whatsoever as an element of the total situation and in relating it to other facts.[5] One can make two remarks about this statement. At first sight this observation can appear paradoxical, for traditional cultures, more than any others, are centred on relations which are established between beings and push to the limit the 'concern for an exhaustive observation and a systematic inventory of relationships'.[6] More than any other, they are characterized by the unity and coherence of their universe. One can even say that in their eyes, no clearly defined element has any existence, that in their world everything is intertwined and related; that fundamentally it constitutes a single whole: desire and reality, knowledge and belief, the possible and the impossible, the sacred and the profane, thought and imagination.[7] But if everything holds together, it is according to the principle of analogy which for Western man is only of secondary importance, while causal, functional, and temporal relations which are predominant in the latter seem less well integrated. The point of view of the traditional Black African is egocentric in the sense that it makes man the centre of the world, in his whole cosmo-biological vision, but also in the attitudes and concrete judgements through which he takes an interest in the environment according to whether it is useful or harmful.

On the other hand, it seems right to point out, as does J. Carothers, the single-minded nature of man's consciousness in the traditional environment. It pays attention to immediate aspects of things, allows itself to be dominated by the image, adopts an attitude of all or nothing which orients it towards impulsive behaviour. The individual pays attention to and shows interest in a situation only to the extent that it touches him personally and arouses his emotion. R. Maistriaux has noted among the Kongo a relative incapacity to handle several conceptual identities simultaneously, and thus to perceive all the aspects of a problem, to disregard a detail or an individual fact in order to command the whole with a panoramic vision.

C. Pairault writes: 'Man trusts nature more than he questions it, feeds and clothes himself with what it provides on the spot, uses without substantial reorganization the available materials.' He is satisfied with a world where an actuated explanation takes precedence over a reasoned inventory of symbols, where constant reference to tradition ('our ancestors have taught it to us', 'we have always done it this way') is to be taken seriously, since for these people there is no other point of reference.[8] M. C. Ortigues says that 'an attitude of participatory contemplation occupies the place elsewhere taken up by an intellectual analysis' which destroys in order to know and to possess.[9] For R. Bastide, the African man is at the opposite pole from a Promethean spirit which separates itself from nature in order to make of it something it can dominate; on the contrary, he cultivates nature and cherishes the bonds which unite him to the world and, beyond, to the deceased: 'He is a poet, not an engineer.'[10] As for L. S. Senghor, the reason of the African is synthetic and sympathetic, living inside the heart of the real, espousing its contours, identifying itself with it. His attitude is one of abandon, assimilation, love, not of domination. The total environment in which he lives and all his intellectual and spiritual education urge him never to stop at appearances but to see in everything a sign or a symbol which should be examined thoroughly in order to discover its meaning, its hidden reality, its surreality.[11] His perception of the world is metaphysical, not scientific. Invisible reality is everywhere near the surface, and is detected and comprehended easily. An object is valuable only on account of what it suggests, its spiritual features. Religion occupies the whole of his life and is identical with it.

Since E. Durkheim and M. Mauss, but especially due to the research of G. Dieterlen, R. Bastide, C. Lévi-Strauss, J. Cazeneuve, and R. Makarius, we have come to know that the thought of primitive peoples presents a strongly categorial and classificatory character. The universe which it comprehends is divided into compartments whose global perception helps those concerned, on the one hand, to place a specific plant, animal, or object in the correct class, and on the other, to relate things which belong to the same category or which occupy the same rank in different categories. Inside each of these classes thought by participation can operate, for each one of them constitutes a field of force by bringing together, according to the principle of analogy, beings steeped in the same metaphysical flow. The entire set of twenty-two categories of Dogon thought appears as a system of coherent cosmo-biological correspondences by which man projects himself into the cosmos and by which the cosmos is found within him.[12]

The principle of participation dear to L. Lévy-Bruhl is counterbalanced by that of partition suggested by R. Bastide: reality is partitioned so that it is not just any being that is in a relationship with any other. To each caste, each confraternity, each clan, is attributed a given sector, a specific compartment within reality for which it is responsible in order that the whole may function properly.

> There is a culture in the sense of education, of institutionalization of a certain manner or form of participation, which tends to create children out of fire or water, men out of the earth or daughters out of the tempest. There is a shaping of affective personalities, quite differentiated, around the Word, the living Word, or around Iron, maker of technical civilization. The African does not dissolve into nature, he does not even vibrate with the whole of the cosmos; he sets up a gallery of particularized characters.[13]

This categorial thought, through the subtle game of correspondences between the different compartments of the real, allows the exercise of a true logic of images. It is these images, more than ideas, which mobilize man by eliciting his imitation.

2. THE QUESTIONING AGE AND RHYTHM OF DEVELOPMENT

Regarding the relationship between mental structure and personality, two series of facts have for too long held the attention of observers for us to pass over them in silence. These problems are: (1) the absence of a questioning-age in the small child, and in general, the scarcity of 'why-questions', and (2) the precociousness which is attributed to the young African in the traditional environment before puberty, and the stagnation which is said to follow it.

In fact, we do not have sufficiently refined and careful studies at our disposal to lead us to affirm that the small child does not pass through a phase in which he has a mania for asking questions. Our own experience would rather lead us to question such an affirmation. But it is just possible that our observations based on the school environment produce a distorted picture. Nevertheless, one can easily concede that the child needs rarely to question the cause of things since he has no difficulty either with reality or with the explanations that the adults give of it. In a technically simple environment and with an educational system which enables the child with all the means at his disposal to participate in the tasks and knowledge of the adults, one must not be surprised if he acquires a great maturity and a remarkable independence at an early age. As a general rule, by the time he is twelve he is able to discharge everyday jobs, and has acquired all the knowledge which he will need for the rest of his life. No important domain of life is unfamiliar to him. Among other things, he is often witness, from his earliest age, to sexual realities by observing the intimate life of his parents. His curiosity is therefore quickly satisfied in this area, in the sublimation of which certain psychologists believe they see the basis for the need of investigation in all its forms.

In the European child the explosion of questions is found in a context where causal research and having a mind attentive to grasping the explanation of things are highly valued, and where the social sphere of the child is by and large cut off from that of the adult, so that he feels little integrated into a world whose every particular completely escapes him, where the adult himself is constantly overtaken by the new acquisitions of science and technology. The most revealing fact is that often he does not even care about the answers given to him, and he is content simply to pester his seniors with questions. That in the African child one does not find such a *libido sciendi* running idle is in line with all the education he has received. One does not try to elicit his reactions; one is even distrustful of a child who is too curious. The environment is more passive. His thought remains more closely based on images and therefore well integrated into the depth of personality. Obviously, this does not prevent questions from cropping up each time a child finds himself in an unusual situation, but these cases are rare.[14]

The theme of child precociousness in the traditional environment has been frequently noticed since the earliest voyages of European exploration. Observers are unanimous in their astonishment at the rapidity of psycho-motor development, which they relate to the cessation—even the regression—of the intellectual capacity at puberty.

In *Urgeschichte der Kultur*, H. Schurtz summarizes a rather long series of observations by saying: 'The fact is that the children of the primitive mature more quickly and lose much earlier that which constitutes the proper nature of the child. There is an age in which Africans and Europeans are equal; then the mental development of the African comes to a halt, while in the European the faculties, and with them the aptitude for regular work, continue to develop.' The works of Franke have dwelt for the most part on the inhibitions and the checks that culture seems to impose on the development of the mind. For a very long time these themes have dominated the psychology of the young African as seen by missionary and teacher, and consequently the mentality of these Europeans who were the only ones to have a prolonged contact with the youth. It is not without interest to consider the opinion of these early observers who have known a traditional environment almost completely free from external influences and where, in particular, initiation institutions were still in full vigour.

In fact, very little has been done to relate initiations to the development of personality. It is indeed difficult to evaluate their exact influence because we tend to limit ourselves to purely psychological considerations and not to see them for what they really are: rites, ontological mutations and spiritual experiences. As astonishing transformation has often been noted by teachers who, knowing the children well, see them return from a stay in the bush changed, physically transformed, and morally mature. One must not forget that during the ceremonies of social puberty, the young become the object and the centre of gravity of the whole society which relives in them its own mystery; for the first time they are put into very close contact with the spiritual life of the adult community. [15]

According to J. Piaget, the social constraints which abruptly fall upon the young person at the time of initiations congeal in some way his childhood mentality, and do not allow his thought to emerge from an egocentric narcissim. Instead of being a liberation, adolescence thus would appear as the moment of definitive crystallization of subjectivity. R. Bastide has shown that this opinion has been based on a too-simplified and inexact conception of education among traditional peoples. There is not an absolute spontaneous development of personality followed at a given moment by an abrupt immobilization brought about with the aid of petrifying ceremonies. Piaget seems to overlook above all the co-operative education within the play groups and children's societies through which the individual learns very early to confront the other person, to put himself in harmony with the common thought, and to respect the rules accepted by all. [16]

Recent research on psychomotor development of early childhood seems to agree about the remarkable precociousness of the African baby until about the age of eighteen months followed by an equally notable stagnation about the time of weaning. [17] However, numerous observations show just the opposite, but these are not based on equally long and rigorous research.

Concerning school-age level, several comparative studies have sought to bring out the fact that the best Africans attain and sometimes even surpass the level of the best Europeans, but that below this elite, performances sink rapidly. [18] In 1934, Gordon tried to test through dynamometric measures of manual strength the hypothesis that Black children are particularly alert, but do not realize at their adolescence the promise they had shown. Up to the age of fifteen, he records performances superior to those of their White counterparts; then their development begins to go down, while among the Europeans one notices this decrease only around the age of twenty.[19] However, these studies are full of ambiguities. The extreme difficulty encountered in comparing in an adequate and scientifically satisfactory manner the intelligence of Whites and Blacks by means of tests devoid as far as possible of any cultural implications makes it obvious that the global context within which intellectual activity is exercised differs too fundamentally from one environment to another to be able to determine a common denominator which is at the same time representative of the global intelligence.

What can we make of all these observations which, even in their methods, seem to lay themselves open to easy criticism? In an educational system where older children are as disposed to transmit knowledge as the younger ones are to receive it, and where in general the child finds himself in quite a favourable affective climate, there is nothing surprising in the fact that he should develop harmoniously and rapidly. But then why this stagnation that one seems to notice everywhere at puberty, this lowering in the educability of the individual in the traditional environment? Initiations can no longer be invoked today. If perhaps they had the effect of congealing the sensibility of candidates, it is not clear how they could so completely paralyse the latters' intellectual aptitudes. Could the cause then be the exercise of the erotic activity, the lack of sublimation in this domain? It seems to us that this reason cannot be ignored, but that it is not the determining factor. In fact, sexual liberty can go hand in hand with a high intelligence, and in general the child does not have to wait until puberty to be initiated into this matter.

The deepest cause must be sought in the fact that beyond the age of twelve or thirteen, the child has generally nothing more to learn either in the technological or social domain. Except where there exists an esoteric teaching to be given during adulthood, the child has in a way arrived at the end of his training. It is this 'arrivist' attitude that F. Ngoma justifiably brings out in his study of initiations. He writes:

> The decrease in learning, and not its absence, is explained by lack of motivation . . . Before being admitted to adult status, the Kongo behaved like uninformed young fellows. Hence, their great interest in learning. After initiation, one does not have much to busy oneself with. A selection takes place and with it a fixation and a stabilization. This same mentality explains a certain abuse and licence in morals: one wants to take advantage of the new freedom.[20]

One must not forget that it is the European teachers who have insisted on the problem of the 'arrested' development of intelligence at puberty. Once back in his place of birth after acquiring in school elements of instruction which do not in any way correspond to his needs and have no bearing, the child does not have occasions for perfecting his learning along the lines opened up by the school, and he is going to forget very quickly what he has learned there. The problem will arise, to be sure, the day this instruction can be pursued beyond childhood or adolescence, the day the environment will have developed sufficiently to allow him to put his acquired skills to normal use,[21] the day the school will give rural children knowledge and know-how they can make use of as adults and which have genuine value in their eyes.

3. SPACE AND TIME [22]

Mental categories, with their system of oppositions, are projected into space in order to organize it. Traditional man disposes of a whole geography of the heart which serves as a support for his beliefs and world view. The layout of the village, of the fields, and of the whole landscape, with the species of plants and animals which inhabit it, not only constitute a setting for life, but also for thought. To move away from it would be to deprive oneself of one's most solid points of support, to impose on oneself a difficult and hazardous internal restructuring; without it one is adrift. Often, an individual finds himself gripped by *Heimweh*, this characteristic nostalgia of people coming from very well established environments. In psychopathology, a case has been described for example of a sick Nigerian who, away from home, hears the trees of his native country calling him; and who will actually be cured when he goes back to them. The habitual monotony of the landscape, the poverty of the soil, the low population density, bring out both the insignificance and the importance of man in the cosmos. We have already emphasized that the importance of body contact during childhood and especially during the nursing period, the non-mediated nature of relationships delays the constitution as well as the pertinence of an intermediary space peopled with objects possessing emotional appeal. [23] The Black man, writes D. Westermann, is not a man of far horizons, but of familiar proximity; he is not a man of the heights or the depths, but of the peaceful plain. [24]

Nor does the way in which the baby is suckled allow it to develop a temporal scheme in relation to the satisfaction of his needs. In principle, never having to wait, receiving whatever he asks, the baby cannot know any other thing but the now. Duration can become a psychological reality only to the extent that desire is not fulfilled immediately, and where it meets with a certain resistance. The frequently capricious attitude of the

African baby is caused by an attempt to short-circuit time in order to obtain immediately that which normally is subjected to delays. Time plays a role for the child only to the extent that the pleasure principle yields to the reality principle. On the other hand, the child is constantly subjected to short and monontonous rhythms: walking or playfully tapping his body.

Before the appearance in Europe of the class as a constitutive cell of the world of learning in the sixteenth and especially in the seventeenth century, the life of the child was not divided into annual segments: one kept the same age for a longer time; the same teacher took pupils of very different ages all together. But in the modern school, each age-year acquires its own personality. The knowledge of one's exact age becomes for an individual as determinant as that of his name in order to be able to place himself socially.[25] In traditional Africa, as in the Europe of yesteryear, the idea of reality which predominates is of a reality that cannot be reckoned with exactitude, but which corresponds to a period of life, clearly characterized by a set of physical traits and traits of dress, by modes of activity, and proper functions. Age is expressed with reference to social events, a year of famine, for example, or the death of a chief. Thus in a general way, time appears to be measured more qualitatively than quantitatively.[26]

Nothing would be more misleading than to present African temporality as perfectly homogeneous, without any fixed markers. Everywhere there are conventional units such as 'weeks' of seven, five, or four days; everywhere economic life is measured by the regularity of market-days, everywhere lucky days alternate with unlucky days; ordinary days with feast-days. The passage of time is not perceived in a mathematical way chacteristic of urban and industrial societies, but in a cosmic way. Obviously, the fundamental unit for the peasant is the season, linked to the annual rhythms of rains and vegetation. The agricultural activity requires a greater sense of forecast as the disparity of seasons is more pronounced. In the Sudanese region where drought sometimes extends for three quarters of the year, man must store up important reserves for himself. In Senegal, according to M. Ortigues, 'the formulation of time, the possibilities for anticipation remain scarce. The consciousness of time remains close to the consciousness of the body and of the emotions.'[27] It seems that most often there are no social points of reference allowing one to identify and mark off long periods, and the temporal horizons of traditional civilizations thus seem quite limited. On the other hand, they have the characteristic of developing a sentiment which tends to enclose the individual and the group within the present.

The society to which the African child is thus introduced, makes of him a man who *has* time and who will never be stingy with it; time for him does not represent a monetary value. The person plunges himself into a slow, minimally modulated, temporality where one may spend hours unhurriedly picking off lice in the sun, where one can give oneself up completely to enjoying the present moment, to waiting, to listening for a long time, to just being there in order to get used to one another slowly, where one takes one's time in case of a conflict in order to arrive, by way of discussion, by mutual concessions and compromises, at a re-establishment of unanimity, while majority rule appertains to a democracy of people in a hurry. The notions of profit and productivity, or of punctuality are of little significance in such a context. Among the Lovedu the same word signifies slowness and virtue. [28] The principle of seniority and the importance of the notions of growth and maturity, which together determine the status and rights of a person, imply a clear perception of time and its dynamics, but according to an essentially relative yardstick. One does not revolt against the course of life and remains calm in the face of death. Duration is perceived through the feasts and the rites which mark it, also through the hierarchy which subjects the youth to the older people, and allows exchanges to take place in one direction only—namely the one which is used by word and tradition in order to transmit itself, and thus to assure a link between the past and the future.

Temporal preoccupations appear in the anxiety which the traditional African manifests for his survival and immortality, which can only be made certain by the bearing of children. These preoccupations also manifest themselves in the practice of divination through which knowledge intrudes into the future, and frees itself from the gravity of time. When African tradition emphasizes continuity, return, the appearance and disappearance of the visible and the invisible, the potential and the actual forces of reality, when it sees life as an endless recommencing and believes it sees in the individual the reactualization of an already old figure, all these elements imply a vision of time which could be called cyclic. But these data must be qualified by others no less important.

Not only are there instances where old beings come out of the whirlpool of life and new beings enter into it, but more profoundly still, with each new existence, with each return, it is only one part of being which is perpetuated and conserved; another remains behind, still another is created on this occasion. The points of departure and of arrival do not coincide exactly, and there is always a time-lag. The image of the loop which closes on itself and of the eternal return are not therefore fitting models for African temporality. We prefer the image of the spiral which links the circle to the vector. Among the Sara, R. Jaulin thinks that one can speak of reincarnation only in the minor sense of the term: it consists in a close link 'between the past and the present in such a way that the two form a homogeneous time—as is the ancestors and the new-born were holding hands around the adults.' A child is given the name of the deceased in his memory. But 'this notion of memory is burdened with an almost

Proustian weight: more than time found again it is time come back.' [29]

In traditional societies, the acts and deeds of the ancestors assume tremendous importance in contemporary life. Pleasure is taken in an irremediably retrospective way of looking a things. One knows that the future of which one seeks to have a glimpse through the good offices of the diviner will not be substantially different from the past. As R. Jaulin puts it: 'The ancestors represent time: they are the past, and they authorize and shape the future.' [30] D. Zahan writes:

> Tomorrow is built up out of the elements of yesterday and yesteryear; it is the expression of the will of those whom time has engulfed, but who continue to give witness of their presence in the multiple combinations of human destiny. One can thus affirm that in the eyes of the African, what-will-be is what-has-already-been, that the future is, in a certain sense, the past and that man is and will be only what he has been. [31]

The new and the unknown can thus only result from the many possible combinations of already existing elements.

In traditional societies, everything happens as if history had exhausted itself in the grandiose mythical events of the beginning, as if one felt the need of projecting all innovations backwards into primordial time. The symbolism of death and resurrection which characterizes the rites of passage reveals a kind of obsession with the absolute beginning. [32]

In fact, traditional societies live essentially in the present. Whether in space or time, their thought hardly goes beyond that history or geography of the heart which encompasses their life and activities. The absence of writing deprives them of continuity, not only mythical, but realistic as well. In a cyclical perspective, the past is in some way the future and the future the past; to know one is to guess the other. The child joins the old man, and birth joins death. The extremes touch, but it is the intermediary state, that of the man of today, adult and procreator, which represents the present in the plenitude of its actuality. The Black man, writes L. V. Thomas, lives and moves in an enlarged present of which he has a keen sense, the present where the relatively distant past and the more or less immediate future, defined by vital projects, meet. Each event is endowed with its proper time. Historical facts, even recent ones, are quickly forgotten: they melt into the mist of the mythical horizon where legend is distinguished from history only with difficulty. To convince oneself of this, one has only to listen to, stories covering the colonial period. Human reality is lived directly as presence and as belonging to a world which is precisely localized. Summarizing his psychotechnical studies, A. Ombredane remarks that if one subjects the intellectual behaviour of the Black man in the traditional environment to tests, it appears in a very striking way that his deficiencies and difficulties have chiefly to do with the activities of numbering, measuring, and analysis of objective space. On the other hand, it seems that the African gives evidence of great capacities for accomodation to everything within rhythmic temporal schemes—to everything which moves, dances, sings, and invites his immediate mimicry.

'In an ecological perspective—where environment and technologies are wedded—the details we have sketched give evidence of a regulated, collective movement, the very opposite of a life which has neither tail nor head.'[33]

12
Permanence and Decline
of Traditional Education

To delineate the problem in all its complexity, it is neccesary, first of all, to make two observations.

1. It is no longer possible to observe traditional education anywhere in a pure state, entirely free from foreign influences. But the modifications which it is undergoing affect it to very different degrees and at very different levels depending on ethnic group, regions, families, and individuals.

2. Nowhere has traditional education completely disappeared to give way to the modern, Western type of education. Even in the most Westernized environment, it is always possible to find some elements of traditional education, and very often it continues to form the background of the educational contribution that the child receives from his family and environment.

1. CAUSES AND CHECKS OF EVOLUTION

Traditional education finds itself competing with schools which are being established everywhere, spreading new ideals and skills—even among those it does not touch directly. But, on the other hand, it has been transformed imperceptibly by the fact that the traditional society which has given birth to it is changing economically, socially, and politically. Thus, people have had to leave home in order to work in ports, plantations, and mines, and can no longer play their role as fathers or uncles according to the old standards. The wife is therefore beginning to assume functions which formerly were not hers: she is becoming the pivotal point of the family as the masculine figures become more marginal. The younger children no longer have the older children beside them. The older people are partially losing their authority, and their knowledge is less sought after. New cultural elements are being introduced into the remotest parts of the countryside: money, means of transport and information, cloth and manners of dress, tools, paraffin lamps, and corrugated iron sheets—all of which modify imperceptibly the style of housing, of exchange, of work, and of leisure. The transistor radio, which is on the way to becoming one of the basic items of a house, will replace the songs which used to give rhythm to everyday life. Christian and Muslim influence on one hand and effective

168

atheism on the other are directly undercutting the old belief systems at the most critical level, that of synthesis.

Attending school is becoming the main criterion for differentiating between the traditionalist and the modernist segments of the population, which are sometimes divided by a deep antagonism.[1] It opens the way for new professions and a way of life based on individual renumeration. In Dahomey, it is said of the children who have gone to school that 'they have seen the light.' In his study on Porto Novo, C. Tardits shows that the school affects the lineages: very unequally the children are deliberately not all sent to school and the length of attendance is very variable. As a result, in the same group or even in the same family, there are literates, semi-literates and illiterates. Among the societies of the Gulf of Benin—where traditionally the economic activity of women was great—the benefit young girls derive from going to school is not obvious, and rather keeps them in a position of inferiority. Going to school strongly upsets earlier habits and creates new needs. Among the Southern Bantu where it is customary for boys to herd flocks, it became necessary to reconcile this economically essential activity with going to school, making a very long day for the children. The result was that among the Basuto, for example, it became easier to send girls to school than boys—an unusual situation in Africa.[2] The first pupils were often torn between two worlds, made to feel different, no longer enjoying the good things of the past, and to suffer from a feeling of incompleteness. For many among them, attending school demanded an extraordinary perseverance in order to hold out in the face of the distrust and negative attitude of the people around them.

From the point of view which concerns us, the colonial school everywhere had the same effect, whatever might have been its doctrine or inspiration: sometimes assimilation and sometimes concern for the preservation of local cultural values. The stages of its implantation correspond to those of the decline of traditional education. A period of resistance—when it was necessary to recruit pupils by force, and when the society manifested its conservatism and hostility—was followed quite quickly by another in which a certain selection took place both in the new culture and in ancestral customs. The gradual acceptance of new ideas and ways of life, and the corresponding disenchantment with the old ones led to a near-unanimous ambition of the young to have access to the teaching given at school. The parents themselves, at first resigned, came to desire, little by little, the spread of modern education, hoping thereby to realize through their children the identification with the White man which they themselves had been unable to achieve. The motivations of both children and parents were based on the observation that the old culture was falling apart, and that only the school was in a position to prepare for entry into the new system taking shape.[3] Then, finally, the African minority who, as a result of their university education have come to attain equal status with the White man, and who are no longer worried about being left behind, have often tried to advocate a return to the sources, a rediscovery of authentically African values, and have shown a determination to integrate them into a universal culture. [4]

But this school towards which everyone is rushing is far from always keeping its promises. As it develops and comes to affect a larger number of pupils, the problem of job openings begins to be felt, at times dramatically. The dreams of advancement for a whole family group that have been built up on the basis of a single individual's entry into school prove illusory. The process which it sets in motion, the urbanization which it encourages, leave the generation of parents perplexed and dissatisfied. A complaint is voiced against the independence it confers on the children, against the crisis of authority that the whole society is experiencing, against the general collapse of values once held dear. All this can lead certain people to react and to send their children to their illiterate relatives, there to be educated according to the traditional norms.[5]

One must also take into account that the school conceived on the European model quickly changes its character once exported from its place of origin. In the day-to-day life of a college in Uganda which he observed, F. Musgrove noticed that tribal aspects play a rather small role, but certain of the pupils' reactions could only be explained by taking into account details of traditional life. Thus their attitude towards the teacher remains very dependent; there is pressure for Africanization, but the pupils prefer to have White teachers. The pupils organize few games among themselves, for with respect to tribal occupations, the school for them has as a whole a playful character. The figure of the White man with which the pupils identify is that of the settler rather than that of the European who is a recent arrival in the country. The former has remained a man of the last century in his mentality and by his very acute sense of social class he is closer to the traditional Bantu mentality than the latter. [6]

The autobiographical novel with which the young African literature abounds gives, without doubt, the most complete and the most lively picture of the education received by the still very small minority of the population which has thoroughly assimilated Western culture. From one novel to another, the part devoted to traditional influences varies enormously. In *The African Child* of the Guinean Laye Camara, this part is considerable. There, even though the school is present, it is a school with rather unorthodox methods, and gives the impression of being a sort of foreign body in an organism. Clearly the centre of gravity is elsewhere: in the contact with a priestly father, with a tender but dominating mother, with the familiar maternal uncles and grandmother, in the visits to the paternal smithy, in the contacts with age-mates, and in the initiation camp.

In *Climbié* of the Ivorian Bernard Dadié, this aspect of things comes infinitely less to the fore than the development of the hero within a society stamped to a greater extent with the colonial imprint. In *Tell Freedom* by Peter Abrahams, old pedagogical methods are occasionally in evidence, but they no longer affect in any way the life of the town dweller.

The traditional educational system is not breaking up uniformly, but by sections and layers. The pedagogical institutions which the traditional society recognizes and which it consciously and explicitly promotes as such, are the first ones to disappear, while the ways of doing things belonging to what we have called unconscious pedagogy put up a stronger resistance to change. The former are more an expression of a system of ideas, and the latter of a system of attitudes, and for that reason touch the personality more profoundly. Initiation pedagogy is the first to disappear, while the practices of child rearing are the last to remain. One can also say that the education given by the mother remains more linked to tradition, while the action exercised by the husband and the society as a whole changes more easily, for by its very nature it is more influenced from outside. Certainly apparently contingent changes can have unexpected consequences in South and East Africa, age-group organizations often had military aims, so that the obliteration of this function after peace had been established has made them lose much of their importance. In connection with this whole problem, it must be remembered that the old cultural models constitute, in the eyes of the people in question, more than a simple pattern of behaviour. They are a true vital force from which one cannot free oneself without endangering one's very existence and survival. Certain close relatives, steeped in tradition, will always command a more or less conspicuous influence, and one which is shed most reluctantly.

2. AN EXAMPLE: THE EVOLUTION OF INITIATION PRACTICES

Among the different elements of the traditional system of education, initiation institutions seem to be the most fragile. They are classically presented as the capstone of traditional education—an opinion which does not always turn out to be exact. But to the extent that they must assure a certain synthesis, it is undeniable that, in their function, they feel the repercussions of any intruding change. In the beginning they appear as the high point and symbol of resistance to modern influences, especially Christianity. Then, suddenly, they fall apart. In the eyes of both parents and pupils, the school takes on more and more importance, and thereby deprives the old people of their prestige as the ultimate depositories of knowedge. Technical know-how is valued more than their wisdom, the written word more than the spoken. The school calendar makes children less available; young people leave the country; the age-group becomes smaller and smaller. The hazing of the bush camps is considered outdated and is no longer accepted. Even if nobody openly attacks initiation institutions, they weaken from the fact that their sociological props break down little by little. One day there is no one left to keep them alive and they disappear without anyone noticing it.

Throughout, initiation rites have developed as a consequence of the evolution of the societies themselves and of the influences that one ethnic tradition exercised on another. More recently they have suffered the effects of the establishment of Christian missions, of the European school, and as a whole, from the more and more generalized adoption of Western cultural models.

It happens that the meeting of cultures leads such a population to promote initiations and to confer on them a new value. Certain cases of pubertal initiations which formerly used to enjoy great prestige have been reinterpreted and given a new form within groupings having a political or a religious character, or even that of dissident Christian churches. In Chad, among the Sara, where the practice of pubertal rites is still very strong, R. Jaulin has shown how they have come to be given a truly political dimension, to be considered as the bulwark of the Black world, the shield against European intrusion, the symbol of secret African union. As Jaulin writes:

> The liberation of Africa was realized at one and the same time by opposing the colonial world and by rejecting traditional customs; initiation therefore finds itself repudiated but nevertheless kept jealously by the modernists. The latter rejected it because they were anxious to adopt the Western culture and its means of domination; they preserved it not only because, having grown up under its law, they were imbued with it, but above all because it symbolized the inviolable citadel of African unity. Initiation does not only express the union between tribes, it also symbolizes the earth and the flesh of the clan. [7]

The author shows—especially with regard to his attempt to take part, as a European, in these rites—how the Chadians who apparently are the most detached from their ethnic traditions, remain in fact prisoners of their symbols.

When one follows the evolution of an ancient but still extant *N'domo* institution—the society of the uncircumcised among the Bambara—one notices that formerly it used to include adolescents up to seventeen and eighteen years of age, while today it is often composed only of seven- to eight-year-old children. This fall in the average age of participants is necessarily accompanied by a loss—at least partial—of the esoteric dimension and of the cultural significance of such a group.

This phenomenon is observed throughout the world: young people collect traditions and rites which at first used to belong to adults, and in the end it is children who assume them once nobody else attaches great importance to them. The children's folklore, their games and their catch-phrases form, in all societies, a kind of remnant of old rites and of old adult practices.

B. Holas followed, among the Ubi of the Ivory Coast, the evolution of the feminine rites of excision as a function of the economic changes which the country has undergone. The seclusion period was shortened to just the time necessary for convalescence, instruction became sketchy, the calendar of festivities was upset by that of the new crops introduced into the region, obstacles became more numerous and fees became too high to afford. This is an example of a flexible evolution, an adaptation which safeguards the essential but which, at the same time, weakens it and makes it relative. [8]

In this decay, the modern school is not the only culprit. In West Africa it has been noted that once the pupils in a Koranic school knew how to recite the Koran by heart, they also considered themselves more educated than the elders, so that a new type of relationship was established between the generations. [9]

The traditional educational model, which accords only a limited role to explanation and to verbalization in the context of an essentially functional pedagogy where one is often content simply to name and to show, is partly responsible for the rapid cultural and religious disintegration which took place upon contact with the modern school, with the missions and with the city. Often school pupils are kept apart from ancient cults for fear that they will not be able to maintain the secrecy which these require. On the other hand, their fathers are not in a position to explain these things to them because it is a matter of practices which are lived rather than commented on. And at school the young people become accustomed to a new scheme of thought in keeping with which they deny the value of anything that cannot be rationally explained. Once the person responsible for a particular cultural function disappears, no one is left to replace him.

Missionaries have unanimously fought against the initiation practices; they strictly forbade Christians and catachumens from going into the camps, and expelled from schools those who underwent initiation. They considered it as the most important pedagogical institution of the traditional society, the one which would lead a person to embrace definitively the pagan mentality, thus barring any other form of education. As H. Ashton says, 'their action came to be regarded as a "true moral infanticide"'.[10] Circumcision was tolerated, but as an isolated practice removed from its ritual context. However, excision and artificial defloration were forbidden to Christians. A more careful and liberal examination of facts has led certain missionaries to reverse their stand where it was not already too late. Here and there bush camp methods were ingeniously Christianized. One even saw priests and catechists organize their own camps. More recently, in a few places young Christians were allowed to take part in tribal initiations.

The first Baptist missonaries adopted an uncompromising attitude of rejection against the Chadian Yondo, since they saw a radical incompatibility between this initiation and Christianity, thus leading the young converts to isolate themselves from the rest of the society, and to suffer from a painful feeling of inferiority with respect to those who had undergone the rites and become authentic Sara. It is only recently that the young Catholic community has reconsidered the attitude which had become traditional among Christians; they have accepted the Yondo for its educational and social value, while seeking a compromise in the strictly religious sphere. Thus, ancient ritual gestures have become purveyors of new contents.[11]

What remains of initiations in evironments undergoing acculturation? Generally speaking, they have become isolated practices, wrenched from their global context, but maintaining a constraining character. The circumcision done during the holidays in a dispensary without even a family ceremony no longer resembles a ritual act; it is, however, considered indispensable for marriage, and any young man who has not gone through it feels inferior and ashamed in front of his friends. We have seen Mossi seminarians demand it firmly. A character in the novel of F. Oyono working as a houseboy for an administrator suddenly becomes conscious of his superiority over his boss when one day he comes upon him unexpectedly in the shower and notices that he is uncircumcised. At puberty, young towngirls are sometimes sent to their kinsfolk to undergo a seclusion period of artificial defloration, or to be subjected to fertility dances. Of the seclusion of Tonga girls, for example, which had the aim of making them fat, there remains only the practice of a thorough wash before marriage. In general, one can say that feminine initiations happen to survive more easily than those of boys. Their more intimate nature, less spectacular, also less harsh, their aspect of domestic celebrations, the importance attached to them for assuring the fertility of young girls, also the fact that women are less prone to factors of change, explain why they have remained popular for a longer time.*

Formerly, on the coast of Benin, stays of months—even years—in 'convents' and sanctuaries were required in order to become possessed by

---

*But the case is different among the Gikuyu, where pubertal initiation for girls has practically ceased. The circumcision of boys still takes place—but in hospital, without being preceded or followed by any rites or instructions. The situation has changed so much that one wonders whether some of the Gikuyu men one meets have undergone circumcision, for the whole subject has become taboo.—Transl.

the divinity, to become a priest or a 'daughter of the gods'. As traditional practices remain deep-rooted even among Christians, and since those who have attended school refuse to submit to the requirements of this initiation, it is, in a town like Porto-Novo, the rural and illiterate branches of lineages which continue to supply the clergy for the family sanctuaries. Generally speaking, Christian or Islamic rites do not displace pagan rites in Dahomey, but exist alongside them, for it is said that a child who has not been subjected to these ceremonies has no family.[12]

Among the Bemba, the traditional Chisungu has become debased as a result of social changes which have intervened. The men go to work in the mines, families are becoming smaller, and it is no longer possible for them to collect the large amounts of food and money which used to constitute their prestige in former days. Regarding the evolution that this whole ritual complex has undergone. A. Richards confirms a hypothesis put forward by Schapera: in contact with the European culture, it is the rites described as 'magic' which survive best, while the properly religious ceremonies associated with moral values, and expressed in prayers to the ancestors and the divinity, tend to fall into disuse more rapidly.

An initiation spirit lives on beyond practices: in whatever domain, knowledge and skill are shrouded in mystery. They are only communicated in silence, and they are transmitted through stages marked by payments in money, in kind, and in service given by the apprentice to the master. The chauffeur, the mechanic, the seamstress, the cook, deliver their knowledge and service to young people to help them have access to a status similar to theirs. This they do only against gifts and payments which are duly calculated and graduated. As F. Ngoma writes:

> It is sufficient to mention marginal spontaneous payments and tips offered to school headmasters. Every good teacher has received, in one visit or another, a nice calabash of wine, eggs, chickens, so that he can transmit true knowledge to children.[13]

Certain forms of popular education or of vulgarization of knowledge meet this obstacle. When, for example, women are taught a bit of sewing at a community centre, one expects that they will, little by little, transmit what they have learned to their companions, and thus help to raise the general standard of living. But, in fact, one generally notices a very great reluctance to transmit without any further ado a skill once acquired.

Such is the spirit of old professional initiations: the divulgation of knowledge always implies something in return which tells the beneficiary what he must furnish in effort proportional to the importance of the instruction received. The secret knowledge of diviners, magicians, and healers continues to be highly valued and dearly paid for even in the most developed environments.

Finally, certain symbolisms of initiations persist. In Katanga, it was observed that the crowd transposed spontaneously a ragging gesture characteristic of bush schools to first communicants as they came out of church. Standing in two rows, the crowd struck children with rods as they passed in between, signifying thereby their accession to the ordeals of adult life.

3. THE CRUMBLING OF THE SYSTEM

With the decay of initiations, a well-defined social institution crumbles. In a traditional environment, this institution represents, with the age-grades intimately related to it, the only genuine pedagogical institution. Its decline can be followed quite accurately, and in many regions it is known when the last assembly took place or when the girls underwent the whole set of rites of passage for the last time. This termination is often associated with the death of the master or mistress of ceremonies for whom no replacement could be found.

The task of observer becomes infinitely more delicate when it comes to evaluating the evolution of attitudes toward the child and of the values which one tries to inculcate in him within the family and the village community. We would like to show that here too, traditional pedagogical elements continue to mould the minds and character of the young.

Let us take the extreme case of the highly acculturated groups living in the great urban areas. Here one witnesses the breaking up of the mediating role which the family unit normally plays between the culture and the individual. But structures evolve only slowly. It is more within the family circles than anywhere else that the use of the mother tongue is maintained, while the categories of thought and feeling are most often shaped by the usage of vernacular and European languages. As the school and the occupations to which it gives rise take up a more important place in the child's existence, a considerable part of the life of the young people tends to escape from all family control. The family does not know which criteria to invoke in order to impose coherent models. Old ideals have become blurred and the motivations underlying the new aspirations still elude it. Many children, even those not in school, receive only crumbs of traditional education; nevertheless it cannot be said that outside of school their training is structured around coherent new models. The school itself is viewed by the people according to the old schemes of thought. The social context tends to weaken considerably the traditional pedagogy, to change it, to decompose it, to the point where, in extreme cases, only a caricature of it remains. But it is very important to note that outside of school, nothing of value takes its place.

A careful, comparative study of two sections of the same population, one in an urban context, the other in a more traditional rural context, brings out the changes which, as a whole, elements and attitudes concerning education undergo. We have shown in Brazzaville that such a central notion as *nsoni* (shame) among the Kongo people is no longer seen in the same way by the urban and rural children; and that the use that the parents make of it is also different. In the urban environement as social control slackens, punishment becomes more arbitrary, more brutal. But the overall structure according to which sanctions are applied is maintained. Children are not well acquainted with the traditional tales of oral literature, but new stories, which integrate many modern elements, are true to type as regards their structure. The evening conversations around the fire continue to influence sensitivity strongly. Far from disappearing, beliefs in witchcraft and evil influences are gaining in vitality where old cultures are breaking up. The phenomenon of street gangs finally takes over from that of the traditional children's society.

It is the practices of child rearing and the way in which the mother treats the baby which seem the most resistant to change. But even here one can already notice some changes. Thus, the period of post-natal abstinence tends to be shortened, and the weaning is earlier. The alimentary and affective transition takes place less abruptly, and births tend to be closer to each other. But, on the whole, the spirit which infuses this first education has hardly changed, and the exercise of strictly feminine functions faithfully follows the traditional models. However, the psychology of the woman, wife and mother, is entering a phase of transformation to the extent that she is becoming conscious of herself as a subject, she refuses to be seen solely as an object of exchange and a bearer of children, the nuclear family is asserting itself and acquiring consistency, there is a transition from a socialized and clan sexuality to one which is more libidinous. But these are profound changes, the consequences of which are felt only gradually. The father gets closer to the baby, openly showing interest and affection, which also is evidence of a change in the relationship between the couple: in the past, this closeness would have been seen as an intrusion into the maternal functions; today it corresponds to a necessary tightening of the family circle around what it perceives as essential.

We have seen in town life the greatest threat to traditonal education. But it must not be forgotten that the majority of children still come from the rural areas, and that more than half of them are not directly touched by the school. The development taking place in crowded cities is not identical to that in the countryside, for the latter still maintain a stronger attachment to the traditional and fundamental values; also, sociological conditions are far from being the same. In order to appreciate the effect that traditional education can at present still have in a particular case, we must use a double criterion: both quantitative, taking into account the number of individuals which it affects either partially or exclusively; and qualitative, taking into consideration the more or less debased form in which it still persists.

Some isolated pedagogical attempts have been made to integrate the traditional elements as fully as possible into modern education so as not to uproot the child and in order to make the education given in school an extension of that given by the family.[14] These initiatives were not imitated. In keeping with the doctrine of direct rule, schools established by the English settler were the most anxious of all to safeguard the values promoted by the environment, and to use mother tongues. The 'rural' schools started by the French in their territories before the Second World War had as their objective to act as a transition, but without emphasizing the indigenous cultural patrimony. African opinion regularly rebelled against these attempts at adaptation, very often rightly seeing them as a way of maintaining the teaching at a inferior level to that of the cities, thus denying the people rapid entry into modern civilization. In order to attain equality, identical education was demanded.

The present state of cultural transition is therefore characterized, in a very general way, by the fact that two pedagogical trends with quite different internal consistencies, and often appearing in a partial and debased form, have come to co-exist within the same society and to shape—each in its own domain—the personality of children. Certainly, it can happen anywhere that the respective contributions of the family, the school, and the street do not agree exactly, and sometimes even diverge appreciably; in a homogeneous society they remain nevertheless complementary, only expressing different aspects of the same cultural universe. But in the case of a society undergoing acculturation, the gulf separating the current trends is much deeper for each reflects a different system, fundamentally divergent in its structure, its orientation, and its ends.

Initiation : Three Accounts from Zaïre

(*AN APPENDIX TO CHAPTER TEN*)

We asked about a hundred psychology and education students of the University of Lubumbashi—representing a cross-section of the people of Zaïre—to tell us about initiation rites in their own regions. On the whole, their knowledge in this matter turned out to be quite superficial. Many had been circumcised, but very few among them had passed through rites which had kept a certain consistency. The following statements are met with repeatedly: 'Unfortunately, I did not go through that'; 'I entered boarding school too early'; 'I was born in the city, but my father told me what used to take place in the past'; 'I must admit that I feel ashamed not to have been able to undergo those ordeals which free us from the state of *non vir*, and admit us to many adult activities.'

For those who have gone through these rites, they know it is a serious experience as shown by the following statements: 'What is described here is only a general view; the essence of initiation cannot be revealed to just anybody. Consequently, there is a certain belief involved—and I would even say a fear. Those who have passed through these rites have taken an oath never to speak about them to anyone, no matter who, and this for fear of falling sick or dying.'

Of the material thus collected, we extract three accounts which appear to us particularly significant.

1. AN ACCOUNT BY A TSHILUBA-SPEAKING STUDENT FROM KANIANIA, EAST KASAI

The rites, in their entirety, are known as 'bukishi'. It was a 'school' about a hundred metres from the village. The initiators, previously initiated people mandated by the elders to perpetuate the tradition, dug a pit 6 m wide, 10-15 m long, and 1.5 m deep. This pit was used as a 'bedroom', and symbolized at the same time the tomb from which the neophytes would emerge victorious on the feast-day. Right near the hole there were huts covered with thatch of branches of trees from top to bottom. These served as shelters for giving instruction in cases of heavy rain or great heat. Instruction was given orally, and lasted about six months. The first neophyte chosen by the elders had to be a lively, fifteen-to seventeen-year-old individual, courageous and enterprising. On the morning of the opening

179

day, the young novice was caught and taken by force to the school; on the way there, he was given instructions to which he was to adhere firmly; otherwise he would die. These were: to keep away from the village, to flee from people, and to keep secrecy. At that moment the drums announced the news to those due for initiation, who thereupon waited to be captured unresisting. Very often, teachers who lived in the village used to come to check on and add to the instruction. The novices neither cut their hair nor washed themselves; they fended for themselves when no food was brought to them. The physical conditions were too hard for the girls, who came for only a few weeks before the closure. On that day, the elders went to the school in traditional costume. The newly-initiated, clad in clean skirts of raffia from hip to ankle, took the oath of allegiance to the traditional customs. From there, the procession set off towards the village where the popular celebrations commenced and continued late into the evening.

I learned all this from a friend who took part in these rites. My own parents did not allow me to be initiated in rites different from those of our own Luba group.

2. AN ACCOUNT CONCERNING THE NGBAKA PEOPLE, UBANGUI DISTRICT, EQUATOR PROVINCE

Among us, the initiation rite for boys is called *Gaza*. It is of a secret nature: women and uncircumcised men cannot take part in it. The neophytes go through several stages:

a. The whip stage: In order to alert you that you are going to be circumcised that year, you are whipped in the morning, and then your body is smeared with a red powder of certain trees mixed with water and oil.

b. The stage of the exhibition dance which takes place in the evening at least five or six times before the circumcision. The leaders order that women and uncircumcised men be driven away; they are even forbidden to hide in the houses and listen to the singing. The men make a circle and hold hands. If the circle breaks, this means that there is a suspect around who must be removed. The initiates-to-be must not lift their heads, for the elders are dancing naked.

c. The stage of the test of courage: Led into the forest, the young men must eat, without crying, some barks which are more stinging than red pepper. In addition, a 'biting' substance is applied to the eyes and nose. If you cry, this means that you are still weak, and the dose is increased. Then, you are led to an ants' nest and asked to put your hand in. All these ordeals take place only once, on the eve of circumcision, to see whether you are brave and capable of bearing suffering. They fortify your will and prevent you from crying.

d. The stage of circumcision: Circumcision takes place in the forest. The first one to go through it is called *bagaza*. Masks to scare the young men are made. Using a pot covered with a goatskin and a pointless arrow which is rubbed on the skin, a terrible noise, similar to the roar of a lion, is produced. Even the people outside the camp who hear this noise are frightened. The whole procedure is accompanied by singing and by beating of the gong.

e. The stage of learning: When everyone has been circumcised, each one receives a teacher (*buna*) who will teach him in the camp. (The camp is called *butu.*) You are taught to respect elders, chiefs, women, and other people's property. You are taught to keep secrets, to start a home, to live with others, and to share what you have. No food brought from outside is eaten by an individual in isolation. In the practical domain, one is taught how to hunt, to fish, to weave mats, to construct houses and to make certain artistic objects. You are also taught a special dance performed to the rhythm of the gong, without singing. If an initiate dies in the forest, the mother cannot be informed before the last day: his father is enjoined to keep it secret.

If people come to the camp without permission, they are presented with graphic signs that they must decipher in order to prove that they have been initiated. If they fail, they are forced to stay in the camp and undergo instruction. (One of these signs is Y-shaped, and represents the support for the circumcised organ.)

f. Coming out is a day of great ceremony. On the previous night, the young people either assume new names or retain their old ones. There is dancing and drinking. They have passed from the old to the new life. In the village, their behaviour changes. They feel transformed.

I am witness to what I have described, for I was subjected to this type of rites. I spent months in the forest and passed through the different stages.

3. AN ACCOUNT CONCERNING THE BASOKO OF THE EASTERN PROVINCE

Circumcision is an important stage in one's life, initiation into true life, a birth into a new life. Before circumcision who is one if not a little woman, a child? Afterwards, one becomes completely man.

The operation takes place away from the village, in a valley traversed by a stream.

Among the elders, there is one who is a specialist in the art of circumcision, and well versed in all the secrets of the medicinal power of plants. He has a very sharp knife which he cleans twice a year, and keeps carefully in a small sheath, hermetically sealed. We call the circumciser *motena mambute.* He is aided by several assistants; they can number as many as six.

At the appointed time, the circumciser gathers together, in the evening, all would-be initiates. These spend the night singing and dancing while the elders drink and enjoy themselves. The village is festive. It is a night of saying farewell for these young men who are going to undergo the hardest of tests and who will be absent from the village for at least three months.

At dawn, one of the assistants starts the march. His terrible whistling makes women, children, and the uncircumcised tremble. The procession advances towards the sacred valley to the rhythm of songs and dances. Gripped with fear and anguish, the young men march shivering with cold, for their only covering is a simple loincloth between the legs in this rainy and humid region.

On arriving at the place, the circumciser and his assistants erect an altar. A goat presented by one of the neophytes is sacrified to God. While passing his right hand lightly from the head to the tail of the victim, the circumciser says a silent prayer. Then, while repeating the same gesture, he says over and over again: 'Saviour Spirit, save us.' In the evening, the victim is consumed by the circumciser and his assistants. After making the sacrifice, the neophytes go to look for branches of trees for constructing a sort of lean-to to serve as shelter. They look for moss which they weave and which serves them both as blanket and mattress. After this is done, a general assembly takes place. The initiates are lined up. Passing from one to the other, one of the assistants cuts their belts. The loin-garment falls off, and the young man will remain naked until he is completely healed. The neophytes all sit on a tree trunk and await the terrible scene. Several assistants seize the young man and keep him standing motionless while the circumciser gets on with his job.

The neophyte shouts in despair! But the merciless assistants sing and beat the drum in order to smother the cry of the patient. An assistant then wraps the foreskin in a soft herb, while the circumciser applies medications to the wound. A herb wrapped around the wound serves as a bandage. During all this time, the educators, i.e. the circumciser and his assistants, will follow the initiates step by step, to teach them and to make adults of them.

This instruction concerns first of all the matrimonial domain. Circumcision has as its principal aim to change the youth and to make an adult of him. Now the common vocation of any adult man is to start a home and to procreate. The circumciser and his assistants teach the young man everything concerning sexual realities.

—'Young man, do not put too much confidence in your wife. If you give a piece of meat to a woman, eat some of it first, for even if you treat her well, she will betray you one day.'

—'In the choice of a wife, do not look at beauty, but at goodness; beauty is not the heart.'

—'Learn to respect the one who gives you your wife: your mother-in-law; your mother-in-law's face is very slippery. Do not stare at it lest you are overcome and commit the worst of crimes.'

—'Do not believe any of the nonsense that your wife tells you, especially when she is priding herself on a virtue.'

—'A young girl with a lively tongue, who boasts of everything, does not know that one day the naked truth might be uncovered. This is the way you must treat your wife. She is inferior to you, and your duty is to keep her in this state. But your wife will give you children.

How must one go about the begetting of children? In this bush school, the educators undertake true sexual initiation. Here is one of the many anecdotes they tell: 'Once upon a time, there lived in a village a very liberated woman. She believed herself superior to her husband, and at night she would always sleep on the front part of the matrimonial bed, while her husband slept at the back against the wall. One night it happened that a lion entered the hut. Gripped with great fear, the virago leaped over her husband and squeezed herself against the wall. Arming himself with all his courage and strength, the husband killed the beast. Since that time the man sleeps on the front part of the bed, on the side nearest the door, and the woman sleeps behind him.'

The assistants and the circumciser teach the initiates many other things concerning the technique of the act of procreation. They are to observe these techniques under pain of committing a sin against the order of nature and of remaining sterile all their lives.

But is it sufficient to have children in order to realize one's destiny as a man? No! One's children must also remain alive. Therefore, they are also taught about all sorts of remedies against sorcery which might endanger their lives. It is good to bring children into the world but the children must also grow up.

Instruction on social matters is given a very important place. In the evening, in the bush, lying on their moss beds, the neophytes listen to the great circumciser or one of the assistants recount the epic history of the tribe. It is at this time that they learn about the vicissitudes of the migrations of their ancestors, how they went to war against the Tolombo, commonly known as the Anyota, how they crossed the river Aruwini and extended their occupation. While the epic is being recited, the newly-circumcised forget their pain and feel their hearts swell with pride and grandeur. At the end of the story, all answer in chorus: 'We shall fight for the soil acquired by our ancestors! We are worthy sons of our ancestors. May their spirits protect us.' The assistants then ask each one of the neophytes to repeat what he has heard, and to recite that beautiful epic with the greatest possible expression. The others pass judgment on the correctness and form of the 'oration'. It is a real competition. Good orators are thus revealed, those who will know how to defend a cause in the assembly of elders.

Another characteristic on which the assistants insist is the sense of adaptation. They teach the initiates how to adapt themselves to different circumstances of life. 'If you are visiting a friend and find him sleeping on ashes, you ought also to sleep on ashes. Learn to share the fate of your friends while visiting them.'

'You must also travel and see the country. A bird which has never left its tree will not know that there is millet elsewhere. However, after travelling in order to enrich your knowledge, return home: do not forget your country of birth. In a foreign country one hardly lives long; in a strange country one does not have a long and happy old age. Where a relative lives distance is of little consequence, for love does not know any frontiers. If you want to be happy during your entire lifetime, choose well those who surround you. When you notice that you are not accepted in a place, take care, for the least of your faults can be made into a great crime: it is always the orphan's potato which extinguishes the fire. If later some of you will occupy high places in society, learn how to respect your subjects: it is through your men that you will be a chief.'

And the list of educational proverbs stretches on. The initiates listen, and take in these wise dictums, for later they will have to transmit them to their children.

In this bush school, the educators also initiate the newly-circumcised into the art of dance. They sing and dance. The dance for the circumcised is called 'Bondonga'. It is this same dance which is used to mourn someone who dies in the valley of circumcision. Later, in the village, if a circumcised man dies, 'Bondonga' will be danced. Through this dance, the avenging spirit of the deceased is calmed. Should the 'Bondonga' take place in the village, no woman or uncircumcised man is allowed to be present.

The young neophytes must also learn the technique of procuring themselves game, fish, and birds. The assistants do not ask them to dig holes for catching elephants or buffaloes. That is the work of specialists. They content themselves with setting traps for small game—wild rabbits, squirrels, antelopes, etc. They learn from their masters the art of weaving basket-traps.

But, let us not forget! Circumcision is a school of harshness and brutality. The neophytes, sometimes without any weapons, pursue game until they catch it. They pick fruit from high trees. Along with the educators, they cross bush and forest. There, they see many different varieties of trees and plants, useful and dangerous shrubs. When they come across a very useful shrub, they stop, and the assistants then explain: 'Do you see that? You will scrape off the bark, then go and boil it. Then you will filter the solution and use it as an enema. It will cure children of stomach ailments. This other plant with greenish leaves can be used to heal your wounds. You will crush these leaves and apply them to the wound.' During these three months in the bush, the initiates learn to recognize most of the plants and their respective uses.

Now let us consider initiation from the religious point of view. We said earlier that the ceremony starts by making a sacrifice to God, the creator. *Jakumba* is his name. He is absolute and transcendent; below him there are the Spirits to whom he has confided the government of the universe. Among them there are some good and some bad ones. It is especially the latter who flog people for their misdeeds. The educators teach their disciples the tricks for escaping from sorcery. In the bush there exists a liliaceous-like herb called 'Lilanga'. They learn how to use the tuber and leaves of this plant against evil spirits and against all men who have concluded a pact with evildoers: sorcerers. Besides this plant, there are certain parts of some rare animals that one must carry on oneself in order to be immunized against evil. The assistants—men with experience—know all the secrets of life, and they pass them on to the neophytes. Once the latter have returned to the village, they will be able to protect their wives, their children and themselves against any danger liable to diminish or destroy their vital force.

But what good is this knowledge required during initiation, if the initiate does not change his behaviour? If he does not act like an adult? In short what use is the intellectual baggage if there is no personality development?

During the period of circumcision, the educators help the young man to think before acting. They watch scrupulously over his words and actions. When a neophyte allows himself to talk nonsense, the teachers intervene directly to correct his speech: 'You are speaking like a bird', or 'How you hold forth like one who, in his early years, was served food in a bird's nest!'

The stories of the Tortoise, the Fox, and the Antelope are here given a special place. This is how it is done. The master starts to relate a story, and when he finishes, he gives the neophytes a moment to reflect. They draw their own conclusion, which they are asked to remember for their future life. 'Heed this advice, young man, and put it into practice, for the proverb says: 'The lamb which does not heed advice will do so when its head is in a pot on the fire.'

But the heart of this teaching is found in the philosophy with which the neophytes are inspired. Before circumcision, the young man was considered as a woman, fearful, weak, cowardly, incapable of enduring anything. From now on, he must be proud of himself for having passed harsh tests. Henceforth, he will take his place in the assembly of elders, and his opinion will be taken into account. In the village his wives will be respected. It will not be said of them: 'The wife of the uncircumcised is the wife of a leper.'

The circumcised young man must behave in society like a man. Later on, in the village, he will have to defend the interest of all and share in the common joys and sorrows. Is there a misfortune which strikes a member of the community? Everybody will sympathize and come to the rescue. Is there somebody who has committed a sin against the intangible order of nature? The whole community will be punished by the spirits. It is at circumcision school that one acquires a sense of life and community responsibilites. If a neophyte points at an antelope, all must run after it until they catch it. They run through brambles and thorns in common solidarity. In this way, they are prepared to suffer for the common cause.

Another very important element is incomporated in this pedagogy: the cultivation of taste and of aesthetic sense. The teachers insist on the art of oratory, especially as regards the history of the tribe. They themselves tell stories and try to introduce in them a maximum of poetry and literary beauty. They ask their pupils in turn to reproduce the same expressions. Each one will try to retell the story in the most moving manner. Then there are songs and dances. Through choreographic art, the neophytes penetrate the mystery of beauty and rhythm, of all those things which speak to the heart.

On a more practical level, each newly-circumcised youth is obliged to make himself a loin-cloth which he will wear at the end of initiation. Here, too, each one tries to make the most beautiful and best decorated loin-cloth.

Initiation in the bush aims above all at shaping the will of the neophyte, to bend it, to mould it, until it is ready to endure any affliction, to face any ordeal at any time. It is a true school of asceticism, renunciation (self-denial) and mortification. Before circumcision, heads are shaved. Circumcision is performed without any anaesthesia. All the pain is therefore felt. The initiate must not speak of his mother or father during the ordeal lest they die. The initiates have neither blankets nor mats for their bed: only a rough moss carpet to protect them against the chill of the night. Each morning they go to take a bath in the river. To heal the wounds of the neophytes, the teachers sometimes use the ashes of banana peels—a very painful treatment. When it comes to food, austerity is absolute: they eat neither meat nor fish until they are healed. The produce of their hunting and fishing is reserved for the chief circumciser and his assistants. No salt or oil is put in their food. During three months they are not allowed to see a woman, and at home their parents must officially observe continence.

Quite often a big fire is lit in the evening. The initiates sit around it. But do not all of us have the experience of a camp-fire? As the fire gets hotter, people move away! But that is not the case with the neophytes. They are forced to remain in the same place in spite of the vivacity of the flames. Is it necessary to mention that this fire causes great pain to their wounds, especially because they are naked?

When everyone has healed, the teachers redden a stick in the fire. A young man is then grabbed and the hot burning stick is directed towards his sexual organ. Those who have self-composure take this as a ruse. But others, more timid, cry out loud and promise the earth—one his sister, another a field, another a part of his father's property.

Here is the very last trial which closes the stay in the bush. In the morning, all the newly-circumcised go to the river. There, an assistant has hidden a ring. The young men must recover the ring from the bottom of the river with their mouths. They can not come out of the river until they have found the ring. The one who finds it is declared the leader of the class.

All these tests are of a painful nature. Thanks to them, the young Musoko has experience of life: hard and ungrateful. One must conquer it, and continually struggle if one wants to remain alive. After circumcision the young man will see himself given great responsibilities. In order to assume them in a worthy manner, he will need patience, courage, perseverance, and endurance. These qualities must manifest themselves as soon as an occasion presents itself. The adult must therefore be continually prepared to act in spite of difficulties and risks. If war should break out with the neighbouring village or tribe, he will be the first to take up his spear and shield and go forward to defend his people. Women and children will live in a climate of peace and security, for they know that their father who fears nothing, braves everything, and succeeds in everything, is there to protect them.

Appendix

MAP OF THE PRINCIPAL PEOPLES TREATED IN THIS BOOK

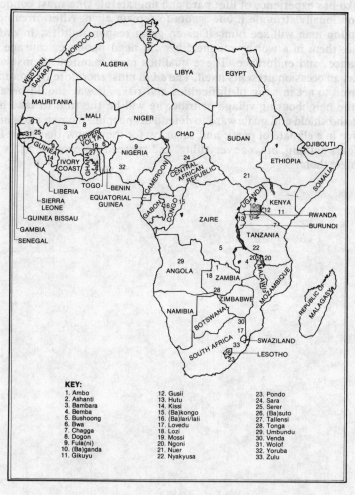

KEY:

1. Ambo
2. Ashanti
3. Bambara
4. Bemba
5. Bushoong
6. Bwa
7. Chagga
8. Dogon
9. Fula(ni)
10. (Ba)ganda
11. Gikuyu
12. Gusii
13. Hutu
14. Kissi
15. (Ba)kongo
16. (Ba)lari/lali
17. Lovedu
18. Lozi
19. Mossi
20. Ngoni
21. Nuer
22. Nyakyusa
23. Pondo
24. Sara
25. Serer
26. (Ba)suto
27. Tallensi
28. Tonga
29. Umbundu
30. Venda
31. Wolof
32. Yoruba
33. Zulu

PRINCIPAL ETHNIC GROUPS: THEIR DISTRIBUTION AND LINEAGE SYSTEMS

ETHNIC GROUP	COUNTRY OR COUNTRIES	LINEAGE SYSTEM
Ambo	Zambia	patrilineal
Ashanti	Ghana	bilineal
Bambara	Mali	patrilineal
Bemba	Zambia	matrilineal
Bushoong	Zaïre	matrilineal
Bwa	Upper Volta	patrilineal
Chagga	Tanzania	patrilineal
Dogon	Mali	patrilineal
(Ba)ganda	Uganda	patrilineal
Fula(ni)	Senegal, Guinea, Nigeria	patrilineal
Gikuyu	Kenya	patrilineal
Gusii	Kenya	patrilineal
Hutu	Rwanda, Burundi	patrilineal
Kissi	Guinea	patrilineal
(Ba)kongo	Zaïre, Congo	matrilineal
(Ba)lari/lali	Congo	matrilineal
Lovedu	South Africa	patrilineal
Lozi	Zambia	patrilineal
Mossi	Upper Volta	patrilineal
Ngoni	Malawi, Zambia, Tanzania	patrilineal
Nuer	Sudan	bilineal
Nyakyusa	Tanzania	matrilineal
Pondo	South Africa	patrilineal
Sara	Chad	patrilineal
Serer	Senegal	bilineal
(Ba)suto	Lesotho	patrilineal
Tallensi	Ghana	patrilineal
Tonga	Zambia	bilineal
Umbundu	Angola	matrilineal
Venda	South Africa	bilineal
Wolof	Senegal, Gambia	matrilineal
Yoruba	Nigeria	patrilineal
Zulu	South Africa	patrilineal

The spelling of ethnic names is that of G. P. Murdoch's *Africa: Its People and their Culture History* (New York: McGraw Hill, 1959). Interested readers may wish to refer to his map 9, page 28, for information on ethnic groups not listed above. In it, areas of patrilineal, matrilineal, double, or bilateral descent are indicated.

Notes

Foreword

1. M. T. Knapen, *L'enfant mukongo*, p. 53.
2. J. Kenyatta, *Facing Mount Kenya*, pp. 98-9. This is not a true quotation, but rather an abridgement of the two pages indicated. As I have mentioned in the preface, all the references to Kenyatta will be to this work and not to *Au pied du Mont Kenya* used by the author.—Transl.
3. A. Moumouni, *L'éducation en Afrique*, p. 12.
4. Ibid., p. 83.

Chapter 1: *Introduction to the Study of Traditional Education*

1. René Hubert, *Traité de pédagogie générale*, p. 5.
2. H. I. Marrou, *Histoire de l'éducation dans l'Antiquité*, p. 17.
3. E. T. Hall, *The silent language*, pp. 83-118.
4. P. H. Diebold, 'Wa dia fua yika dio', *Proverbes des Balari*.
5. J. Kenyatta, *Facing Mount Kenya*, p. 112.
6. D. Zahan, *Sociétés d'initiation bambara, le Ndomo, le Koré*.
7. E. Jensen-Krige and J. D. Krige, *The realm of a rain queen*, p. 124.
8. P. Erny, *L'enfant dans la pensée traditionnelle de l'Afrique Noire*.
9. A. Métraux, *Religions et magies indiennes d'Amérique du Sud*, p. 122.
10. A. Varagnac, *Civilisation traditionnelle et genre de vie*, p. 22ff.
11. Text of A. Siegfried; cited in Varagnac, *Civilisation traditionnelle*, p. 33.
12. Cf. also R. Redfield, 'The folk society', pp. 293-308.
13. P. Fougeyrollas, *Modernisation des hommes*, p. 8ff.
14. Ibid., pp. 35-6.

Chapter 2: *Ritual Pedagogy*

1. This need of identifying someone at the beginning of his career is found, for example, in the rite of crowning the *Bour* of Sine in Senegal. In fact, the king who is being crowned is a baby in his new function and in the personality which he must assume. He is asked: 'Who are you? What is your name?' Then he will be struck violently in order to awaken his memory: he must recall the name under which he has already lived and reigned during a previous existence. See H. Gravrand, *Dynamique interne de la famille sérèr*, pp. 95-122.
2. See M. Houis, *Les noms individuels chez les Mossi*.
3. M. Eliade, *Naissances mystiques*, p. 61.
4. G. Dieterlen, *Essai sur la religion bambara*, p. 64; D. Zahan, *Sociétés d'initiation bambara*, pp. 49, 126. It is especially these authors who, following M. Griaule, have analysed the theme of androgyny as it is found in the valley of the Niger. For more information, see H. Baumann, *Das doppelte Geschlecht*.
5. E. Beuchelt, *Kulturwandel bei den Bambara von Segou*, p. 209. The author describes as 'foreign to development' the conception of the person in this ethnic group.

190

6. This appears very clearly in the observations recorded by M. C. and E. Ortigues, *Oedipe africain*: 'Culpability is little interiorized or constituted as such. Everything happens as if the individual could not bear to see himself internally divided and moved by conflicting desires. The "evil" is always situated outside the self, belonging to the domain of fate or of God's will' (p. 128). 'In pedagogical consultations one hardly hears the words: "It is his fault", which are very common in France. "He is bad" means rather that "he is attacked or inhabited by something bad." The child is not held guilty or evil in himself, and no one bears him a grudge' (p.129).* Another very common remark is: 'It is very difficult to obtain from parents descriptions of children's behaviour. What is given is rather a trait of character having a value of social status and of prognosis. The term "badly educated" does not connote only a character trait but also a status generally felt as irreversible' (p. 131).

7. D. Westermann, *Der Afrikaner heute und morgen*, p. 49.

8. Among the Bambara, children must go to greet their parents each morning before they wash their faces. By doing so, children are supposed to imbue themselves with the power which emanates from the parents. This power diminishes after washing, being carried away by water. See D. Zahan, 'La littérature orale en Afrique Noire', p. 38.

9. G. Gusdorf, *Pourquoi des professeurs?*, p. 22.

Chapter 3: *The First Discovery of the Other*

1. For a more detailed study, see P. Erny, *Les premiers pas dans la vie de l'enfant d'Afrique Noire*.

Chapter 4: *Vertical Integration in the Lineage*

1. L. S. Senghor, *Liberté I*, p. 74.

2. It is in this respect that the father-mother-children constellation in Rwanda and Burundi appears similar to that in traditional rural Europe. (M. Vincent, *L'enfant au Ruanda-Urundi*, pp. 106-7.)

3. R. Clignet, 'Les attitudes de la société à l'égard de la femme en Côte d'Ivoire', p. 143.

4. R. Bastide, 'La sexualité chez le primitifs', p. 70.

5. L. Thore, *Langage et sexualité*, p. 83.

6. J. Vansina, 'La famille nucléaire chez les Bushoong', p. 98.

7. In M. Gluckman, *Custom and conflict in Africa*, p. 78.

8. M. T. Knapen, *L'enfant mukongo*, p. 94. In a cross-cultural study, W. Stephens has shown that by keeping members of the married couple at a distance, this form of marriage brings the mother closer to her offspring. He has brought out the positive correlations between the variables of 'dilution' and the dependence of the child, the leniency of others towards him, the intensity of taboos and the phobias in sexual matters, and the constraint on the boys to reside elsewhere at the onset of puberty. (W. Stephens, *The Oedipus complex*.) Other authors have made the comparison with initiations and the degrees of severity which characterize them in their object of snatching the future men from the maternal universe. (J. Whiting,

*See also E. B. Castle, *Growing up in East Africa* (London: Oxford University Press, 1966). —Transl.

R. Gluckhohn, A. Anthony, 'The function of male initiation ceremonies at puberty', pp. 359-70.)

9. Vansina, 'La famille nucléaire', p. 101.

10. M. Fortes, 'Social and psychological aspects of education in Taleland', p. 64.

11. 'The youth or girl cannot advance from one stage to another without the parents' will and active assistance. The satisfaction of all a boy's longings and ambitions depends on the father's and family's consent. Without it he cannot be circumcised. Without it he cannot be married, for he has no property of his own, and marriage involves gifts or exchanges which only the two families can arrange. He cannot even join in a meat feast, kĩruũgu, or a beer-drinking party without his father's permission' (J. Kenyatta, Facing Mount Kenya, p. 113).

12. D. Paulme, Une société de Côte d'Ivoire hier et aujourd'hui, p. 68.

13. E. Colson, Marriage and the family among the plateau Thonga of Northern Rhodesia, p. 224.

14. M. C. Ortigues recounts the words of a Senegalese mother: 'When he becomes big, two years, three years, he is a boy, and he must go away from me in order to learn how things are done. If he stays around, he will say to himself: "My father and mother are there", and he knows that whatever he wants he will get.' Among the matrilineal Serer, fifty per cent of the boys are still brought up by their maternal uncles even today. Among the Wolof, it is preferred to confide the education of a child, especially of a boy, to uncles or aunts. (M. C. and E. Ortigues, Oedipe africain, pp. 24, 33. In a matrilineal society, custom often forces a child to go to his maternal uncle's place at a given age in order to live among his 'own', the people of his lineage. The Umbundu insist above all that children should spend one to two years at their mother's brother's or at their father's sister's. Formerly, it used to be arranged for them to spend some time in the king's capital. Among friends and blood brothers, it is customary to exchange children. (G. M. Childs, Umbundu kinship and character, p. 105). Among the Gourmantché, the child was almost automatically taken charge of and educated by his father's older brother. Today, that custom has evolved somewhat, and one often sees two brothers who entrust their children to each other. (M. Cartry, 'Attitudes familiales chez les Gourmanthcé', p. 47.

15. P. Erny, Aspects de l'univers affectif de l'enfant congolais, p. 158. In Lagos, according to the research of P. Marris, hardly fifty per cent of the children interrogated live with their parents, and twenty per cent live neither with their father nor with their mother. (P. Marris, Family and social change in an African city, p. 56)

16. Ph. Ariès has shown that it was usual in the Europe of yesteryear up to the fifteenth century to send children of seven to fourteen years to other families so that they could learn good manners, while one received children of strangers in one's house. This practice of going to be educated in strange families seems to have been widespread in medieval Europe. (Ph. Ariès, L'enfant et la vie familiale sous l'ancien régime, pp. 408-9.) Domestic service was bound up with apprenticeship, and sharing the professional life involved sharing the private life from which it could hardly be dissociated.

16a. The author was able to observe among the Mossi people the case of one of his twelve-year-old pupils whose father used to leave home quite regularly to go and work in Ghana. While the father was at home, the boy did very well in school, but during the rest of the time his performance was nothing but mediocre, and he was unable to concentrate.

17. L. V. Thomas, 'L'enfant et l'adolescent diola'.

18. Everywhere it is observed that the worst insult—even to the child—is to mention with contempt the person or the name, and especially the sexual organs of one's mother. To erase such an insult, a single combat is inevitable.

19. It is in this respect that M. Leblanc notes after a projective test that 'women describe themselves as not being appreciated by their children except in their role of feeders. Moreover, the mother is the object of the aggressiveness of the child, who dares not adopt a similar attitude towards his father.' (M. Leblanc, *Personnalité de la femme katangaise*, p. 261.)

20. E. Smith, 'Indigenous education in Africa', p.326.

21. Among the Ambo, where the boy has scarcely any contact with the mother after five or six years of age, the attachment which he has for her is nevertheless very strong. (B. Stefaniszyn, *Social and ritual life of the Ambo of Northern Rhodesia*, p. 10.)

22. L. de Heusch, *Essai sur le symbolisme de l'inceste royal en Afrique*, p. 155.

23. The consequence of this is that the boys, having had the experience of a close mother, are led to seek a heterosexual partner, whereas the girls, having known a severe and reserved father, will abhor heterosexuality and will be more inhibited in their sexual conduct. These dispositions explain to a certain degree the frequency of abduction, and therefore a sado-masochistic type of heterosexuality. (R. A. Levine, 'Gusii sex offences'.)

24. Vansina, 'La famille nucléaire', p. 104.

25. Vincent, *L'enfant au Ruanda-Urundi*, p. 201.

26. E. Hopen, *The pastoral Fulbe family in Gwandu*, p. 121.

27. J. Kenyatta, *Facing Mount Kenya*, p. 10.

28. A. Richards, *Chisungu*, p. 132.

29. Hopen, *The pastoral Fulbe*, p. 135.

30. 'The small Dogon boy, as soon as he is able to "sit up alone", and no longer follows his mother to the house of menstruating women—that is to say, as soon as he no longer needs constant maternal care—leaves the family court. Very proud of his son, the father takes him by the hand, leads him to the public place where the *toguna* (men's shelter) is located. The child will attend long conversations of men, some seated on the ground against the pillars of the *toguna*, the others underneath the thick mat of millet stalks covering the *toguna*. The children sit there completely silent. Certain children, at the age of four or five, seem to follow the conversations with much interest. Sometimes they pose their elders questions which the latter take quite seriously.' (D. Paulme, *Organisation sociale des Dogon*, p. 465.)

31. Among the Kongo, they say that scraping the bottom of pots in order to get the left-over food makes boys feeble-minded.

32. J. Hallaire, 'Chrétiens africains face à l'initiation ancestrale', p. 486.

33. A. R. Radcliffe-Brown and D. Forde (eds.), *Systèmes familiaux et matrimoniaux en Afrique*, pp. 121-2.

34. Vincent, *L'enfant au Ruanda-Urundi*, pp. 111-12: 'The mother forms the other pole, ready to receive all those the father will not have selected. By so doing she increases still more by that tutelage the impression of security that the father does not give.'

35. M. Fortes, *Oedipus and Job*; Gluckman, *Custom and conflict*, p. 55. 'In case of a serious dispute between an older man and a junior, both of the same kinship (the extreme case being the dispute between father and son), it is always the older member who is considered offended, even if in fact he be in the wrong. Never has one the right to reproach an older person in front of young people. It would be ruinous to side with a child against his father, for this kind of reversing of generations would cause disorder in the world.' 'The child does not have the truth,' says the proverb, 'it is the father who has it.' (G. Calame-Griaule, *Ethnologie et langage*, p.274.)

36. H. Gravrand, 'Dynamisme interne de la famille sérèr', pp. 103-4.

37. Cf. Erny, *L'univers affectif*, pp. 110-59.

38. Vansina, 'La famille nucléaire', p. 103.
39. Colson, *Marriage and the family*, p. 288.
40. R. and L. Makarius, *L'origine de l'exogamie et du totémisme*, pp. 62-3.
41. E. Beuchelt, *Traditionelle und moderne Jugenderziehung*, p. 151.
42. de Heusch, *L'inceste royal*, p. 222.
43. This is an expression of the Ngoni. See M. Read, *Children of their fathers*, p.81.
44. Kenyatta, *Facing Mount Kenya*, p. 16.
45. Ibid., p. 15.
46. Paulme, *Les gens du riz*, p. 118.

Chapter 5: *Horizontal Integration in the Society of Equals*

1. The classification based on the principal of seniority can, however, be corrected by other criteria, as we learn from F. Ngoma, *L'initiation bakongo et sa signification*, p. 133: 'Even at the age of twelve, a Mukongo boy who, by his judgement and conduct shows a real social effectiveness, is considered more highly than the one who is twenty but whose social conduct leaves much to be desired.'
2. M. Read, *Children of their fathers*, p. 86.
3. See S. Balde, 'Les associations d'âge chez les Foulbé du Fouta-Djallon', pp. 89-109.
4. K. Weule, 'Negerpädagogik', p. 65.
5. See M. M. Edel, *The Chiga of Western Uganda*, and D. Paulme, *Les gens du riz*, p. 114.
6. B. Stefaniszyn, *Social and ritual life of the Ambo of Northern Rhodesia*, p. 87.
7. J. Ki-Zerbo, 'La crise actuelle de la civilisation africaine', p. 129.
8. L. Frobenius, *Paideuma*, p. 55.
9. H. Schurtz, *Alterklassen und Männerbünde*, p. 83.
10. J. Kenyatta, *Facing Mount Kenya*, p. 116: 'The fellowship and unity of these age-groups is a rather remarkable thing. It binds men from all parts of the country, and though they may have been circumcised at places hundreds of miles apart, it is of no consequence. They are like old boys of the same school, though I question whether the Europeans have any association with the same high standards of mutual obligation except perhaps in time of national emergency.'
11. L. S. Senghor, *Liberté I*, p. 172.
12. M. Wilson, *Good company*, pp. 19-21.
13. Read, *Children of their fathers*, pp. 91-7.
14. Ibid., pp. 100-102.
15. See D. Zahan, *Sociétés d'initiation bambara, le Ndomo, le Koré*.
16. See Balde, 'Associations d'âge'.
17. Being relatively less free, the young girls ask the permission of an old woman to stay at her place in small groups.
18. M. Fortes, 'Social and psychological aspects of education in Taleland', pp. 7, 17, 35.
19. R. A. Levine, 'Nyansongo', p. 17.
20. M. Vincent, *L'enfant au Ruanda-Urundi*, pp. 68-9.
21. J. van Wing, *Etudes bakongo*, p. 29.
22. M. Hunter, *Reaction to conquest*, pp. 180-84.
23. If a young couple have been together for a long time, they may, by mutual consent, go as far as *coitus interruptus*, but this may be punished. (Kenyatta, *Facing Mount Kenya*, p. 159.)
24. A. Schaeffner, 'Les rites de circoncision en pays kissi', p. 28.
25. Zahan, *Sociétés d'initiation*, p. 48.

26. In order to avoid the creation of an erogenous zone around the clitoris, which will later be excised, according to Kenyatta, *Facing Mount Kenya*, p. 162.

27. Read,*Children of their fathers*, pp. 181, 120.

28. R. Alt, *Vorlesungen über die Erziehung auf frühen Stufen der Menschheitsentewicklung*, p. 173.

29. One may wonder whether there exists a correlation between the attitudes of adults towards children and that of older children towards younger ones: do the gentleness and indulgence of the former elicit the same type of conduct among the latter or just the opposite?

30. E. Jensen-Krige and J. D. Krige, *The realm of a rain queen*, p. 107.

31. See P. Hazoumé, *Le pacte du sang au Dahomey*.

32. Read, *Children of their fathers*, pp. 90, 102.

33. B. Gutmann, *Die Stammeslehren der Dschagga*, vol. 1, pp. 12-13.

34. Senghor, *Liberté I*, p. 172.

35. Here education is being viewed more as an 'enrolment' ('Einreihung') than as an 'initiation' ('Einweihung').

36. The class of 'lions' has as an emblem the rhombus; that of toads a small friction drum; that of 'birds' the reed-pipe; that of 'guinea-fowl' a hoe and a door key; that of 'dogs' a perforated gourd. (See Zahan, *Sociétés d'initiation*.)

37. See J. Capron, 'Quelques notes sur la société du Do chez les populations bwa du cercle du San', pp. 81-129.

38. Kenyatta, *Facing Mount Kenya*, p. 115.

39. The Tale child will say the same thing when speaking about his father's co-wives: 'This is my younger mother or my older mother.' See M. J. Fortes, *The web of kinship among the Tallensi*.

40. Speaking about the Kissi, D. Paulme, in *Les gens du riz*, p. 114, notes: 'Even though all the children of the "court" and of the lineage live together, it is the bond between consanguines which is felt more particularly: the older child takes care of the younger child, seeing to it that he does not fall even in the most violent games. The brother and sister live together until the older one is nine or ten, when he or she goes to look for a companion of the same sex outside the family circle.'

41. E. Colson, *Marriage and the family among the plateau Thonga of Northern Rhodesia*, p. 48: 'Once they have become adults, their relation will be one of both avoidance and intimacy. A brother cannot treat his sister harshly, and a quarrel ought not to arise between them. At the death of her husband the sister will go back to live with her brother.'

42. Vincent, *L'enfant au Ruanda-Urundi*, p. 117.

43. Read, *Children of their fathers*, p. 86.

44. M. J. Field, *Religion and medicine of the Ga people*, pp. 166, 177.

45. Colson, *Marriage and the family*, p. 249.

46. In royal families one sometimes used to witness bloody conflicts.

47. For example, it is noted that formerly among the Ambo, the older brother could reduce his own sister or one of her children to slavery in order to redeem an adultery or a manslaughter. But, on the other hand, he is considered—after the brother of his mother—as the guardian of his sister. He must pay costs in case she divorces or commits adultery. (See Stefaniszyn, *Life of the Ambo*, p. 9.)

48. A. Richards, *Chisungu*, p. 83: 'In matrilineal societies where the children belong to the relatives of the wife, the conjugal bond is weak, the family unstable, and divorce frequent. During a quarrel, the woman will side with her brother against her husband; a man will confide in his sister more easily than in his wife: "Your sister will always be your sister; tomorrow your wife could be someone else's." ' (D. Paulme, 'Structures sociales traditionnelles en Afrique Noire', p. 25). In A. R. Radcliffe-Brown and D. Forde (eds.), *Les systèmes familiaux et matri-*

moniaux en Afrique, one finds among different researchers analogous statements regarding very different ethnic groups. Among the Nyakyusa, 'the sister is the equal and intimate friend of her brother more than the latter's wife will ever be.' However, 'this tendency to liken the brother and sister is limited at each instance by the difference of sex. The brother and sister show much less familiarity between them than two brothers or two sisters' (M. Wilson, p. 167). Among the Ashanti, 'a man will discuss confidential subjects such as those concerning property, money, official duties, the future of his children, matrimonial difficulties, etc. with his sister, being quite sure that she will not tell it to anyone' (M. Fortes, p. 143). Among the Lozi, 'a man will seek the company of his men friends, and a woman that of her women friends. Except in the intimacy of the conjugal bed, it is difficult for a man to enjoy the company of a woman. In this respect, a Zulu is more free than a Lozi. He can spend his time with his sister, whom he will refer to as "my brother"' (M. Gluckmann, p. 237).

49. Cf. F. L. K. Hsu (ed.), *Psychological anthropology*, p. 438.

50. In societies where the father-son axis predominates, there is a tendency to concentrate on the past. Modern civilisation, where the husband-wife axis is strong, is oriented towards the future.

51. R. and L. Makarius, *L'origine de l'exogamie et du totémisme*, p.80.

52. L. de Heusch, *Essai sur le symbolisme de l'inceste royal en Afrique*, pp. 164-5, 228-9.

Chapter 6: *Social Integration and Personality*

1. P. Parin, F. Morgenthaler, and G. Parin-Mattey, *Les Blancs pensent trop*, p. 431.

2. M. C. and E. Ortigues, *Oedipe africain*, pp. 129-30: 'African psychopathology is still a stammering discipline, but there are numerous observations which show the depth of attachments which unite the individual to the group. Thus J. C. Carothers, *Psychologie normale et pathologique*, p. 181, shows how hysterical manifestations, which in Europeans result from an internal mental conflict, explode among Africans during a conflict with the group. In general, it appears that the clear distinction which exists among Europeans between the "conscious" and "unconscious" elements of psychism is non-existent among rural Africans. The place of "censure" is occupied by the sorcerer, and the personality splits are vertical, not horizontal.'

H. Collomb and H. Ayats, 'Une étude psychopathologique sur les migrants', p. 91, show that in Dakar the 'unusual, the discomforting, the bad news, require an immediate solution which can only come from the group or from certain socio-cultural techniques. An isolated individual, incapable of surmounting the situation by himself, suddenly becomes aware of this isolation which is lived as a fragmentation, with vital catastrophic consequences. Certain pathological manifestations such as zoopathic possession appear related to wrongly personified self-image.'

M. C. Ortigues also reports the case where sexual impotence is lived as a collective family problem, where it affects the group inasmuch as it affects the individual. Impotence makes social insertion impossible, and condemns the individual to solitude, to being nobody (*Oedipe africain*, p. 94f.).

3. M. J. Field poses the question whether this reversal—which comes quite some time after the birth of a sibling, and affects paternal as well as maternal behaviours—is not the source of the feeling of persecution that one generally meets among adults. See Field, *Search for security*, p. 28.

4. Ortigues, *Oedipe africain*, p. 233.

5. G. Roheim, *Psychoanalysis and anthropology*, p. 422.

6. It is to be noted in this connection that this rivalry probably has not only a sexual but also an oral component. In fact, according to the data collected by J. F. Ritchie,

the child believes that during the resumption of the sexual relations, the father approaches the mother in order to be suckled. The child therefore takes the mother as a renegade who gives to another the milk which till then was reserved for him exclusively.

7. On the other hand, in the myths, traditions, and beliefs which are at the root of the Rwandese kingdom, the heir appears as a rival associated with his father's ritual murder. Once on the throne, the new Mwami raised his mother, who until then was merely the wife of the king, to the dignity of queen. (L. de Heusch, *Essai sur le symbolisme de l'inceste royal en Afrique*, p. 59)

8. See M. J. and F. Herskovits, *Sibling rivalry*.

9. P. Tempels, *La philosophie bantoue*, pp. 40-41.

10. Ortigues, *Oedipe africain*, p. 58.

11. O. Mannoni, *Psychologie de la colonisation*, p. 53.

12. Ibid., p. 48.

13. Ortigues, *Oedipe africain*, pp. 101, 104, 109, 126.

14. Ibid., pp. 126, 58, 147.

15. One can find at times a sort of collective but institutionalized revolt of the young against the older people; cf. Nazi Boni, *Crépuscule des temps anciens*.

16. G. Calame-Griaule, *Ethnolgie et langage*, p. 289. Regarding analogous terms, C. Pairault notes that among the Goula Iro, 'any possession within the family—ordinary or exceptional—is first of all inherited by the younger child from the older one. Everything takes place as if the succession operates preferably on the horizontal axis. In another particular case—that of the levirate—even the substance of the inheritance forbids the axis of succession tò bend towards the younger generation, i.e. to descend from the youngest "brother" to the oldest "child".' (See *Boum-le-Grand*.)

17. See Parin et al., *Les Blancs pensent trop*.

18. F. Morgenthaler and P. Parin, 'Observations sur la genèse du Moi chez les Dogon', p. 42.

19. Ibid., p. 43.

20. H. Collomb, 'Psychiatrie et culture', p. 267.

Chapter 7: *Learning of Facts and Skills*

1. D. Zahan, 'La littérature orale en Afrique Noire', p. 45: 'Once ripe, the fruit of the silk-cotton tree scatters its floss. The mistletoe symbolizes the child; it is a particle of the spirit symbolized by the silk-cotton tree.'

2. See M. Griaule, 'Le savoir dogon', pp. 27-42.

3. See E. Smith, 'Indigenous education in Africa'.

4. J. Kenyatta, *Facing Mount Kenya*, p. 109.

5. M. Fortes, 'Social and psychological aspects of education in Taleland', p. 44.

6. H. Hedenus, 'Wesen und Aufbau der Erziehung primitiver Völker', p. 128.

7. D. Westermann, *Der Afrikaner heute und morgen*, p. 46.

8. See, for example, M. Griaule, *Jeux dogons*; C. Béart, *Jeux et jouets de l'Ouest-Africain*; S. Comhaire-Sylvain, 'Jeux congolais', pp.351-62; T. Centner, *L'enfant africain et ses jeux dans le cadre de la vie traditionnelle au Katanga*.

9. Kenyatta, *Facing Mount Kenya*, p. 101.

10. Cf. M. T. Knapen, *L'enfant mukongo'*, p. 171.

11. E. Franke, *Die geistige Entwicklung der Negerkinder*, p. 216.

12. See D. Kidd, *Savage childhood*.

13. G. M. Childs, *Umbundu kinship and character*, p. 121.

14. Kenyatta, *Facing Mount Kenya*, p. 105.

15. Ibid., pp. 120-21.

16. Griaule, *Jeux dogons*, p. 27.
17. Fortes, 'Education in Taleland', p. 15.
18. M. C. and E. Ortigues, *Oedipe africain*, p. 13.
19. See M. Géber, 'Développement psycho-moteur de l'enfant africain'.
20. Knapen, *L'enfant mukongo*, p. 157.
21. R. Maistriaux, *L'intelligence noire et son destin*, pp. 186, 191.
22. Knapen, *L'enfant mukongo*, p. 76: 'The structuring of the first mother-child relation develops in such a way that, on the side of the child, it is mainly his passive dependence which is developed. From the observations that we were able to make, it appears that this relative passivity is a characteristic which persists into the later years of early childhood. Moreover, it is typical that prehension is less developed as it appears from a comparison of behaviours observed with the aid of models proposed by Gesell. When a bright object is swung in front of a baby's eyes (from the age of six months), he attentively looks at every movement and follows it with his eyes in all directions. But it is only in about half of the cases that the object is seized.' A. Richards, *Hunger and work in a savage tribe*, p. 41, reports similar observations: 'I was myself surprised to see how little babies several months old seem to observe by keeping their eyes on a bright object as do our own children. I came to the conclusion that that was due to the fact that none of those stimuli was related to the satisfaction of their needs.'
23. Maistriaux, *L'intelligence noire*, p. 186.
24. Knapen, *L'enfant mukongo*, p. 76.
25. Griaule, 'Le savoir dogon', pp. 39, 41.
26. Kenyatta, *Facing Mount Kenya*, p. 103.
27. F. Ngoma, *L'initiation bakongo et sa signification*, p. 35.
28. B. Gutmann, *Die Stammeslehren der Dschagga*, p. 59.
29. J. van Wing, *Etudes bakongo*, pp. 288-9.
30. D. Paulme, *Organisation sociale des Dogon*, p. 461.
31. At the stage of early childhood among the Lovedu, E. Jensen-Krige observes, willingness to be helpful and useful is appreciated more than work done to perfection. 'To a little girl who gives help, the mother will say, "Thank you, Madam"—praise which implies that she has already reached maturity and knows how to make herself useful as a young woman. In this society, young girls of eight to ten already know how to do housekeeping as well as cook, but the brewing of beer is only confided to them after puberty. At around the age of ten they are put in charge of a small garden' (see *Realm of a rain queen*, p. 105). M. Vincent observes that in Rwanda and Burundi, if a Hutu child refuses to help his parents, the latter punish him. However, conflicts are rare, as from a very early age the child has learnt to render service. An observer is surprised to see how much, in the practical domain, the child gives evidence of a remarkable maturity of behaviour. (See *L'enfant au Ruanda-Urundi*, p. 138.)
32. Fortes, 'Education in Taleland', pp. 15, 33-4.
33. Kidd, *Savage childhood*, p. 164.
34. Griaule, *Jeux dogons*, p. 22.
35. M. Read, *Children of their fathers*, p. 98.
36. R. Fettweis, *Das Rechnen der Naturvölker*.
37. E. Smith, 'Indigenous education in Africa', p. 325.
38. But with this difference: that metal is soft when hot and hard when cold, while clay, at first soft, is hardened by fire.
39. Zahan, 'La littérature orale', p. 28: 'The character of a blacksmith also connotes the idea of truth because he works on hard material difficult to deform. Among the Bambara, he is the master of the society of the *Komo* where exact relations of man and knowledge are taught. As such, he is opposed to the griot who, as a poet, has

the role of embellishing, of going beyond the truth, and thus appears as a "liar" excluded from all the societies of initiation whose end is to seek truth.'

40. R. Cousinet, *Pédagogie de l'apprentissage*, pp. 15-17.
41. L. and R. Makarius, *L'origine de l'exogamie et du totémisme*, p. 116.
42. See O. F. Raum, 'Some aspects of indigenous education among the Chaga'.
43. G. Calame-Griaule, *Ethnologie et langage*, p. 257.
44. F. Ngoma, *L'initiation bakongo*, pp. 50-51.

Chapter 8: *Entry into the Universe of the Word*

1. R. Jaulin, *La mort sara*, p. 271.
2. Cf. especially G. Calame-Griaule, *Ethnologie et langage* and D. Zahan, *La dialectique du verbe chez les Bambara*.
3. Calame-Griaule, *Ethnologie et langage*, pp. 29-31.
4. J. van Wing, *Etudes bakongo*, p. 228.
5. Calame-Griaule, *Ethnologie et langage*, p. 256.
6. Zahan, *La dialectique du verbe*, pp. 31, 49.
7. Calame-Griaule, *Ethnologie et langage*, p. 256: 'When a small girl has had her nose pierced, she has completed her education in the word; she is supposed to be able to speak and understand the word better. The placing of these different rings corresponds to a real teaching (which, by the way, she has received in the meantime). From now on she is ready for adult life, and in particular for assuming her essential function in society: marriage and procreation.'
8. Zahan, *Dialectique du verbe*, p. 66
9. M. Read, *Children of their fathers*, p. 102.
10. Zahan, 'La religion africaine', p. 11.
11. Zahan, *Dialectique du verbe*, p. 68.
12. Laye Camara, *L'enfant noir*, p. 35.
13. E. Jensen-Krige and J. D. Krige, *Realm of a rain queen*, pp. 109-10.
14. E. Beneviste, *Tendances récentes en linguistique générale*, pp. 133-4.
15. A. Martinet, *Eléments de linguistique générale*, pp. 16, 25.
16. Calame-Griaule, *Ethnologie et langage*, p. 111.
17. Ibid., p. 492.
18. Read, *Children of their fathers*, p. 127.
19. J. Kenyatta, *Facing Mount Kenya*, pp. 99-100.
20. J. Struyf, 'Märchenschatz der Bakongo', p. 742.
21. From the marrying age among the Dogon.
22. Calame-Griaule, *Ethnologie et langage*, p. 463.
23. Calame-Griaule, 'Signification ésotérique des contes dogons', p. 341.
24. Zahan, *La dialectique du verbe*, pp. 110, 114-15.
25. Calame-Griaule, 'L'art de la parole dans la culture africaine', p. 76.
26. L. Frobenius, *Paideuma*.
27. Zahan, *La dialectique du verbe*, p. 67.
28. Ibid., pp. 101-106.
29. Read, *Children of their fathers*, p. 97.
30. F. Dufay, 'Lieder und Gesang bei Brautwerbung und Hochzeit', pp. 847-78.
31. W. S. and K. Routledge, *With a prehistoric people*, p. 192.
32. Read, *Children of their fathers*, p. 97.
33. Zahan, *La dialectique du verbe*, p. 196.
34. Ibid., p. 60.
35. Ibid., pp. 11, 121-2.
36. Ibid., p. 122.
37. R. Allier, *Le non-civilisé et nous*, p. 254.

38. Zahan, *La dialectique du verbe*, p. 167.

39. Examples of this are given by the author in his *Sociétés d'initiation bambara*, pp. 103-104, of which the following is an extract: 'Which small one? The small one which is knowledge. Which knowledge? The knowledge which is tiny. Which tiny? The tiny which is teaching. Which teaching? The teaching which is pleasant. Which pleasant? The pleasant which is canary. Which canary? The canary which is a pond. Which pond? The pond which is a nest. Which nest? The nest which is the sun', etc., the conclusion often not being explicit.

40. In *Tradition et modernisme en Afrique Noire*, p. 24.

41. See M. Eliade, *Traité d'histoire des religions*.

Chapter 9: *Assimilation of Moral Values*

1. L. S. Senghor, *Liberté I*, pp. 277-8.

2. E. Durkheim, *Les formes élémentaires de la vie religieuse*, p. 603.

3. R. Hubert, *Traité de pédagogie générale*, pp. 404, 413.

4. G. Gurvitch, *Traité de sociologie*, vol. 2, pp. 137-72..

5. C. Pairault, *Boum-le-Grand*, p. 314.

6. F. Ngoma, *L'initiation bakongo et sa signification*, p. 36.

7. A. Richards, *Chisungu*, p. 19.

8. J. Kenyatta, *Facing Mount Kenya*, cf. pp. 119, 157.

9. R. Bureau, 'Sorcellerie et prophétisme en Afrique Noire', pp. 467-81.

10. Ibid., p. 478.

11. P. Erny, 'Aspects de l'univers affectif de l'enfant congolais', p. 300.

12. M. C. and E. Ortigues, *Oedipe africain*, p. 127.

13. A. Ombredane, *L'exploration de la mentalité des Noirs au moyen d'une épreuve projective*, p. 19.

14. Hubert, *Traité*, p. 411.

15. E. Jensen-Krige and J. D. Krige, *The realm of a rain queen*, p. 104.

16. In this connection, A. Hesnard speaks of an attitude of *preculpability*, characterized in the child who feels himself abandoned by an 'ethical' reaction of personal devaluation. 'The mother's refusal, the withdrawal of the object so desperately desired, these are associated so precociously and so intimately with threat, reprimand and imminent punishment that it would be surprising indeed if the forsaken child's reaction were not generally aroused by this ignominious prospect as much as by the simple lack of satisfaction or by the simple absence of parasitic contact which has become a need and a condition of his vital equilibrium. This is why the growing child quickly feels, or, if you prefer, expresses weaning as a *punishment* imposed by the chosen one for a "bad" organic demand: he then behaves as though it is wrong and punishable to demand the protective presence; and this preculpability keeps developing and establishing itself firmly to the full extent that the unsatisfied tension survives (in any shape) within him: every affective frustration will henceforth give rise to an attitude of indignation.' (A. Hesnard, *L'univers morbide de la faute*, p. 319-20). Neumann speaks of *primal culpability*: 'The lack of love felt at the moment when the primal relationship is disrupted, and the need to compensate for it, do not lead to a rebuke addressed by the child to mankind and the universe but to a feeling of guilt . . . which is expressed by the conviction that not being loved is equivalent to being abnormal, sick, fit to be rejected, condemned. [This feeling] is constituted according to the following formula: to be good is to be loved by one's mother; but you are bad because your mother doesn't love you.' (E. Neumann, *Das Kind*, pp. 95-6.)

17. Cf., for example, G. Ballandier, *Sociologie actuelle de l'Afrique Noire*, p. 381.

18. See R. A. Levine, *The internalization of political values in stateless societies*,

pp. 51-8; also M. Vincent, *L'enfant au Ruanda-Urundi*, p. 131.
19. Durkheim, *L'éducation morale*, p. 115.
20. M. Edel, *The Chiga of Western Uganda*, pp. 181-3.
21. E. Mangin, *Les Mossi*.
22. M. Hunter, *Reaction to conquest*.
23. M. Read, *Children of their fathers*, p. 88.
24. G. Calame-Griaule, *Ethnologie et langage*, p. 389: 'The holders of words of authority make compliments and utter reproaches. The Dogon believe that whoever has a difficult task to accomplish needs encouragement, for it increases his strength. But one must know how to distribute compliments and reproaches so that authority will remain effective. A father who only knows how to blame is not respected by his children.'
25. Ngoma, *L'initiation bakongo*, p. 38.
26. D. Kidd, *Savage childhood*, pp. 113-16.
27. See M. Griaule, *Jeux dogons*.
28. See P. Erny, 'Note dur l'image du Blanc chez l'enfant congolais'.
29. _____. 'Aspects de l'univers affectif de l'enfant congolais', p. 220.
30. Durkheim, *L'éducation morale*, p. 162.
31. Griaule, in *Jeux dogons*, pp. 16-17, says that 'ragging is fruitful. The Dogon practise it with indefatigable zeal. The peers impose it among themselves at all times and according to well regulated occasions. It provides them with the concept of the individual facing the group, defenceless before it, beaten without reason, then taken inside it again.'
32. Ortigues, *Oedipe africain*, p. 31.
33. Durkheim, *L'éducation morale*, pp. 157-8.
34. See the opening chapter of Cheik Hamidou Kane, *L'aventure ambiguë*.
35. In the biography of a Bushman cited by D. Westermann, one reads: 'If today we beat our children it is because the White men have taught it to us, for they even beat adult Bushmen.'
36. Similar observations have been made elsewhere, for example, among the Tonga; see E. Colson, *Marriage and the family among the plateau Thonga of Northern Rhodesia*, p. 224.
37. D. Zahan, 'La religion africaine'.
38. Calame-Griaule, *Ethnologie et langage*, p. 370: 'Similarly, if a Dogon girl cries during defloration she is overwhelmed by shame, and the fault is reflected on her mother who has failed to teach her properly' (ibid., p. 312).
39. The songs exalt the courage of those to be circumcised and warn them of the shame that would fall upon their families if they failed to master pain.
40. G. Vieillard, 'Notes sur deux institutions propres au populations peules d'entre Niger et Tchad: le soro et le gerewol', pp.85-93.
41. Read, *Children of their fathers*, p. 90.
42. D. Paulme, *L'organisation sociale des Dogon*, p. 475.
43. Kenyatta, *Facing Mount Kenya*, p. 159.
44. Zahan, 'La religion africaine', p. 47.
45. Calame-Griaule, *Ethnologie et langage*, pp. 374, 375.
46. Zahan 'La religion africaine', pp. 6, 22.

Chapter 10: *Initiation Pedagogy and Spiritual Experience*

1. E. H. Ashton, *The Basuto*, p. 54.
2. D. C. Simmons, 'Sexual life, marriage, and childhood among the Efik'.
3. Cf. M. Eliade, *Naissances mystiques*.
4. R. Guénon, *Aperçus sur l'initiation*, p. 112.

5. F. Ngoma, *L'initation bakongo et sa signification*, pp. 162-3.

6. In the intitiation code of Lokele it is said: 'Do not quarrel. Do not fight. Do not complain about the quantity of food given to you. Do not refuse to give food to a man when you are eating. Do not laugh when you go to the village. Do not look at a woman lower than the waist. Do not make indecent movements when you are dancing', etc. (In J. Ruytinx, *La morale bantoue et le problème de l'éducation morale au Congo*, p. 29.) E. Anderson, 'Contribution à l'ethnologie des Kuta', has noted the following formulae: 'You must not commit adultery. When your wounds have healed, you should get married. You must not steal. You must now look after the members of your clan. Now that you are circumcised, you must help those who are hungry.' Among the Beti of Cameroon, the enumeration of nine precepts is preceded by the following words: 'God has tied nine loads; it is the law. Whoever neglects even one of them has committed a sin.'

7. Cf. A. C. Hollis, *The Nandi*, p. 57: The Nandi attach a strap to the little finger and pull sharply on it, nearly tearing it off, when an important question is asked.

8. 'A serious anthropological study shows that clitoridectomy is a bodily mutilation considered in some ways as the *conditio sine qua non* for receiving a complete moral and religious teaching'; cf. J. Kenyatta, *Facing Mount Kenya*, p. 133.

9. A. Richards, *Chisungu*, p. 60. Cf. also H. Cory, *African figurines*; Schoffield, 'Pottery images or *mbusa* used at the Chisungu of the Bemba people of North-Eastern Rhodesia'.

10. Later, these initiation songs could be repeated on occasion to remind a young woman of her obligations, of the duties which they invoke in a picturesque manner, and which were taught to her by a specific emblem during the rite. They thus become means of exerting pressure in the hands of the group.

11. Richards, *Chisungu*, p. 164.

12. Ibid., pp. 165, 201, 206, 212.

13. For the girl, the doll is 'an exemplary summary of her bodily and emotional development, of her rights and duties, of latent antagonisms, and of complementarities of the lineages, the givers and receivers of women, of consanguines and those related through marriage. It represents a harmonious and healthy compromise as well as a synthesis of the imaginary and the real, of physical and social needs, a dialectic of the relations of the ego and the external world conceived as a dialectic of microcosm and macrocosm. This doll illustrates a common feature we have constantly observed: the remarkable wisdom and tolerance of African humanism expressed here by a lived symbol actualising all the powers of symbolic language.' (See P. Roumeguère and J. Roumeguère-Eberhardt, 'Poupées de fertilité et figurines d'argile', pp. 205-24.

14. D. Zahan, *Sociétés d'initiation bambara, le Ndomo, le Koré*, pp. 238-55.

15. 'Basically, Black children's games are theatrical, played by actors unconscious of their role and unaware of the meaning of the themes treated therein. Through these amusements, children are at first plunged into an organized world whose meaning their minds cannot grasp. Above all, the 'script' of these skilful constructions escapes them completely. Unconsciously, the children steep their psyches in the world of games and, by identifying themselves with their own activity, they espouse progressively their hermetic and obscure character. They themselves become hidden, dissimulated, interior . . .' (Zahan, 'La religion africaine', p. 11).

16. Initiation and circumcision did not therefore have any relation to physiological puberty, since small children and old people were treated in the same way. However, there exists in this ethnic group an individual rite of puberty: at his first ejaculation, the boy goes to wash in the river and rubs himself with a special root. (E. Jensen-Krige and J. D. Krige, *The realm of a rain queen*, p. 115.)

17. J. Hallaire, 'Chrétiens africains face à l'initiation ancestrale', p. 487.

18. G. Lapassade, *L'entrée dans la vie*, p. 95.
19. Eliade, *Naissances mystiques*, p. 274.
20. E. Mveng, *Personnalité africaine et catholicisme*, pp. 173-4.
21. R. Jaulin, *La mort sara*, p. 258: 'The Whites distance themselves from death with the truism: Death is death and life is life.' The African way of dominating death is quite different. One does not forget or reject it; it is even affirmed with exaggeration. Death is life—lost, badly played. Life is death—subdued, not at the biological but at the social level.'
22. E. Beuchelt, *Kulturwandel bei den Bambara von Ségou*, p. 240.
23. Y. Cohen, *The transition from childhood to adolescence*, p. 105.
24. R. Schurtz, *Alterklassen und Männerbünde*, p. 100.
25. Comparable, *mutatis mutandis*, to that of the European child who discovers his father is Santa Claus, in whom he had firmly believed. In *Soleil Hopi*, Don Talayeswa describes the sentiments which he experienced when the true nature of *Katchinas* was revealed to him.
26. C. Pairault, *Boum-le-Grand*, pp. 44, 127-8, 307-8.
27. R. Alt, *Vorlesungen über die Erziehung auf frühen Stufen der Menschheitsentwicklung*, p. 189.
28. J. Capron: 'Quelques notes sur la société du Do chez les populations bwa du cercle de San', p. 116.
29. Richards, *Hunger and work in a savage tribe*, pp. 173-4.
30. See Roumeguère and Roumeguère-Eberhardt, 'Poupées de fertilité'.
31. See G. Bataille, *L'érotisme*.
32. Zahan, 'La religion africaine'. p. 2.

Chapter 11: *Problems of Mental Structure*

1. W. H. Bentley, *Pioneering on the Congo*, cited in R. Allier, *Le non-civilisé et nous*, p. 256.
2. H. Dieterlen, *Journal des Missions évangéliques*, quoted in Allier, *Le non-civilisé*, pp. 175-6.
3. L. Frobenius, *Paideuma*, p. 47.
4. See F. Nadel, 'Experiments on culture psychology'.
5. J. C. Carothers, *Psychologie normale et pathologique de l'africain*, p. 102.
6. C. Lévi-Strauss, *La pensée sauvage*, p. 107.
7. D. Westermann, *Der Afrikaner heute und morgen*, p. 201.
8. C. Pairault, *Boum-le-Grand*, p. 302.
9. M. C. and E. Ortigues, *Oedipe africain*, p. 141.
10. R. Bastide, 'L'homme africain à travers sa religion traditionnelle', p. 37.
11. L. S. Senghor, *Liberté I*.
12. J. Cazeneuve, *La mentalité archaïque*, p. 79; Dieterlen, 'Classification des végétaux chez les Dogon', p. 115.
13. Bastide, 'L'homme africain', p. 38: 'The mystical trance is the apex in which this feeling is expressed: its richness derives from the fact that it constitutes an experience of this very particular sector of the real.'
14. This context recalls the one described by G. A. Richards among the Navaho: in the Navaho family, learning the trade of weaver and jeweller is done by example: for the young native, to look is to learn. Hence, the complete absence of asking too many unnecessary questions as is done in the West. More than any other, this habit is responsible for giving the native the strange opinion that the White man is foolish. (See *Navaho religion*, p. 674.)
15. 'The purification of memories through induced amnesia restores, in some way, virginity to consciousness. It delivers consciousness from its earlier links with

manifestations which have become insufficient or obsolete with regard to the world and to other people. The superficial "I" can become erased, and thus allow the deeper levels of interior being to emerge. Thanks to the rites of passage, the eternal present of a sensitivity entirely invested by a myth consumes and transforms the stains accumulated by the individual and collective history.' (See R. Alleau, *Les sociétés secrètes, leurs origines et leur destin*, p. 67.)

16. See Bastide, *Sociologie et psychanalyse*, pp. 185-7.

17. Corresponding results were obtained in this respect by M. Géber in Uganda and South Africa, Falade in Dakar, M. T. Knapen in the Congo, and Vouilloux in the Cameroons.

18. Cf. Carothers, *Psychologie normale et pathologique*, p. 101, and the works of R. Maistriaux.

19. Carothers, *Psychologie normale et pathologique*, p. 98.

20. F. Ngoma, *L'initiation bakongo et sa signification*, pp. 163-4.

21. Cf. A. Ombredane, 'Etudes psychologiques des Noirs Asalampasu', pp. 29-30.

22. The content of this section has already been published in *Revue de psychologie des peuples*, 1 (1970), pp. 67-74.

23. Ortigues, *Oedipe africain*, p. 140.

24. Westermann, *Der Afrikaner heute und morgen*, p. 56.

25. Ph. Ariès, *L'enfant et la vie familiale sous l'ancien régime*, pp. 13, 189.

26. 'The hours which a piece of work takes count less, for example, than how many times one had worked on it, or at what moment-event one started work, at what time one finished.' (Ngoma, *L'initiation bakongo*, p. 57.)

27. Ortigues, *Oedipe africain*, p. 141.

28. E. Jensen-Krige and J. D. Krige, *The realm of a rain queen*, p. 291.

29. R. Jaulin, *La mort sara*, pp. 241-2.

30. Ibid., p. 268.

31. D. Zahan, 'La religion africaine'.

32. M. Eliade, *Naissances mystiques*, p. 12.

33. Pairault, *Boum-le-Grand*, p. 178.

Chapter 12: *Permanence and Decline of Traditional Education*

1. J. Kenyatta, *Facing Mount Kenya*, p. 120: The system of mutual help and tribal solidarity 'is less practised among those Gikuyu who have been Europeanized or detribalized. The rest of the community looks upon these people as mischiefmakers and breakers of the tribal traditions, and the general disgusted cry is heard: "The White man has spoiled and disgraced our country."'

2. E. H. Ashton, *The Basuto*, p. 58.

3. D. Westermann, *Der Afrikaner heute und morgen*, p. 235: 'African tribal life and modern education are, in their present forms, irreconcilable. The old Africans see this very clearly. If they still send their children to school, it is because they see the futility of opposing a tidal wave. So, they find it better—or at least more convenient—to let events take their course.'

4. M. Read, *Education and social change in tropical areas*, pp. 106-9.

5. P. Marris, *Family and social change in an African city*, p. 56.

6. F. Musgrove, 'A Uganda secondary school as a field of culture change'.

7. R. Jaulin, *La mort sara*, pp. 127-8.

8. B. Holas, 'L'évolution du schéma initiatique chez les femmes Oubi (Côte d'Ivoire).

9. E. Beuchelt, 'Traditionelle und moderne Jugenderziehung im West-Sudan'.

10. Cf. Ashton, *The Basuto*, p. 54.

11. A discussion of this problem may be found in J. Hallaire, 'Chrétiens africains

face à l'initiation ancestrale', pp. 482-94; R. Sastre, 'La confirmation et les actes d'initiation en Afrique Noire', pp. 63-6; J. de Reeper, 'Les rites d'initiation'; and in A. V. Murray, *The school in the bush*.

12. C. Tardits, *Porto-Novo*.

13. F. Ngoma, *L'initiation bakongo et sa signification*, p. 166.

14. One can refer, for example, to the experience described by W. B. Mumford, 'Malangali School', pp. 265-90.

Bibliography

KEY TO ABBREVIATIONS

A.O.F.: Afrique Occidentale Française
B.I.C.E.: Bureau International Catholique de l'Enfance
C.E.P.S.I.: Centre d'Etudes des Problèmes Sociaux Indigènes
I.F.A.N.: Institut Fondamental d'Afrique Noire (formerly Institut Français d'Afrique Noire)
T.A.T.: Thematic Apperception Test
P.U.F.: Presses Universitaires de France

Alapini, J. 'L'éducation traditionnelle du Dahomey', *L'éducation africaine*, 38 (1956), pp. 51-61.
Albert, E. M. 'Une étude de valeurs en Urundi', *Cahiers d'études africaines*, 2 (1960), pp. 147-60.
Alleau, R. *Les sociétés secrètes, leurs origines et leur destin*. Paris: Denoel, 1963.
Allier, R. *Psychologie de la conversion chez les peuples non-civilisés*. Paris: Payot, 1925.
_____. *Le non-civilisé et nous*. Paris: Payot, 1927.
Alt, R. *Vorlesungen über die Erziehung auf frühen Stufen der Menschheitsentwicklung*. Berlin: Volk und Wissen, Volkseigener Verlag, 1956.
Ammar, H. M. *Growing up in an Egyptian village: Silwa, province of Aswan*. London: Kegan Paul, 1954.
Anderson, E. 'Contribution à l'ethnographie des Kuta, I', *Studia ethnographica upsaliensia*, VI. Uppsala, 1953.
Ankermann. 'Negerzeichnungen aus Ostafrika und Kamerun', *Zeitschrift für Ethnologie*, 1913, p. 636.
Appia, B. 'La représentation humaine dans les dessins d'enfants noirs', *Bulletin de l'I.F.A.N.*, 2-3 (1939), pp. 405-11.
Ariès, Ph. *L'enfant et la vie familiale sous l'ancien régime*. Paris: Plon, 1960.
Arnoux, A. 'Quelques notes sur les enfants au Ruanda et à l'Urundi', *Anthropos*, XXVI (1931), pp. 341-51.
Ashton, E. H. *The Basuto*. London: Oxford University Press, 1952.
Balandier, G. 'L'enfant chez les pêcheurs lébou du Sénégal', *Enfance*, 4 (1949), pp. 285-303.
_____. *Sociologie actuelle de l'Afrique Noire. Dynamique des changements sociaux en Afrique Centrale*. Paris: P.U.F., 1955.
Bagge, S. 'The circumcision ceremony among the Naivasha Masai', *Journal of the Royal Anthropological Institute*, 34 (1904), pp. 167-9.
Balde, S. 'Les associations d'âge chez les Foulbé du Fouta-Djallon', *Bulletin de l'I.F.A.N.*, 1, 1 (1939), pp. 89-100.
_____. 'L'éducation de la fille dans l'ancienne famille foulah', *Outre-Mer*, IX (1937), pp. 322-30.
_____. 'L'éducation de l'enfant foulah', *Bulletin d'informations et de renseignements*, 165 (1937), pp. 4-5.
Bardet, C., Moreigne, F., Senegal, J. 'Application du test de Goodenough à des écoliers africains de 7 à 14 ans', *Enfance*, 2 (1960), pp. 199-208.

206

Barry, H., Child, I. L., Bacon, M. K. 'Relations of child training to subsistence economy', *American Anthropologist*, 61, 1 (1959), pp. 51-63.

Bartlett, F. C. 'Psychological methods and anthropological problems', *Africa*, X, 4 (1937), pp. 401-20.

————. *Psychology and primitive culture*. London: Cambridge University Press, 1923.

Bastide, R. 'La sexualité chez les primitifs'. In *Sexualité humaine*. Paris: Lethielleux, 1966, pp. 57-72.

————. *Sociologie et psychanalyse*. Paris: P.U.F., 1950.

————. 'L'homme africain à travers sa religion traditionnelle', *Présence africaine*, XL (1962), pp. 32-43.

Bataille, G. *L'érotisme*. Paris: Editions de Minuit, 1957.

Baumann, H. 'Die Mannbarkeitsfeiern bei den Tschokwe (N.O. Angola) und ihren Nachbarn', *Baessler Archiv*, XV (1932), pp. 1-54.

————. *Das doppelte Geschlecht. Ethnologische Studien zur Bisexualität in Ritus und Mythos*. Berlin: Reimer, 1955.

Baumann, H. and D. Westermann. *Les peuples et les civilisations de l'Afrique. Les langues et l'éducation*. Paris: Payot, 1948.

Beart, C. *Jeux et jouets de l'Ouest-Africain*, 2 vols. Dakar: I.F.A.N., 1955.

————. 'Jouets et dessins d'enfants de Casamance et du Sine', *Notes africaines*, 17 (1950), pp. 70-71.

———— 'Adolescence', *Présence africaine*, 8-9 (1950), pp. 261-9.

Bellin, P. 'L'enfant saharien à travers ses jeux', *Journal de la Société des Africanistes*, 33 (1963), pp. 47-104.

Benedict, R. 'Continuities and discontinuities in cultural conditioning', *Psychiatry*, 1, 1 (1938), pp. 161-7.

Benoist, L. *L'ésotérisme*. Paris: P.U.F., 1965.

Beneviste, E. 'Tendances récentes en linguistique générale', *Journal de psychologie normale et pathologique*, 1-2 (1954), pp. 130-45.

Bernard, M. 'Enquête sur les connaissances en calcul des enfants africains à leur entrée à l'école', *L'éducation africaine*, 40 (1957), pp. 11-34.

Bernardi, B. 'The age-system of the Nilo-Hamitic peoples', *Africa*, 22 (1952), pp. 316-32.

Bestermann, T. 'The belief in rebirth among the natives of Africa (including Madagascar)', *Folk-Lore*, XLI, pp. 43-94.

Beuchelt, E. *Kulturwandel bei den Bambara von Segou. Gesellschaftsordnung. Weltanschauung. Sozialweihen*. Bonn: Schroeder, 1962.

————. 'Traditionelle und moderne Jugenderziehung im West-Sudan', *Soziologus*, XI, 2 (1961), pp. 147-60.

Beyer, G. 'Die Mannbarkeitsschule in Südafrika, speziell unter den Sotho in Nordwest Transvaal', *Zeitschrift für Ethnologie*, 58 (1926), pp. 249-61.

Beyries, J. 'Note sur l'enseignement et les moeurs scolaires indigènes en Mauritanie', *L'éducation africaine*, 92 (1935), pp. 245-55.

Biesheuvel, S. *African intelligence*. Johannesburg: South African Institute of Race Relations, 1943.

————. *Race, culture and personality*. Johannesburg: South African Institute of Race Relations, 1959.

B.I.C.E. *L'enfant africain. L'éducation de l'enfant africain en fonction de son milieu de base et de son orientation d'avenir*. Paris: Fleurus, 1959.

Bilz, J. *Menschliche Reifung im Sinnbild. Eine psychologische Untersuchung über Wandlungsmetaphern des Traumes, des Wahns und des Märchens*. Leipzig: Hirzel, 1943.

Bittinger, D. W. *An educational experience in Northern Nigeria in its cultural setting*. Elgin, Illinois: Brethren Publishing House, 1941.

Blacking, J. *Black background: the childhood of a South African girl*. New York: Abalard-Schuman, 1964.

Blanluet, J. 'Enquête sur l'enfant noir en A.O.F. L'enfant gourounsi', *Bulletin de l'enseignement en A.O.F.*, XXI, 78 (1932), pp. 8-9.

Bleeker, C. J. ed. *Initiation*. Leiden: E. J. Brill, 1965.

Bohannan, P. 'Circumcision among the Tiv', *Man*, 54 (1954), pp. 2-6.

Bossard, J. H. S. and Boll, E. S. 'Rite of passage, a contemporary study', *Social Forces*, 26 (1948), pp. 247-55.

Boni, Nazi. *Crépuscule des temps anciens*. Paris: Présence africaine, 1962.

Boullagui, Fadiga. 'Une circoncision chez les Markas du Soudan', *Bulletin du Comité d'études historiques et scientifiques de l'A.O.F.*, XVII (1934), pp. 564-77.

Brameld, I. *Cultural foundations of education: an interdisciplinary exploration*. New York: Harper, 1957.

_____. *Philosophies of education in cultural perspective*. New York: Holt-Rinehart-Winston, 1955.

Brewster-Smith, M. 'Cross-cultural education as a research area', *Journal of Social Issues*, 12, 1 (1956), pp. 3-8.

Brinker, P. H. 'Ursprung und Bedeutung der Beschneidung unter den Bantu-stämmen', *Globus*, 62 (1892), pp. 41ff.

Brookes, E. H. *Native education in South Africa*. Pretoria: Van Schaik, 1930.

Brown, J. K. 'A cross-cultural study of female initiation rites', *American Anthropologist*, 65 (1963), pp. 837-53.

Brown, J. T. 'Circumcision rites of the Bechwana tribes', *Journal of the Royal Anthropological Institute*, 51 (1921), pp. 419-27.

Brownlee, F. 'The circumcision ceremony in Fingoland', *Bantu Studies*, 3, 2 (1928), pp. 179-83; and in *Man*, 21 (1931), pp. 251-4.

Bryck, F. *Die Beschneidung bei Mann und Weib, ihre Geschichte, Psychologie und Ethnologie*. Neubrandenburg: Feller, 1931.

Bugeau, F. 'La circoncision au Kikouyou', *Anthropos*, 6 (1911), pp. 616-27.

Bureau, R. 'Sorcellerie et prophétisme en Afrique Noire', *Etudes* (1967), pp. 467-81.

Calame-Griaule, G. *Ethnologie et langage: la parole chez les Dogon*. Paris: Gallimard, 1965.

_____. 'Signification ésotérique des contes dogons'. In *Présence africaine*, 14-15 (1957), pp. 335-42 (contribution to the first congress of Black writers and artists).

_____. 'L'art de la parole dans la culture africaine', *Présence africaine*, 47 (1963), pp. 73-91.

Callaway, H. *Nursery tales, traditions and histories of the Zulus*. Springvale, Natal: 1866.

Camara, Laye. *L'enfant noir*. Paris: Plon, 1953.

Capron, J. 'Quelques notes sur la société du Do chez les populations bwa du cercle de San', *Journal de la Société des Africanistes*, 27, 1 (1957), pp. 81-129.

Carothers, J. C. 'A study of mental derangement in Africans and an attempt to explain its particularities more especially in relation to the African attitude to life', *East African Medical Journal*, 25, 4 (1948), pp. 47-86.

_____. *Psychologie normale et pathologique de l'Africain. Etude ethnopsychiatrique*. Geneva: World Health Organisation, 1954.

Carrington, J. F. 'The initiation language of the Lokele tribe', *African Studies*, 6, 4 (1947).

Cartry, M. 'Attitudes familiales chez les Gourmantché', *L'Homme*. 6, 3 (1966), pp. 41-67.

Cazeneuve, J. *Les rites et la condition humaine d'après des documents ethno-graphiques*. Paris: P.U.F., 1958.

————. 'La connaissance d'autrui dans les sociétés archaïques', *Cahiers internationaux de sociologie*, 25 (1958), pp. 75-99.

————. *La mentalité archaïque.* Paris: Colin, 1961.

Centner, T. *L'enfant africain et ses jeux dans le cadre de la vie traditionnelle au Katanga*. Elisabethville: C.E.P.S.I., 1963.

Ceuterick, P. 'Evolution psychologique du Noir', *Bulletin du C.E.P.S.I.*, 14 (1950), pp. 59-65.

Chadwick, G. C. 'Initiation rites among the Basuto', *African World* (Feb. 1958), pp. 9-10.

Chamberlain, A. F. 'Die Entwicklungshemmungen der Kinder bei den Naturvölkern', *Zeitschrift für pädagogische Psychologie und Pathologie*, II (1900).

Cheveneau, R. 'La circoncision chez les Sanga-Sanga', *Pro Medico*, I (1931), pp. 4-7.

Chéron, G. 'La circoncision et l'excision chez les Malinké', *Journal de la Société des Africanistes*, 3, 2 (1939), pp. 297-303.

Childs, G. M. *Umbundu kinship and character. A description of the social structure and individual development of the Umbundu of Angola*. London: Oxford University Press, 1949.

Clarke, A. S. 'Ba-Wemba initiation', *Man*, XXX (1930), p. 148.

Clarke, F. 'The double mind in African education', *Africa*, 5, 2 (1932), pp. 158-68.

Clerq, A. de. 'La peur et la honte chez les Noirs Baluba', *Congo* (1928), pp. 588-601.

Clignet, R. 'Les attitudes de la société à l'égard de la femme en Côte d'Ivoire', *Revue internationale des sciences sociales*, 14, 3 (1962).

Cohen, Y. A. *The transition from childhood to adolescence. Cross-cultural studies of initiation ceremonies, legal systems and incest taboos*. Chicago: Aldine, 1964.

————. *Social structure and personality*, New York: Holt-Rinehart-Winston, 1961.

————. 'The establishment of identity in a social nexus: the special case of initiation ceremonies and their relationship to value and legal systems', *American Anthropologist*, 66 (1964).

Colin, R. *Les contes noirs de l'Ouest africain, témoins majeurs d'un humanisme*. Paris: Présence africaine, 1957.

Collomb, H. 'Psychiatrie et culture: quelques considérations générales', *Psychopathologie africaine*, 2, 2 (1966), pp. 259-75.

Collomb, H. and Ayats, H. 'Une étude psychopathologique sur les migrants', *Afrique-Documents*, 67 (1963), pp. 71-95.

Colson, E. *Marriage and the family among the plateau Thonga of Northern Rhodesia*. Manchester: Manchester University Press, 1958.

Comhaire-Sylvain, J. *Food and leisure among the African youth of Leopoldville*. Cape Town, 1950.

Comhaire-Sylvain, S. 'Jeux congolais', *Zaïre*, 6 (1952), pp. 351-62.

————. 'Jeux des enfants noirs à Léopoldville', *Zaïre*, 3 (1949), pp. 139-52.

————. 'Quelques devinettes des enfants noirs de Léopoldville', *Africa*, XIX, 1 (1949), pp. 40-52.

Cory, H. 'Figurines used in the initiation ceremonies of the Nguu of Tanganyika', *Africa*, XIX, 8 (1944), pp. 459-64.

————. *African figurines. Their use in puberty rites in Tanganyika*. London: Faber, 1956.

Costier, M. 'La formation coutumière de l'enfance noire', *Bulletin du C.E.P.S.I.*, 44 (1949), pp. 92-6.

Cousinet, R. *Pédagogie de l'apprentissage*. Paris: P.U.F., 1959.

Croce-Spinelli, M. *Les enfants de Poto-Poto*. Paris: Grasset, 1967.

Cyrille, G. 'Enquête sur l'enfant noir en A.O.F.—Le petit Dahoméen', *Bulletin de l'enseignement de l'A.O.F.*, XXI, 79 (1923), pp. 79-90.

Dadie, Bernard. *Climbié*. Trans. Karen.C. Chapman. London: Heinemann, 1971.

Dean. R. F. A. 'The pattern of development of African children'. In A. F. C. Wallace, *Men and cultures*. Philadelphia, 1960.

Delano, I. O. 'The Yoruba family as the basis of Yoruba culture', *Odu*, 5, n.d. pp. 21-7.

Denis, L. 'Jeux des enfants bakongo', *Congo* (1937), pp. 412-26.

Devers, R. 'Le rite d'initiation kizungu dans le Sud de la Lulua', *Bulletin des juridictions indigènes et du droit coutumier congolais*, 2 (1934).

Diakhate. 'Passe-temps de l'enfant djallonkais', *Education africaine*, 19 (1953).

Diebold, P. M. 'Wa dia fua yika dio', *Proverbes des Balari*. Brazzaville: Imprimerie Saint-Paul, n.d.

Dieterlen, G. 'Classification des végétaux chez les Dogon', *Journal de la Sociéte des Africanistes*, XXII, 1-2 (1952), pp. 115-58.

_____. *Essai sur la religion bambara*. Paris: P.U.F., 1951.

Dooley, C. T. 'Child training among the Wanguru (Tanganyika)', *Primitive Man*, VII, 2 (1934), pp. 22-31; VIII, 4 (1935), pp. 73-80; IX, 1 (1936), pp. 1-12.

Doresse, J. 'Enfances africaines', *Table ronde*, 114 (1957), pp. 132-40.

Driberg, J. H. 'African systems of education', *Man*, XXXII (1932), pp. 122-3.

_____. 'The institution of age-grades'. In *Congrès de l'Institut international des langues et civilisations africaines* (1931), pp. 199-208.

Durkheim, E. *L'éducation morale*. Paris: P.U.F., 1934 (1963).

_____. *Les formes élémentaires de la vie religieuse: le système totémique en Australie*. Paris, 1912.

Dufay, F. 'Lieder und Gesang bei Brautwerbung und Hochzeit in Mulera Ruanda', *Anthropos*, IV (1909), pp. 847-78.

Edel, M. M. *The Chiga of Western Uganda*. London: Oxford University Press, 1957.

Edme, P. 'Scenes de la vie noire; des jeux et des ris', *Bulletin du C.E.P.S.I.*, 4 (1946-7), and 24 (1954).

Eilers, A. 'Die soziale Beziehungen des Kindes bei den Bantunegern', Thesis, Hamburg, 1927.

Eiselen, W. 'Initiation rites of the Bamasemola', *Annals of the University of Stellenbosch*, X, sect. B, 2 (1932).

Eisenstadt, S. N. 'African age groups. A comparative study', *Africa*, XXIV, 2 (1954), pp. 100-113.

_____. *From generation to generation. Age groups and social structure*. London: Routledge & Kegan Paul, 1956.

Eliade, M. *Naissances mystiques; essai sur quelques types d'initiation*. Paris: Gallimard, 1959.

Erikson, E. H. *Kindheit und Gesellschaft*. Stuttgart: Klett, 1961.

Erny, P. *L'enfant dans la pensée traditionnelle de l'Afrique Noire*. Paris: Le Livre Africain, 1968.

_____. *Les premiers pas dans la vie de l'enfant d'Afrique Noire: naissance et première enfance; éléments pour une ethnologie de l'éducation*. Paris: Le Livre Africain, 1972.

_____. 'Aspects de l'univers affectif de l'enfant congolais: milieu, expérience enfantine, personnalité', Mimeographed thesis, Strasbourg, 1965.

_____. 'L'enfant noir: jalons pour une païdologie africain', *Afrique-Documents*, 92 (1967), pp. 151-73.

_____. 'Aspects de l'éducation morale en Afrique Noire', *Afrique-Documents*, 96 (1968), pp. 35-43.

_____. 'Situation oedipienne chez l'enfant mukongo?', *Psychologie africaine*, II, 1 (1969), pp. 139-50.

_____. 'Notes sur l'image du Blanc chez l'enfant congolais', *Revue de psychologie des peuples*, 3 (1966), pp. 365-75.

_____. 'La perception de l'espace et du temps en Afrique Noire', *Revue de psychologie des peuples*, 1 (1970), pp. 67-74.

_____. 'Symbolisme religieux et affectivité chez le jeune Congolais', *Parole et mission*, 35 (1966), pp. 643-58.

Evans, J. M. *Social and psychological aspects of primitive education*. London: Golden Vistas, n.d.

Evans-Pritchard, E. E. *Kinship and marriage among the Nuer*. Oxford: Clarendon Press, 1960.

Fettweis, R. *Das Rechnen der Naturvölker*. Berlin, 1927.

Feuilloley, B. 'Un coin de l'âme nègre: l'initiation', *Revue anthropologique*, XLVIII (1938), pp. 69-79.

Field, M. J. *Religion and medicine of the Ga people*. London: London University Press, 1961.

_____. *Search for security: an ethnopsychiatric study of rural Ghana*. London: Faber, 1960.

Forsbrook, H. A. 'The life of Justin: an African autobiography translated and annotated', *Tanganyika Notes and Records*, 41 (1955), pp. 31-57; 42 (1956), pp. 19-30.

Fortes, M. J. 'Social and psychological aspects of education in Taleland', *Africa*, XI, 4 (1938).

_____. *Oedipus and Job in West African religion*. Cambridge: Cambridge University Press, 1959.

_____. *The web of kinship among the Tallensi*. London: Oxford University Press, 1949.

Fougeyrollas, P. *Modernisation des hommes: l'example du Sénégal*. Paris: Flammarion, 1967.

Franke, E. *Die geistige Entwicklung der Negerkinder: ein Beitrag zur Frage nach den Hemmungen der Kulturentwicklung*. Leipzig: Voigtländer, 1915.

_____. 'Die geistige Entwicklung und Erziehung bei Negerkindern'. In *Jubiläumsfestschrift der 2. Realschule zu Leipzig*, 1926.

_____. 'Bemerkungen über Berufsauslese und Berufserziehung bei Naturvölkern, insbesondere über die Ausbildung zum Zauberer', *Mitteilungsblatt der Gesellschaft für Völkerkunde*, 6 (1935), pp. 5-23.

_____. 'Neuere Forschungen über die Erziehung und die Entwicklung des Kindes bei Naturvölkern'. In O. Rechte, *In Memoriam K. Weule*, Leipzig: 1929.

_____. 'Zeichnungen von Kindern und Jugendlichen aus dem Waldlande von Nord-Liberia. Form und Psychologie der Zeichnungen', *Ethnologische Studien* (1929), pp. 90-96.

Frobenius, L. *Paideuma: Umrisse einer Kultur- und Sittenlehre*. Düsseldorf: Diederich, 1953.

Froelich, J. C. 'Les sociétés d'initiation chez les Moba et les Gourma du Nord-Togo', *Journal de la Société des Africanistes*, XIX, 2 (1949), pp. 99-143.

Gbaguidi, F. 'L'enfant au sein de la famille traditionnelle'. In *Enfance et jeunesse togolaises, Rencontres*, 3 (1953).

Gbaguidi, B. 'Enquête sur l'éducation dans la société indigène: généralités', *L'Education africaine*, 96 (1937), pp. 48-57.

Géber, M. 'Problèmes posés par le développement du jeune enfant africain en fonction de son milieu social', *Travail humain*, XXIII, 1-2 (1960), pp. 97-111.

————. 'Développement psycho-moteur de l'enfant africain', *Courier*, VI, 17 (1956).

————. 'Tests de Gesell et de Terman-Merril appliqués en Uganda', *Enfance*, 1 (1958), pp. 62-7.

Geigy, R. and Holtker, G. 'Mädcheninitiationen im Ulanga-Distrikt von Tanganyika', *Acta Tropica*, 8 (1951), pp. 289-344.

Germann, P. 'Zeichnungen von Kindern und Jugendlichen aus dem Waldlande von Nord-Libera. Entstehung und Inhalt der Zeichnungen', *Ethnologische Studien* (1929), pp. 75-90.

————. 'Afrikanische Puppen'. In O. Rechte, *In Memoriam K. Weule*. Leipzig, 1929.

Gluckman, M. 'The roles of the sexes in the Wiko circumcision ceremonies'. In M. Fortes, ed., *Social structure: essays presented to A. R. Radcliffe-Brown*, New York: Russell & Russell, 1949 (1963).

————. *Custom and conflict in Africa*. Oxford: Blackwell, 1960.

————. 'Les rites de passage'. In *Essays on the ritual of social relations*. Manchester: Manchester University Press, 1962, pp. 1-52.

Goody, J. 'The mother's brother and the sister's son in West Africa'. *Journal of the Royal Anthropological Institute*, 89, 1 (1959), pp. 61-88.

Graft-Johnson, J. C. de. 'African traditional education', *Présence africaine*, 7 (1956), pp. 50-55.

Gravrand, H. 'Dynamisme interne de la famille sérèr', *Afrique-Documents*, 85-6 (1966), pp. 95-122.

Griaule, M. 'Le savoir dogon', *Journal de la Société des Africanistes*, XXII, 1-2 (1952), pp. 27-42.

————. *Jeux dogons*. Paris: Institut d'ethnologie, 1938.

————. 'Remarques sur l'oncle utérin au Soudan', *Cahiers internationaux de sociologie*, XVI (1954), pp. 35-49.

————. 'Etendue de l'instruction traditionnelle au Soudan', *Zaïre* (1952), pp. 563-8.

————. 'Le problème de la culture noire'. In *L'originalité des cultures*. Paris: UNESCO, 1953.

————. 'Note sur la circoncision chez les Sonray de Gao', *Journal de la Société des Africanistes*, XIII (1943), pp. 215-17.

Griffith, A. W. M. 'Primitive native education in the Bukoba district'. *Tanganyika Notes and Records*, 1 (1936), pp. 87-9.

Guena. 'La circoncision chez les Bakouélés', *Bulletin de la Société de recherches congolaises* (1938), pp. 169-74.

Guénon, R. *Aperçus sur l'initiation*. Paris: Les Oeuvres Traditionnelles, 1946.

Gurvitch, G. *Traité de sociologie*, 2 vols. Paris: P.U.F., 1963.

Gusdorf, G. *Pourquoi des professeurs? Pour une pédagogie de la pédagogie*. Paris: Payot, 1963.

Gutmann, B. *Die Stammeslehren der Dschagga*, 3 vols. Munich: Beck, 1932.

————. 'Kinderspiele bei den Wadschagga', *Globus*, XCV (1909).

Hall. E. T. *The silent language*. New York: Doubleday, 1959.

Hallaire, J. 'Chrétiens africains face à l'initiation ancestrale', *Etudes* (1967), pp. 482-94.

Hambly, W. D. 'Tribal initiation of boys in Angola', *American Anthropologist*, 37 (1935), pp. 36-40.

_____. *Origins of education among primitive peoples*. London: Macmillan,1926.

Hammon-Tooke, W. D. 'The attainment of adult status among the Mount-Frere Bhaca', *African Studies*, 17, 1 (1958), pp. 16-20.

Hampaté Ba, A. and Dieterlen, G. *Koumen. Texte initiatique des pasteurs peuls*. Paris-La Haye: Mouton, 1961.

Hanry, P. 'La clitoridectomie rituelle en Guinée, motivations, conséquences', *Psychopathologie africaine*, 1, 2 (1965), pp. 161-267.

Harries, L. 'The initiation rites of the Makonde tribe'. In *Communications from the Rhodes-Livingstone Institute*, 3 (1944).

Hart, C. W. M. 'Contrasts between prepubertal and postpubertal education'. In G. D. Spindler, ed., *Education and Anthropology*, pp. 127-62.

Haward, L. R. C. 'Extra-cultural influences on drawings of the human figure by African children', *Ethnos*, 21, 3-4 (1956), pp. 220-30.

Hazoumé, P. *Le pacte de sang au Dahomey*. Paris: Institut d'ethnologie, 1956.

Heckel, B. 'The Yao tribe, their culture and education', *Studies and Reports*, 4 (1935), pp. 7-42.

Hedenus, H. 'Wesen und Aufbau der Erziehung primitiver Völker', *Baessler Archiv*, XVI (1933), pp. 105-63.

Henry, J. 'A cross-cultural outline of education', *Current Anthropology*, 1, 4 (1960), pp. 267-305.

_____. 'More on cross-cultural education', *Current Anthropology*, II, 3 (1961), pp. 255-64.

Hermann, S. N. and Schild, E. 'Contexts for the study of cross-cultural education', *Journal of Social Psychology*, 52, 2 (1960), pp. 231-49.

Hermann, F. *Symbolik in den Religionen der Naturvölker*. Stuttgart: Hiersemann, 1961.

Herskovits, M. J. 'Freudian mechanisms in primitive Negro psychology'. In E. E. Evans-Pritchard et al., eds., *Essays presented to C. G. Seligman*. London: Kegan, 1934, pp.75-84.

Herskovits, M. J. and F. 'Sibling rivalry, the Oedipus complex and myth (Dahomey)', *Journal of American Folklore*, 71 (1958), pp. 1-15.

Hervouet, L. 'Préformation scolaire des jeunes Africains', *Afrique et Asie*, 55 (1961), pp. 35-40.

Hesnard, A. *L'univers morbide de la faute*. Paris: P.U.F., 1949.

Heusch, L. de. *Essais sur le symbolisme de l'incest royal en Afrique*. Brussels: Institut de sociologie Solvay, 1958.

Hoernle, R. F. A. 'Native education at the cross-roads in South Africa, *Africa*, XI (1938), pp. 389-411.

Hoernle, A. W. 'An outline of the native conception of education in Africa', *Africa*, IV, 2 (1931), pp. 145-63.

Hofmayr, W. *Die Schilluk: Geschichte, Religion und Leben eines Niloten-Stammes*. Anthropos, 1925.

Holas, B. 'L'évolution du schéma initiatique chez les femmes Oubi (Côte d'Ivoire)', *Africa*, XXVII, 3 (1957), pp. 241-50.

Hollis, A. C. *The Nandi: Language and folklore*. London: Oxford University Press, 1909.

Hopen, E. *The pastoral Fulbe family in Gwanda*. Oxford: Oxford University Press, 1958.

Houis, M. *Les noms individuels chez les Mossi*. Dakar: I.F.A.N., 1963.

Hsu, F. L. K., ed., *Psychological anthropology: approaches to culture and personality*. Homewood, Illinois: The Dorsey Press, 1961.

Hubert, René. *Traité de pédagogie générale*. Paris: P.U.F., 1970.

Hugot, S. 'Enfance saharienne', *Bulletin de liaison saharienne*, X, 36 (1959), pp. 331-4.

Hunter, M. *Reaction to conquest: effects of contact with Europeans on the Pondo of South Africa*, 2nd ed. Oxford University Press, 1960.

Imbert, Y. 'Enquête sur l'enfant noir: l'enfant malinké', *Bulletin de l'éducation en A.O.F.*, XX, 75 (1921), pp. 3-19.

Izzett, A. 'The fears and anxieties of delinquent Yoruba children', *Odu*, 1 (1955).

Jahn, J. *Muntu: l'homme africain et la culture néo-africaine*. Paris: Seuil, 1961.

Jahoda, G. 'Immanent justice among West African children', *Journal of Social Psychology*, 47, 2 (1958), pp. 241-8.

_____. 'Boys' images of marriage partners and girls' self-images in Ghana', *Sociologus*, VIII, 2 (1958), pp. 155-69.

_____. 'Child animism, I: a critical study of cross-cultural research', *Journal of Social Psychology*, 47, 2 (1958), pp. 197-212; 'II: a study in West Africa', ibid., pp. 213-22.

Jaulin, R. *La mort sara: l'ordre de la vie ou la pensée de la mort au Tchad*. Paris: Plon, 1967.

Jensen, A. E. *Beschneidung und Reifezeremonien bei Naturvölkern*. Stuttgart: Strecker und Schröder, 1933.

Jensen-Krige, E. and Krige, J. D. *The realm of a rain queen: a study of the pattern of Lovedu society*. Oxford: Oxford University Press, 1943.

Junod, H. *Les moeurs et coutumes des Bantous: la vie d'une tribu sud-africaine*. 2 vols. Paris: Payot, 1936.

_____. 'La seconde école de circoncision chez les Ba-Khaba du Nord du Tansvaal', *Journal of the Royal Anthropological Institute*, LIX (1929), pp. 231-47.

Kane, I. 'Enquête sur l'enfant noir en A.O.F.—l'enfant toucouleur', *Bulletin de l'enseignement en A.O.F.*, XXI, 79 (1932), pp. 91-102.

Kane, Cheikh H. *L'aventure ambiguë*. Paris: Julliard, 1961.

Kawaters, P. H. 'Reifezeremonien und Geheimbund bei den Babli-Negern von Ituri', *Der Erdball*, V (1931), pp. 452-64.

Kaye, Barrington. *Bringing up children in Ghana: an impressionistic survey*. London: Allen & Unwin, 1962.

Kenyatta, J. *Facing Mount Kenya: the tribal life of the Gikuyu*. London: Secker & Warburg, 1938.

_____. *Au pied du Mont Kenya* (French translation of the same). Paris: Maspero, 1960.

Kidd, D. *Savage childhood: a study of Kafir children*. London, 1906.

Ki-Zerbo, Joseph. 'La crise actuelle de la civilisation africaine', In *Tradition et modernisme en Afrique Noire*. Paris: Editions du Seuil, 1965, pp. 117-43. (Rencontre Internationale de Bonaké)

Klages, J. 'Negerkinder', *Atlantis*, 26 (1954), pp. 47-54.

Klemke, O. 'Die Erziehung bei Eingeborenengruppen in Ruanda-Urundi'. Thesis, Bonn, 1962.

Kluckhohn, C. 'Theoretical bases for an empirical method of studying the acquisition of culture by individuals', *Man*, 89 (1939).

Knapen, M. T. 'Some results of an enquiry into the influences of child-training practices on the development of personality in a Bakongo tribe', *Journal of Social Psychology*, 47, 2 (1958), pp. 223-9.

_____. *L'enfant mukongo: orientations de base du système educatif et développement de la personnalité*. Louvain: Publications universitaires, Nauwelaerts, 1962.

Knops, P. 'L'enfant chez les Sénoufos de la Côte d'Ivoire', *Africa*, XI, 4 (1938), pp. 482-92.

_____. 'L'enfant chez les Noirs du Cercle de Kong (Côte d'Ivoire); réponses brèves à un questionnaire', *Anthropos*, XXVI (1931), pp. 141-55.

Koppers, W. 'Pädagogik in der Urkultur', *Oesterreichische Pädagogische Warte*, XXII (1927).

Kuntz, M. 'Education indigène sur le Haut-Zambèze', *Cahiers de foi et de vie—Le monde non-chrétien*,3 (1932), pp. 101-8.

―――――. 'Jeux sur le Haut-Zambèze', *Journal de la Société des Africanistes*, XII (1942), pp. 94-116.

Lacoste, Y. 'Un problème carrefour dans les pays sous-développés: la signification économique de l'enfant', *Les Carnets de l'enfance*, 7 (1968), pp. 27-37.

Lagrave, R. 'Quelques remarques sur les dessins spontanés d'écoliers du Nord-Caméroun', *Etudes camérounaises*, 55 (1957), pp. 16-33.

Lambert, H. E. 'A note on children's pastimes', *Swahili* (1959), pp. 74-8.

Lamy, R. 'Enquête sur l'enfant noir en A.O.F.—l'enfant agni', *Bulletin de l'enseignement en A.O.F.*, XXI, 80 (1932), pp. 199-220.

Lapassade, G. *L'entrée dans la vie*. Paris: Editions de Minuit, 1963.

Laurent, D. *Les problèmes de l'enfance en Afrique Equatoriale française*. Paris: Vigot, 1938.

Laydevant, P. 'Childhood among the Basuto', *Annali Lateranensi* (1948).

Leakey, L. S. B. 'The Kikuyu problem of the initiation of girls', *Journal of the Royal Anthropological Institute*, IX (1930), pp. 185-209.

Lebeuf, J. F. 'Jeux et jouets des enfants noirs', *La Revue française*, V, 42 (1953).

―――――. 'Notes sur la circoncision chez les Kouroumba au Soudan français', *Journal de la Société des Africanistes*, XI (1941), pp. 61-84.

―――――. 'Poupées d'Afrique Noire (Fali), *Marco-Polo*, 22 (1956), pp. 58-65.

Leblanc, M. *Personnalité de la femme katangaise: contribution à l'étude de son acculturation*. Louvain: Publications universitaires, Nauwelaerts, 1960.

―――――. 'Problèmes de l'éducation de la femme noire', *Revue nouvelle*, 13, 3 (1957), pp. 257-77.

―――――. 'Une adaptation africaine et comparaison interculturelle d'une épreuve projective: test de Rosenzweig', *Revue de psychologie appliquée*, VI, 2 (1956), pp.91-109.

Le Coeur, C. and M. 'Initiation à l'hygiène et à la morale de l'alimentation chez les Djerma et les Peuls de Niamey', *Bulletin d'I.F.A.N.*, 8 (1946), pp. 164-80.

Leenhardt, M. 'L'initiation chez les Venda et les Soutos', *L'Anthropologie*, XL (1930), pp. 463-4.

Le Goff, G. 'L'éducation des filles en A.O.F.: l'éducation d'une fillette indigène par sa famille', *Overseas Education*, 18, 4 (1947), pp. 547-63.

Lehmann, F. R. 'Bermerkungen zu einer neuen Begründung der Beschneidung', *Soziologus*, 7 (1957), pp. 57-74.

Leiris, M. 'Rites de circoncision namchi', *Journal de la Société des Africanistes*, IV, 1 (1934), pp. 63-80.

Leiris, M. and Schaeffner, A. 'Les rites de circoncision chez les Dogon de Sanga', *Journal de la Société des Africanistes*, VI (1936), pp. 141-62.

Lestrange, M. de. 'Jeuness coniagui', *Journal des voyageurs*, 73 (1947), pp. 1448-51.

―――――. 'Mère et enfant en Afrique Noire', *Le Concours médical*, 47 (1954), pp. 367-70.

Levine, R. A. 'Nyansongo: a Gusii community in Kenya'. In B. B. Whiting and J. L. Fischer, eds., *Six cultures: studies of child rearing*. New York: John Wiley, 1963.

―――――. 'Africa'. In F. L. K. Hsu, ed., *Psychological anthropology: approaches to culture and personality*. Homewood, Illinois: The Dorsey Press, 1961, pp. 48-92.

_____. 'Gusii sex offences: a study in social control', *American Anthropologist*, 61 (1959), pp. 965-90.

_____. 'The internalization of political values in stateless societies', *Human Organization*, 19 (1960), pp. 51-8.

Levine, R. A. and Sangree, W. H. 'The diffusion of age-group organization in East Africa: a controlled comparison', *Africa*, XXXII, 2 (1962), pp. 97-110.

Levine, R. A. and B. B. 'Studying child rearing and personality development in an East African community', *Annals of the New York Academy of Sciences*, 96, 2 (1962), pp. 620-8.

Lévi-Strauss, C. *La pensée sauvage*. Paris: Plon, 1962.

Leyder, D. 'Dessins d'enfants au Congo Belge', *Les Vétérans coloniaux*, 19, 6 (1947), pp. 3-9.

Ligers, Z. 'Pirogues d'enfants bozo', *Notes africaines*, 79 (1958), pp. 85-98.

Linton, R. *The cultural background of personality*. London: Routledge & Kegan, 1947.

Lynd, H. M. *On shame and the search for identity*. New York: Harcourt-Brace, 1958.

Lystad, M. H. 'Paintings of Ghanaian children', *Africa*, XXX, 3 (1960), pp. 238-42.

_____. 'Traditional values of Ghanaian children', *American Anthropologist*, 62, 3 (1960), pp. 454-64.

Mahlobo, G. W. K. and Krige, E. J. 'Transition from childhood to adulthood amongst the Zulu', *Bantu Studies*, VIII (1934), pp. 157-91.

Mair, L. P. 'The anthropologist's approach to native education', *Overseas Education*. VI (1935), pp. 53-60.

Mairlot, F. 'De quelques aspects de la psychologie profonde du Noir congolais', *Bulletin du C.E.P.S.I.*, 34 (1956), pp. 22-52.

Maistriaux, R. *L'intelligence noir et son destin*. Brussels: Editions Problèmes d'Afrique Centrale, 1957.

_____. 'La sous-évolution des Noirs, sa nature, ses causes, ses remèdes', *Revue de psychologie des peuples*, 2 and 4 (1955), pp. 167, 397; 1 and 2 (1956), pp. 80, 134.

_____. 'Réflexions sur l'intelligence des Noirs et des Blancs à propos d'une épreuve simple de classement', *Bulletin du C.E.P.S.I.*, 31 (1955), pp. 29-57.

Makarius, R. and L. *L'origine de l'exogamie et du totémisme*. Paris: Gallimard, 1961.

Malinowski, B. *The father in primitive society*. New York: Norton, 1927.

Mangin, E. *Les Mossi: essai sur les us et coutumes du peuple mossi au Soudan occidental*. Vienna: Anthropos, 1916.

Mannoni, O. *Psychologie de la colonisation*. Paris: Seuil, 1950.

_____. 'La personnalité malgache: ébauche d'une analyse des structures', *Revue de psychologie des peuples* (1948), pp. 263-81.

Marie-André du Sacré-Coeur (Sr.). 'La mère et l'enfant en A.O.F.', *L'Ethnographie*, 37 (1939), pp. 71-82.

Marris, P. *Family and social change in an African city: a study of rehousing in Lagos*. London: Routledge & Kegan Paul, 1961.

Marrou, H. I. *Histoire de l'éducation dans l'antiquité*. Paris: Seuil, 1948.

Martinet, A. *Eléments de linguistique générale*. Paris: Colin, 1960.

Matthews, Z. K. 'The tribal spirit among educated South Africans', *Man*, XXXV, (1935), pp. 26-7.

Matota, H. 'Influence des membres masculins de la famille sur l'enfant Mukongo', Thesis, Louvain: Institut de psychologie appliquée et de pédagogie, 1958.

_____. 'Le problème du mal et mes compatriotes Bakongo', *Revue du clergé africain* (1946), pp. 136-44.

M'baye, G. 'L'enfant bassari', *Education africaine*, 30 (1955), pp. 43-55.

McGlashan, N. 'Indigenous Kikuyu education', *African Affairs*, LXIII, 250 (1964), pp. 47-57.

Mead, M. 'Adolescence in primitive and in modern society'. In E. MacCoby et al., eds., *Readings in social psychology*. New York: Holt-Rinehart-Winston, 1958.

Meister, R. 'Anfänge und Frühformen der Erziehung', *Beiträge zur Kulturgeschichte und Linguistik*, 9 (1952), pp. 244-58.

Métraux, A. *Religions et magies indiennes d'Amérique du Sud*. Paris: Gallimard, 1967.

Minturn, L. and Lambert, W. *Mothers of six cultures: antecedents of child rearing*. New York: J. Wiley, 1964.

Monyenye, S. 'Indigenous education among the Abagusii', Thesis, Nairobi: University of Nairobi, 1979.

Morgenthaler, F. and Parin, P. 'Observations sur la genèse du Moi chez les Dogon, *Revue francaise de psychologie*, XXXI, 1 (1967), pp. 29-58.

Moumouni, A. *L'éducation en Afrique*. Paris: Maspero, 1964.

Muehlmann, W. 'Die Problematik des Kindes in ethnologischer Sicht', *Kölner Zeitschrift für Soziologie*, VI, 3-4 (1953-4), pp. 150-8.

Mulagò, V. 'L'union vitale bantoue', *Rythmes du monde*, 3 (1956), pp. 27-35.

Mumford, W. B. 'Malangali School: a first year's work in the development of a school from native custom and looking towards adjustment to European culture', *Africa*, 3, 3 (1930), pp. 265-90.

Murray, A. V. *The school in the bush*. London: Cass & Co. Ltd., 1967.

Musgrove, J. 'A Uganda secondary school as a field of culture change', *Africa*, XXII (1952).

Mveng, E. *Personnalité africaine et catholicisme*. Paris: Présence africaine, 1962.

Mylius, N. 'Ehe und Kind im abflusslosen Gebiet Ostafrikas', *Archiv für Völkerkunde*, 3-4 (1948-9).

Nadel, S. F. 'Experiments on culture psychology', *Africa*, X, 4 (1937), pp. 421-35.

Namfei, L. 'L'éducation chez les Baya de Bossangoa', *Liaison*, 64 (1958), pp. 32-9.

Ndongmo, A. 'L'éducation en pays bamiléké', *Etudes camérounaises*, 47-48 (1955), pp. 43-51.

Neumann, E. *Das Kind: Struktur und Dynamik der werdenden Persönlichkeit*. Zurich: Rhein-Verlag, 1963.

_____. *Ursprungsgeschichte des Bewusstseins*. Zurich: Rascher, 1949.

Ngoma, F. *L'initiation bakongo et sa signification*. Elisabethville: C.E.P.S.I., 1963.

Nicoli, J. 'Enquête sur l'enfant noir en Afrique Occidentale française', *Bulletin de l'enseignement en A.O.F.*, XX, 74 (1931), pp. 7-29.

Nissen, H. W. and Kinder, E. F. 'A study of performance tests given to a group of native African Negro children', *British Journal of Psychology*, XXV, 3 (1935), pp. 308-55.

Ocitti, J. P. *African indigenous education as practised by the Acholi of Uganda*, Kampala: East African Literature Bureau, 1973.

Offonry, H. K. 'Age-grades: their power and influence in village life (ibo), *West African Review*, 19, 255 (1948), pp. 178-9.

Ombredane, A. 'Etude du problème psychologique posé par les Noirs congolais', *Revue de l'Université de Bruxelles*, IX, 2-3 (1957), pp. 183-97.

_____. 'Principes pour une étude psychologique des Noirs du Congo Belge', *Année psychologique* (1951), pp. 521-47.

_____. *L'exploration de la mentalité des Noirs congolais au moyen d'une épreuve projective: le Congo T.A.T.* Brussels: Institut royal coloniale belge, 1954.

_____. 'Présentation d'un mémoire intitulé: l'exploration de la mentalité des Noirs congolais au moyen d'une épreuve projective', *Bulletin des séances*, XXIII (1952), pp. 375-88.

_____. 'Etude psychologique des Noirs Asalampasu'. In *Mémoire de l'Académie royale des sciences coloniales*, IV, 3 and 7. Brussels, 1956, 1958.

_____. 'Etude psychologique des Baluba'. In *Mémoire de l'Académie royale des sciences coloniales*, VI, 5. Brussels, 1957.

Ominde, S. H. *The Luo girl, from infancy to marriage*. London: Macmillan, 1952.

Ongantsang, J. M. 'L'éducation dans la famille congolaise, hier et aujourd'hui', *Pour servir*, 3 (1962), pp. 7-24.

Ortigues, M. C. and E. *Oedipe africain*. Paris: Plon, 1966.

Pages, A. 'La vie intellectuelle des Noirs du Ruanda', *Congo* (1934), pp. 357-89.

Pairault, C. *Boum-le-Grand: village d'Iro*. Paris: Institut d'ethnologie, 1966.

Palau Marti, M. 'Métaphysique noire et psychologie', *Revue de psychologie des peuples*, XI (1956), pp. 174-80.

Parin, P., Morgenthaler, F. and Parin-Mattey, G. *Les Blancs pensent trop: treize entretiens psychanalytiques avec les Dogon*. Paris: Payot, 1966.

_____. 'Considérations psychanalytiques sur le moi de groupe', *Psychopathologie africaine*, III, 2 (1967), pp. 195-206.

_____. 'Aspekte des Gruppen-Ich: eine ethnopsychologische Katamnese bei den Dogon von Sanga', *Schweitzerische Zeitschrift für Psychologie*, 27, 2 (1968), pp. 133-54.

Parin, P. and Morgenthaler, F. 'Charakteranalytischer Deutungsversuch am Verhalten "primitiver Afrikaner"', *Psyche*, X, 5 (1956-7), p. 328.

Parin, P. 'Die Anwendung der psychoanalytischen Methoden auf Beobachtungen in Westafrika', *Acta Tropica*, 91 (1961), pp. 142-67.

_____. 'Einige Charakterzüge "primitiver Afrikaner"', *Psyche*, XI, 11 (1957-8), pp. 692-706.

_____. 'Eine scheinbare Schamkultur; psychologische Betrachtungen über die Regulatoren des Verhaltens im Gesellschaftsgefüge der Dogon in Westafrika', *Kölner Zeitschrift für Soziologie und Sozialpsychologie*, XVI, 1 (1963), pp. 94-107.

_____. 'Orale Eigenschaften des Ich bei Westafrikanern', *Schweitzerische Zeitschrift für Psychologie*, XXIV, 4 (1965).

Paulme, D. 'La notion de parenté dans les sociétés africaines', *Cahiers internationaux de sociologie*, XV (1953), pp. 150-74.

_____. *Les gens du riz: Kissi de Haute-Guinée française*. Paris: Plon, 1954.

_____. *Une société de Côte d'Ivoire hier et aujourd'hui: les Bété*. Paris: Mouton, 1962.

_____. 'Structures sociales traditionnelles en Afrique Noire', *Cahiers d'études africaines*, 1 (1960), pp. 15-27.

_____. ed., *Femmes d'Afrique Noire*. Paris: Mouton, 1960.

_____. *Organisation sociale des Dogon*. Paris: Domat-Montchrestien, 1940.

_____. *Classes et associations d'âge en Afrique de l'Ouest*. Paris: Plon, 1971.

Perham, Y. *Ten Africans*. London: Faber, 1936.

Person, Y. 'Brèves notes sur les Logba et leurs classes d'âge', *Etudes dahoméennes*, 17 (1956), pp. 35-49.

Philips, A., Mair, L. and Harries, L., eds. *Survey of African marriage and family life*. London: Oxford University Press, 1953.

Piddington, R. 'Some aspects of native education and culture contact', *Africa*, XI, 2 (1938), pp. 229-32.

Pierre, E. 'L'enfant Djerma-Songhai de 7 ans; première phase de bilan psychologique', *Travaux de la section de recherche de la Télévision scolaire du Niger*.

Niamey, 1966, pp. 105-15.
Piers, G. and Singer, M. B. *Shame and guilt, a psychoanalytic and cultural study.* Springfield: C. Thomas, 1953.
Ponsionen, J. A. 'L'enfant en Afrique dans les divers milieux sociaux', *Les Carnets de l'enfance*, 5 (1966), pp. 21-7.
Porteus, S. D. *Primitive intelligence and environment.* New York: Macmillan, 1937.
Prins, H. A. J. *East African age-class systems.* Groningen: Wolters, 1953.
Quenum, M. *L'Afrique Noire, rencontre avec l'Occident.* Paris: Nathan, 1958.
Rachewiltz, B. de. *Eros noir: moeurs sexuelles de l'Afrique de la préhistoire à nos jours.* Milan: Longanesi and Editions de la Jeune Parque.
Radcliffe-Brown, A. R. and Forde, D., eds., *Systèmes familiaux et matrimoniaux en Afrique.* Paris: P.U.F., 1953.
Ramseyer, P. 'La circoncision chez les Basuto', *Revue d'ethnologie et des traditions populaires*, IX (1928), pp. 40-70.
Rattray, A. 'The African child in proverb, folklore and fact', *Africa*, VI, 4 (1933), pp. 456-72.
Raum, O. F. 'Education in an African tribal society', *Colonial Review*, X, 3 (1957), pp. 71-5.
_____. 'Some aspects of indigenous education among the Chaga', *Journal of the Royal Anthropological Institute*, LXVIII, pp. 209-21.
_____. 'Educational psychology in the speech of the Chaga', *Bantu Studies*, XIII, 3 (1929), pp. 237-41.
_____. 'Female initiation among the Chaga', *American Anthropologist*, 41 (1939), pp. 554-65.
_____. *Chaga childhood: a description of indigenous education in an East African tribe.* London: Oxford University Press, 1940.
Raux, M. 'Crise d'adolescence dans l'Uganda', *Bulletin des missions*, XI, 2 (1932), pp. 94-105.
Read, M. *Children of their fathers: growing up among the Ngoni of Nyasaland.* New Haven: Yale University Press, 1960.
_____. *Education and social change in tropical areas.* London: Nelson, 1955.
_____. *Education and cultural tradition* (inaugural lecture on the study of child-training in non-literate societies) Evans, 1950.
Redfield, R. 'The folk society', *The American Journal of Sociology* (1947), pp. 293-308.
Reeper, J. de. 'Les rites d'initiation', *Eglise vivante*, IX, 6 (1957).
Reichard, G. A. *Navaho religion: a study of symbolism*, 2 vols. New York: Pantheon Books, 1950.
Reik, Th. *Ritual.* London: Hogarth Press, 1931.
Remondet, A. 'Deux formes primitives d'éducation au Soudan français', *Bulletin du Comité d'études historiques et scientifiques de l'A.O.F.*, XIV, 1-2 (1931), pp. 1-26.
Remondet, L. 'Une enquête sur l'enfant noir en A.O.F.', *Outre-Mer*, VII, 3-4 (1935), pp. 128-49.
Richards, A. *Chisungu: a girl's initiation ceremony among the Bemba of Northern Rhodesia.* London: Faber, 1956.
_____. *Hunger and work in a savage tribe: a functional study of nutrition among the Southern Bantu.* London: Routledge, 1932.
Ritchie, J. F. *The African as suckling and as adult.* Manchester: Rhodes-Livingstone Institute, 1943.
_____. 'The African as grown-up nursling', *The Rhodes-Livingstone Journal*, 1 (1944), pp. 55-60.
Roelens, V. 'Esquisse psychologique du Noir', *Etapes*, 24 and 25 (1947), pp. 319-

23; 384-5.

Roheim, G. *Psychoanalysis and anthropology*. New York: International University Press, 1950.

Roovere, J. de. 'L'adolescent congolais dans son milieu', *Grands lacs*, 3 (1953).

Roumeguère, P. and Roumeguère-Eberhardt, J. 'Poupées de fertilité et figurines d'argile: leurs lois initiatiques', *Journal de la Société des Africanistes*, XXX, 2 (1960), pp. 205-24.

Ruytinx, J. *La morale bantoue et le problème de l'éducation morale au Congo*. Brussels: Institut de sociologie Solvay, 1960.

Sachs, W. *Black Hamlet: the mind of an African Negro revealed by psychoanalysis*. London: Geoffrey Bles, 1937.

————. *Black anger*. Enlarged edition of Black Hamlet. New York: Grove Press, 1957.

Sastre, R. 'La confirmation et les actes d'initiation en Afrique Noire', *Bulletin du Cercle Saint-Jean Baptiste* (1957), pp.63-6.

Satge, P. 'Les conditions de vie de l'enfant dakarois: problèmes et esquisses de solutions', *Les Carnets de l'enfance*, 5 (1966), pp. 233-62.

Schaeffner, A. 'Les rites de circoncision en pays kissi', *Etudes guinéennes*, 12 (1953).

Scheler, M. *Die Wissensformen und die Gesellschaft*. Leipzig, 1926.

Schmitz, J. C. 'L'éducation des enfants et des adolescents noirs', *Bulletin du C.E.P.S.I.*, 10 (1949).

Schoffield. 'Pottery images or *mbusa* used at the Chisungu of the Bemba people of North-Eastern Rhodesia', *South African Journal of Science*, XLI (1945).

Schott, R. 'Ahn und Enkel bei Naturvölkern', *Sociologus*, VII, 2 (1957), pp. 130-41.

Schulien, P. M. 'Die Initiationszeremonien der Knaben bei den Atchwabo'. In *In Memoriam K. Weule*, Leipzig, 1929, pp. 179-239.

Schurtz, H. *Altersklassen und Männerbünde: eine Darstellung der Grundformen der Gesellschaft*. Berlin: Reimer, 1902.

Sciascia, G. 'L'éducation et l'instruction en Afrique: éléments constitutionels d'unité', *Civilisations*, XVI, 3 (1964), pp. 202-8.

Scott, H. S. 'Native authorities and education', *Africa*, XV, 4 (1945), pp.173-82.

Seabury, R. I. *Daughter of Africa*. Boston: Pilgrim Press, 1945.

Senghor, L. S. 'De la négritude: psychologie du Négro-Africain', *Diogène*, 37 (1962), pp. 3-16.

————. *Liberté I, négritude et humanisme*. Paris: Seuil, 1964.

Shann, G. N. 'The early development of education among the Chagga', *Tanganyika Notes and Records*, 45 (1956), pp. 21-31.

Sharp, E. *The African child*. London: Longmans, 1931.

Shelton, A. J. 'Proverbs and education in West Africa', *Overseas Education*, XXXIV, 4 (1963), pp. 181-6.

Sieber, D. and J. 'Das Leben des Kindes im Nsungli-Stamm', *Africa*, XI (1938), p. 208.

Simmons, D. C. 'Sexual life, marriage and children among the Efik', *Afrika*, 30 (1960), pp. 153-65.

Smith, M. F. *Baba of Karo: a woman of the Muslim Hausa*. London: Faber, 1956.

Smith, E. 'Indigenous education in Africa'. In E. E. Evans-Pritchard et al., eds. *Essays presented to C. G. Seligman*. London: Routledge & Kegan Paul, 1934, pp. 319-34.

Spitz, R. A. 'Frühkindliches Erleben und Erwachsenenkultur bei den Primitiven', *Imago*, XXI (1935), pp. 367-87.

Stefaniszyn, B. *Social and ritual life of the Ambo of Northern Rhodesia*. London: Oxford University Press, 1964.

Steinmetz, R. 'Das Verhältnis zwischen Eltern und Kindern bei den Naturvölkern', *Zeitschrift für Sozialwissenschaft* (1898), p. 623.
————. *Ethnologische Studien zur ersten Entwicklung der Strafe.* Leiden, 1892.
Stephens, W. *The Oedipus complex: cross-cultural evidence.* New York: Free Press of Glencoe, 1962.
Struyf, J. 'Märchenschatz der Bakongo', *Anthropos*, III (1908), p. 742.
Tardits, C. *Porto-Novo: les nouvelles générations africaines entre leurs traditions et l'Occident.* Paris: Mouton, 1958.
Tempels, P. *La philosophie bantoue.* Paris: Présence africaine, 1949.
Tessmann, G. 'Die Kinderspiele der Pangwe', *Baessler Archiv*, II (1912).
Thomas, L. V. 'Note sur l'enfant et l'adolescent diola', *Bulletin de l'I.F.A.N.*, XXV, 1-2 (1963), pp.66-79.
————. 'Remarques sur la mentalité des Diola', *Revue de psychologie des peuples*, XIV, 3 (1959), pp. 253-72.
————. 'La frustration chez les Diola', *Bulletin de l'I.F.A.N.*, XXIII, 3-4 (1961), pp. 518-72.
————. 'Étude technique de la personnalité diola'. Thesis, Paris, 1959.
————. 'Temps, mythe et histoire en Afrique de l'Ouest', *Présence africaine*, 39 (1961), pp. 12-68.
Thore, L. 'Langage et sexualité'. In *Sexualité humaine.* Paris: Lethielleux, 1966, pp. 73-104.
Thurnwald, R. 'Primitive Initiation und Wiedergeburtsriten', *Eranos Jahrbuch*, VII (1940), pp. 321-98.
Traore, M. 'Jeux et jouets des enfants foula', *Bulletin de l'I.F.A.N.*, 1-2 (1940), pp. 237-48.
Tucker, A. N. 'Children's games and songs in the Southern Sudan', *Journal of the Royal Anthropological Institute*, 63 (1933), pp. 165-87.
Turner, J. C. 'African education and character', *South African Outlook*, LXXII, 849 (1942), pp. 8-10.
Turner, V. W. 'Three symbols of passage in Ndembu circumcision ritual'. In M. Gluckman, ed., *Essays on the ritual of social relations.* Manchester: Manchester University Press, 1962, pp. 123-73.
Vallois, H. 'Poupées d'Afrique occidentale', *L'Anthropologie*, XLIV (1943), pp. 216-17.
Van Bulck. 'Le problème du mal chez quelques populations d'Afrique Noire', *Rythmes du monde*, III, 2 (1955), pp. 93-111.
Vansina, J. 'La famille nucléaire chez les Bushoong', *Africa*, XXVIII, 2 (1958), pp. 95-108.
————. 'Initiation rituals of the Bushoong', *Africa*, XXV, 2 (1955), pp. 138-53.
Varagnac, A. *Civilisation traditionnelle et genres de vie.* Paris: Michel, 1948.
Verhaegen, P. and Leblanc, M. 'Quelques considérations au sujet de l'éducation primaire de l'enfant noir', *Revue pédagogique congolaise*, 31 (1955), pp. XVII-XXXII.
Vieillard, G. 'Note sur deux institutions propres aux populations peules d'entre Niger et Tchad: le soro et le gerewol', *Journal de la Société des Africanistes*, II (1932), pp. 85-93.
Vincent, M. *L'enfant au Ruanda-Urundi.* Brussels: Institut royal colonial belge, 1954.
————. 'L'enfance noire', *La femme et le Congo*, 28, 161 (1958), pp. 2-6.
Vollbehr. 'Kinderzeichnungen aus den deutschen Kolonien', *Umschau* (1912), p. 759.
Waldow, A. von. 'Mädchenerziehung bei den Zaramo (Tanganyika), *Afrika und Uebersee*, XLV, 4 (1962), pp. 291-305.

Walk, L. 'Die Erziehung bei den Naturvölkern'. In F. X. Eggersdorfer, *Handbuch der Erziehungswissenschaft*. Munich, 1934, pp. 23-99.

_____. 'Initiationszeremonien und Pubertätsriten der südafrikanischen Stämme; ein Beitrag zum Studium des Erziehungswesens und der Mysterienkulte der Naturvölker', *Anthropos*, XXIII (1928), pp. 861-6.

_____. 'Initiationszeremonien und Pubertätsriten der südafrikanischen Stämme', *Mitteilungen der anthropologischen Gesellschaft in Wien*, XII (1929), pp. 19-32.

_____. 'Die ersten Lebensjahre des Kindes in Südafrika', *Anthropos*, XXIII (1928), pp. 38-109.

Wandira, A. *Indigenous education in Uganda*. Kampala: Makere University Press, 1971.

Ward, E. 'The parent-child relationship among the Yoruba', *Primitive Man*, IX (1936), pp. 56-63.

Weule, K. 'Negerpädagogik', *Jahrbuch des städtischen Museums für Völkerkunde*, Leipzig, IX (1928).

Westermann, D. *Autobiographies d'Africains*. Paris: Payot, 1943.

_____. *Der Afrikaner heute und morgen*. Essener Verlagsanstalt, 1937.

Whiting, B. B., Fischer, J. L. et al. *Six cultures: studies of child rearing*. New York: John Wiley, 1963.

Whiting, J. W. M. *Field manual on child training studies*. Harvard University Press, 1955.

_____. 'Socialization process and personality'. In F. L. K. Hsu, ed., *Psychological anthropology: approaches to culture and personality*. Homewood, Illinois: The Dorsey Press, 1961.

Whiting, J. W. M. and Child, I. *Child training and personality: a cross-cultural study*. New Haven: Yale University Press, 1953.

Whiting, J., Kluckhohn, R., and Anthony, A. 'The function of male initiation ceremonies at puberty'. In E. M. MacCoby et al., eds., *Readings in social psychology*. New York: Holt-Rinehart-Winston, 1958, pp. 359-70.

Wilson, M. *Good company: a study of Nyakyusa age-villages*. London: Oxford University Press, 1951.

_____. *Rituals of kinship among the Nyakyusa*. London: Oxford University Press, 1957.

van Wing, J. 'Enfants noirs', *Congo*, II, 2 (1930), pp. 173-81.

_____. 'Nzo-longo ou les rites de la puberté chez les Bakongo', *Congo*, 6 (1920). pp. 229-46; 1 (1921), pp. 48-60; 3 (1921), pp. 365-89.

_____. *Etudes bakongo: sociologie, religion et magie*. Paris: Desclée de Brouwer, 1959.

_____. 'L'homme congolais', *Bulletin des séances*, Institut royal colonial belge, XXIV, 4 (1953), pp. 1102-21.

Winter, E. H. *Beyond the mountains of the moon: the lives of four Africans*. London: Routledge & Kegan, 1959.

Wintringer, G. 'Considérations sur l'intelligence du Noir africain', *Revue de psychologie des peuples*, 1 (1955), pp. 37-55.

Young, F. 'The function of male initiation ceremonies: a cross-cultural test of an alternative hypothesis', *American Journal of Sociology*, 67 (1962), pp. 379-91.

Zaborowski, M. 'De la circoncision des garçons et de l'excision des filles comme pratique d'initiation', *Bulletin de la Société d'anthropologie de Paris*, V (1894), pp. 81-104.

Zahan, D. 'Formes de la connaissance en Afrique Noire'; 'Littérature orale'; 'La religion africaine' (mimeographed notes of the Strasbourg Institute of Ethnology).

_____. *Sociétés d'initiation bambara, le Ndomo, le Koré*. Paris: Mouton, 1960.

_____. 'Ataraxie et silence chez les Bambara', *Zaïre*, XIV, 5-6 (1960), pp. 491-505.

_____. *La dialectique du verbe chez les Bambara*. Paris: Mouton, 1963.

_____. ed. *Réincarnation et vie mystique en Afrique Noire*. Paris: P.U.F., 1965.

_____. *Religions, spiritualité et pensée africaines*. Paris: Payot, 1971.

Zempléni-Rabain, J. 'Modes fondamentaux de relations chez l'enfant wolof; du sevrage à l'intégration dans la classe d'âge', *Psychopathologie africaine*, II, 2 (1966), pp. 143-78.

_____. 'L'aliment et la stratégie de l'apprentissage de l'échange avec les frères chez l'enfant wolof', *Psychopathologie africaine*, IV, 2 (1968), pp. 297-312.

Ziegle, H. 'Notes sur la psychologie des Bantous de l'Afrique Centrale', *Les Cahiers d'Outre-Mer*, 13 (1951), pp. 23-38.

General Index

acculturation   xviii-xix, 174, 178
age   7-9, 53-6, 123, 159, 160, 161, 164
age fraternity   53, 55-6, 62, 64-6, 123
age-group   7, 16, 56ff., 63-5, 147, 150, 194
age-set   54-6, 66
ancestor   17-18, 19, 36-7, 47, 75-7, 122-3, 133, 152-3, 154
androgyny   21-2, 150
art   98

blacksmith   99, 100, 136, 149, 198
breast-feeding   7, 28-31, 127, 136, 141; *see also* weaning

castration   74, 78, 145
circumcision, male and female   21-3, 49, 83, 99-100, 136, 140-41, 149, 150, 151, 154, 173-4, 180-87, 192, 194; *see also* initiation
culpability   127, 200

dance   97-8. 116, 117, 180, 202-3
death   19, 65, 112, 116, 123, 148-9, 150ff., 153-5, 166
dependence   31, 36, 41, 67-8, 70-71, 75, 78, 121-2, 149, 170, 198
doll   145, 202
dormitory   54, 56, 57-8, 63, 72

esotericism   23, 64, 81-3, 99-100, 116, 172

flocks, keeping of   56-7, 60, 62-3, 97, 169
food   27, 45, 63, 98, 101-2, 124-5, 128, 148, 153-4, 169

games   39, 54, 57, 60-62, 84, 86, 97-8, 146, 170, 202
grandparents   41-2, 50, 51(n), 111, 115-16, 153, 170
greetings   102-3, 126

history   110-11, 142, 151
homosexuality   60, 62-3

identity   16-18, 42, 48, 49-50, 63, 77, 78-80, 83, 108, 169-70

imitation   xiv, xv, xvi, 60, 83-4, 87, 100, 101-2
initiation   xv, 3, 8-9, 16, 21-3, 27, 44, 54, 55, 56, 58, 61, 62-3, 64-6, 72, 82-3, 86, 98-100, 101, 107-8, 110, 112, 132, 136, 139ff., 147, 148, 149, 150, 151-4, 161, 162, 170, 171ff., 176 179-87, 195, 202; *see also* circumcision
Islam   10, 12, 42, 134, 168, 173, 175

kinship   35ff., 37, 46, 101-2, 109, 123
knowledge   xiv-xv, 2-3, 8, 12, 22, 27, 34, 36, 82, 85, 111, 112, 118, 130, 142, 143-4, 146, 153, 154, 155, 163, 164, 168, 171, 175

language   9, 14, 38, 105-9
  secret   107-8, 142, 143, 150
life, military   57, 64, 82, 97, 99, 104, 141
litanies   118, 126

marriage   7, 8, 22, 24, 37, 38, 43, 60, 62, 64, 68, 82, 115, 129, 141, 144, 151
mastery   22, 125, 128, 135-7, 146, 201
masturbation   60, 61-2
maxim   6, 8, 112, 114-16, 131
mockery   103-6, 131
moralization   112-13
myth   47, 68, 82, 85, 87, 110, 112-13, 114, 142
mystery   8, 82-3, 110, 112, 117-18, 141-2, 146, 154; *see also* esotericism

name   16ff., 36, 51(n), 63, 78, 79, 92, 148, 152-3, 165
nudity   148, 151

Oedipal situation   33, 47, 71ff., 145
old age   8, 11-12, 19, 115-16, 155

paidology   9, 10, 27
passivity   88-9, 92-3, 159-60
past   11-12, 36, 166
profession   11, 99-100, 175, 184
proverbs   6, 44, 67, 110, 114-16, 157, 184
punishment   33, 41, 53, 57, 63, 127-8,

225

Index of Authors

Index of Ethnic Groups